FAN

Over the years the a messages from LDS members, missionaries and non-Mormons from all over the globe. Below are excerpts from some of those communications and fan mail.

Brother Pennington, I just wanted to take a minute to write and thank you for the *Mr. Mormon* CDs. You are truly amazing and they spark many discussions, discussions I love. I am so grateful that you have been willing to share your thoughts and insights with us. I learn something new each time I listen to them. I was especially excited about your Evolution vs. Creation CD. We have a son who is very intelligent and especially loves the sciences. He loves biology, chemistry and is planning to go to medical school to become a genetic researcher. He has come to us with many questions about creation vs. evolution and has gone away confused, frustrated and feeling that something is missing in the debate between science and God. **Your CD was a great help to him.** I thank you for that. Keep being the great person that you are and using the gifts that you have been given to bring clarity and thought to the mysteries of God. Your musings are a blessing to me. ---*Sister T. R. in Sandy, Utah*

I have to dash off a quick note to tell you how much I have enjoyed your *Mr. Mormon* series. I considered myself fairly well-read when it came to Mormon doctrine but **you have really blown my mind with the simple and practical answers to questions** that have been on my mind. You have even indirectly answered a few questions without intending to! I can't wait to get through the book a second time.
----*Brother B.B in Salt Lake City, Utah*

Your CD's are awesome. I am in the buckle of the Bible Belt. My companion and I will listen to one chapter during companion study **and take millions of notes**.
----*Elder C. West Virginia Charleston Mission*

Dear John, You are like "John the Beloved." He had a gift for writing and so do you. He wrote the Book of Revelation and you have been inspired in your writings. You have a special gift of expressing your thoughts. Thanks for inspiring me to have the desire to study and learn.   ----*Sister O. of Alberta, Canada*

Brother Pennington, I am a missionary in the Houston, Texas Mission and received your CDs unexpectedly about a month ago. When I got the *Mr. Mormon* CDs, I was struggling a bit with my companion. He'd acquired some doubts concerning some doctrines of the Church. The doubts had grown so much that he had called the Mission President to finalize his decision to return home after eight months of service. I had tried every trick in the book to help him. I have been exposed to a lot of anti-Mormon literature, so I thought I'd be able to help him when the Mission President asked me if I would try to help him stay on his mission. The hand of God was heavily involved, but I want to let you know that your commentary was an **immense factor** with my companion's decision to stay on his mission. We are still together tearing it up out here doing the Lord's work. I really enjoyed the CDs you sent and have full intentions of buying the remainder of your work when I return home in another month. Every missionary serving in the south should hear your work. I don't know how I was selected as the recipient of your gift, but I definitely know why.
                    ----*Elder C.S. Houston, Texas Mission*

Hello Brother Pennington, my name is I.C. I am a young English convert who has just returned from serving a mission in the England London South Mission. I came across your audio sermons during my service and just wanted to email you to thank you for publishing them. They have been a great help to me in my quest to understand the plan of salvation and my part in it. I believe that one key to being able to understand doctrine is **being able to organize** it and that is what you have helped me do.   ----*Elder I.C. in England*

I want to thank you for strengthening my testimony and my knowledge of the restored gospel! I am a brand new convert and am strengthened by the testimonies of others and love for the truth. I love that you reference the Bible. It will help as **I try to get my father, who is a Baptist Pastor, to believe and understand why I have made the decision to join the Church.** I have hope that my family will see the light and truth in my life enabling them to one day seek the true gospel! Thank you.

----*Sister L.N. in Colorado*

I have listened to the *Mr. Mormon* Chapter 12 and liked it. You helped me understand the story of Adam and Eve from a different perspective. I am looking forward to Chapter 13! Thanks.   ----*Brother A. S. in New Zealand*

Dear John, we dropped our son William at the airport yesterday and he flew straight to the London England Mission Training Center to start his two year LDS mission. We were listening to the *Mr. Mormon* CDs in the car on the way to the airport. **He has really enjoyed the discussions you share.**

----*Sister D.W. in Virginia*

Dear Dad and Mom: Do you remember those audio books from John Pennington you sent me? Yeah, well me and **almost all of the missionaries in KL zone have listened to them** and are excited for the next chapters to come out! Ha, ha, ha, we really enjoyed listening to them and Brother Pennington's views and the stories in the scriptures. I always knew he was scripture smart, but not like this! He is fun to listen to. You should let him know.   ----*Elder T.H. in Indonesia*

Brother Pennington, I understand the gospel more and more every day and I thought I really knew it all. However, after listening to your *Mr. Mormon* chapters on the gospel, I guess I still have a lot to learn. **The CDs are truly amazing to listen to.** I thank you for putting in the time and effort to publish them.

----*Elder E. H.*

Dear John Pennington, My name is Elder S.M.C; I am a missionary currently serving in the Ghana Cape Coast Mission in West Africa. I recently got your audio book *Mr. Mormon* in a package from my aunt L.B. I am from Draper Utah, graduated from the same High School as your son Bridger. I have been listening to your audio book for the past three days. I have been on my mission for a little over a year and your book has helped me to answer a few of the gospel questions that I have had in the back of my mind. Sometimes people here in Africa ask us crazy questions. Your CDs have helped me to know that "The simplest answer is always the best answer." Thanks for writing the book. **It has been very useful over here**. The Church is true. Serving a mission is the best thing I have ever done. Thanks for helping me strengthen my testimony and to add to my knowledge of the gospel.

----Elder S.M.C. in the Ghana Cape Mission

John, I have to tell you that **your stuff (*Mr. Mormon*) is just awesome**. I use parts of it for lessons here and there in the priest quorum. We need more folks like you around here. Thank you.

----Brother J.T. in Sandy Utah

Hi Brother Pennington, I served a mission in the State of Washington and studied your first seven chapters while I was there. I am now back home in New Zealand and am waiting for your next chapters to come out. **The first seven chapters really sparked my interest in studying the gospel**.

----Elder A.S. Washington Everett Mission

Brother Pennington, the timing of receiving the *Mr. Mormon* CDs in the mail was perfect. There is a man investigating the church for eighteen years and he has always had a problem with the three degrees of glory, the scriptures that you used in the 1st chapter **helped him out greatly**.

----Elder J.D. of Louisville, Kentucky

Dear John, I have thought of you so many times, and just wanted to let you know that I finished listening to all your *Mr. Mormon* CDs. They are fantastic. I am truly impressed with the depth of history that you detailed in presenting all this fabulous information. I loved every one of them, but I would have to say that if I had to pick a favorite, it would be the one about the apostles (Chapter 5). You are a very smart man – a man on a mission – actually a lifetime mission – and it shows loud and clear in these CDs. God bless you, and your family.

----From a Non-Mormon in Alabama

Dear John, We want to thank you for publishing your *Mr. Mormon* chapters. As we listened to the CDs (specifically Chapter 12) we were amazed at your keen thoughts and your questions about Adam and Eve and the Garden. We think this was right there at the top of the list. We are grateful for you **and the impact you are for having in our lives and the lives of missionaries.** *----Brother W.O. Alberta, Canada*

Brother Pennington, I don't know why or who ordered me your CDs while I was serving as a missionary, but one day in the field I received them in the mail and have loved listening to them. Many of my missionary companions and other missionaries around the mission loved listening too. So thank you for sharing your knowledge and testimony in such a special way. I can't even remember how many missionaries I shared them with. I was a Zone Leader almost that whole time period and our main focus was the *Preach My Gospel* lessons with our investigators, but when I talked to LDS members about your CDs many of them said that they really enjoyed them. One member downloaded every chapter from your website and listened to them over the next few days as he worked. They are wonderful and were such a blessing to me on my mission. **You have a special ability to teach and testify of the doctrine of Christ in a very clear way.** So again, Thank You!

---Elder S.R. Macon Georgia & South Carolina Mission

Dear Brother Pennington, I love your CDs. I gave your Chapter Three (the Solar System and the Scriptures) to an atheist friend of mine and to my surprise **he absolutely loved it**. Now we are having continual conversations about God and Jesus Christ. Thanks so much for putting this audio book together. I absolutely love it.   ---*Brother J. Salt Lake City, Utah*

Dear Brother John Pennington, Hi, your book truly strengthened my faith. My favorite chapters are Eight and Twelve. As a new convert, a lot of the questions I had for the missionaries are pointed out here. The conclusions make so much sense, and I love how you relate back to the Bible. I sent a few of your older chapters to my father who does not like me being a Mormon. The fact that you referred to Bible references kept him listening until the end. The Book of Mormon he couldn't even get through the first couple chapters, unfortunately. I'm praying about sending him your Chapter Eight. I love that it is perfect for someone like my Dad. Also, Chapter Twelve is great as it points out different scenarios for the fall of Adam; points that I have never thought about. Like you say, "it feels right to my soul." You truly strengthen and inspire me. As I prepare to go to the temple in two weeks to get my endowments and be sealed I have been listening to your chapters constantly. The Holy Spirit truly tells me it's true. Thank you for what you do!   ----*Sister H.*

Dear Mr. John Pennington, I am friends with your son Bridger, He and I are in the same district. He noticed that my faith is not where it should be so he proceeded to share your *Mr. Mormon* CDs with me. At first I was a bit skeptical. I am a physics major, and for many years I have struggled over science and faith. While I believe both can be used in unity, my colleagues and teachers believe otherwise. While I believe that there are still challenges and gaps, I do find your arguments refreshing. I appreciate your comparisons that I personally would never have thought of. I like your references from the Bible and enjoy your passion for the scriptures. Thank you.   ----*Elder J.R.B. in Taiwan*

Everyone loves the *Mr. Mormon* CDs. Elder B. saw them and wanted to listen and so he and his companion borrowed them. They listened to all of them! Then my companion was super interested and he listened to them every night and every morning. They are amazing!   ---*Elder B. P. in Taiwan*

Brother Pennington, I have enjoyed so much being able to listen to the *Mr. Mormon* CDs as my companion and I have driven around Germany together, learning more from your insights. I especially wanted to simply thank you for the chapter on "God's Multiple Methods of Communication." What you said about prayer and the point of asking "How can I do this?" or "How can I be better?" has been the long awaited answer to my prayers. I had been so lost and confused as to why God wasn't answering my prayers and why my prayers had no effect on me. What you said in that chapter **ultimately changed my life**. I can now see the power of prayer and God's desire to help me. So thank you! I cannot emphasize that enough.   ----*Elder A.D. in Germany*

Brother John, I have loved listening and learning from your voice. The way your CDs explain the gospel lessons is easy to understand and **they have helped me as I teach investigators**. My favorite chapter is number four, the one on the priesthood. It has helped me make sense of the story of Moses and the Israelites and why the Levites had the priesthood. Thank you once again.   ---*Elder J.J. in Sherman, Texas*

Brother Pennington: My companion and I used your "plan of salvation" layout in Chapter One, "What About the Boy in China," It got us pumped **and it was our best lesson about the plan of salvation on my mission!!!** You have a great speaking voice.   ----*Elder M. Las Vegas Nevada Mission*

These CDs are amazing--- let me tell you. They have helped me so much. The whole time I was listening, I was blown away. It is wonderful, now, being able to explain and teach the gospel better. **Your CDs have increased our key investigators and baptisms.** Thank you for helping me be a better missionary. Every time I go on exchanges or get a new companion, I listen to them again and all the missionaries LOVE IT. Well, you're the man.   ----*Elder L. in Oak Harbor, Washington*

These CDs have helped me understand the gospel more clearly and have given me a new perspective (better than my own) about the doctrines. They have helped me teach more effectively. These CDs are awesome.   ----*Elder C. in Australia*

Brother Pennington, I just wanted to send you a quick email, to say thank you! My companion and I have continued to listen to the entire audio book! We finished it all in about a week, listening to it every chance we got! My companion is a convert of less than two years and so it really gave both of us a lot of clarity about the gospel! It also helped us see how things fit into God's plan for us! **It also gave us scriptural backing on things we knew were true, but we just didn't know how to explain it to people.** We have even recommended your book to several members to listen! Thank you again for reaching out.
     ----*Elder P. T. Ohio Columbus Mission*

Mr. Mormon

Advanced Discourses for
Latter-day Saints, Mere-Mortals
& Super-Mormons

John S. Pennington Jr.

Author of the Mr. Mormon audio book series

Mr. Mormon

Publisher Penny10, LLC

11552 Lexington Hills Circle

Sandy, Utah, USA

Website – www.mrmormon.com

Copyright © 2010 John S. Pennington Jr.

Printed in the United States of America

ISBN-13: 978-1517526092
ISBN-10: 1517526094

All rights reserved, except as permitted under the U.S. Copyright Act of 1976.

No part of this publication may be reproduced, distributed, or transmitted in any form or by any means, or stored in a database or retrieval system without the written permission of the publisher or author. Portions of this book (specifically Chapter 14) are not under copyright by the publisher or the author.

The publisher is not responsible for websites (or their content) that are not owned by the publisher or the author.

This book is adapted from the original script for the audio book, titled *Mr. Mormon*, published in the year 2010 by the same author. For an audio copy go to www.mrmormon.com.

In both written and audio book forms, the author is in no way, shape, or form claiming to present any official doctrine of The Church of Jesus Christ of Latter-day Saints. The author maintains that he is not a gospel scholar by any measurement; he just enjoys talking about and discussing scriptural concepts and reserves the right to change his opinion on any subject at any time in the future.

DEDICATION

The inception of this book began when I recorded my thoughts and stories onto audio CDs for my three sons. Our family has always regularly attended church and we've had many discussions about scripture, doctrine, and philosophy. However, I wanted to record some of my knowledge from years of study and experience. If I were to die young, I wanted my children to understand how much I loved the gospel of Jesus Christ. I expect that most people long to leave a legacy of some kind; a remnant of having lived earnestly and offering a glimpse of their own unique personality to their posterity.

I am blessed that my parents are (as of this writing) alive, but my grandparents and great-grandparents are deceased. How I would love to hear their voices again, to remind me of their characters and knowledge! I believe and hope that the Mr. Mormon audio recordings and written text will permit my children and grandchildren, to hear my voice, catch a twinkle of my personality, enjoy my humor and appreciate my dedication to Christ.

Once I placed my thoughts onto an audio recording; my three sons—John Stephen Pennington, Bo James Pennington and Bridger Olsen Pennington—often listened to them for hours as they lay in bed before they went to sleep. They also shared them with their friends; their friends shared them with their parents; their parents shared them with missionaries.

Soon I uploaded the audio recorded files to the website www.mrmormon.com and made them available to anyone who wanted to listen, but particularly for young LDS missionaries. My hope was to give them a teaching model that was backed by scripture and a new way to share the gospel wherever they might be on earth. The stories, scriptures, sources and analogies encourage logical thinking, curiosity, digging deep for explanations to big questions and asking questions until an answer is satisfactory.

I am no biblical scholar by any means. I just enjoy exploring and talking about the scriptures. My thoughts and conclusions do not represent any official view of The Church of Jesus Christ of Latter-day Saints and I reserve the right to change my opinion or my thoughts at any time in the future.

As my sons grew into men, the recordings became very popular with missionaries. I received hundreds of letters and tens of thousands of visits to my website. However, many requested my thoughts in a written form.

The lure of being a published author seems glamorous and important; a worthy dream and goal. However, the difference between the spoken word and written is mystifying and making that transition took much more effort than I expected. My concentration had to wrangle the stream-of-consciousness, off-the-hip original scripts into a readable manuscript for a book.

My wife Jane is a remarkable mother and the love of my life, and I want to be a husband of whom she can be proud. The book you hold in your hands was inspired by our sons, but is dedicated to the mother who carried them.

John Samuel Pennington Jr.

CONTENTS

	Acknowledgments	i
1	What about the Boy in China?	1
2	Why Was There a War in Heaven?	17
3	The Solar System & the Scriptures	29
4	Why Was the Priesthood Restricted?	51
5	What Happened to the Apostles?	67
6	Secret Names of Angels	87
7	Why Do Christians Celebrate Halloween?	103
8	Atheists, Agnostics & Anti-Mormons	117
9	Who Created Satan?	137
10	God's Multiple Methods of Communication	155
11	Do You Really Want the Truth?	173
12	Was Adam Set Up To Fail?	195
13	Evolution vs. Creation	217
14	Joseph Smith's Greatest Speech	241
	About the Author	261

ACKNOWLEDGMENTS

The editing and formation of a book like this is an immense amount of work. The following people need to be recognized for their insights, acute understanding of the written word and knowledge of the scriptures. They truly added quality and detail, for the publication of this book.

Teresa Jane Pennington
John Stephen Pennington
Carol Ann Ewing
Rebecca Lynn Ewing
Elizabeth Drake-Boyt

CHAPTER 1
WHAT ABOUT THE BOY IN CHINA?

If a boy lives in China and never hears about Jesus Christ, then how can he be saved? If everyone must be baptized to go to heaven, then what about the boy in China? This is the question I asked my pastor when I was nine years old and a member of a Protestant church. I asked my pastor about people in China who have never been baptized. He looked into my twinkly-young eyes and said, "The boy in China is in God's hands." That was all he said. I respected him and I accepted his answer. However, this simplistic approach gnawed at me.

A few years later when I was fourteen, I cornered him in his office and asked him again about the boy in China, but it went a little more like this: "Listen, I believe that Jesus is the Christ and I believe that everyone has to be baptized to go to heaven. However, I have a hard time believing that there are children in China or Mongolia who will live, die and never even hear of Jesus. If everyone has to be baptized in order to go to heaven, then is that fair to a boy in China who never had the chance to hear Jesus Christ's name?"

My religious leader looked at me and said, "I don't know, but I do know they are in God's care and He has a plan for them." My pastor was one of the most righteous men I ever knew, and I respected him a great deal. This time, I reluctantly accepted his answer, because I knew that they were God's children. Even though I accepted his answer, I still yearned to understand His plan for them.

Years passed and I couldn't let my question go. I visited other faiths and I asked the same question. Those pastors, teachers, deacons, rabbis and elders all had pretty good answers, but none—not a single one—completely answered my question. There were classmates and friends of the Mormon faith who wanted to help me in my quest and they sent missionaries to teach me. By the time I sat down with Elder Sandbakken and Elder Stakkeland, I had a list of questions ready for them. I could articulate my dilemma with precision and also how the answers I'd been given so far were not completely reconciled in my mind and heart. I was living in Las Vegas, Nevada when the Mormon Elders came to my home each week and taught me the gospel over about a three-month period of time. To my angst regarding the boy in China, this is how they responded: "First we are going to tell you the end of the story and then go back and fill in the blanks." "Great. Go for it, whatever you need to do," I said.

They then handed me a book and said, "Read this verse."

So, I read:

> I knew a man in Christ above fourteen years ago, (whether in the body, I cannot tell; or whether out of the body, I cannot tell: God knoweth;) such an one caught up to the **third heaven**.   *2 Corinthians 12:2*

I then said out loud, "What third heaven?" I closed the book to look at the cover; to my amazement, it was the King James Version of the Bible, the same book I had been reading my whole life. I had never read, nor had anyone ever told me about a "third heaven." I read it again to make sure I had read it correctly, but there it was—staring right back at me in black and white. Astonished, I said to the missionaries, "Are you guys trying to tell me that there are three heavens?" And they said (as all good missionaries say), "We are not telling you that there is a third heaven, the Bible is telling you that there is a third heaven." My reply was, "Oh, yeah. I'd just read it and that is what the Bible says. OK. Got it."

Then they said to me, "Once you realize that there is a third heaven, you'll start finding threes in the Bible, or three different states of existence, or three levels of things." They turned to First Corinthians and handed the Bible back to me. So, I read:

> There are also celestial bodies, and bodies terrestrial: but the glory of the celestial is one, and the glory of the terrestrial is another. There is one glory of the sun, and another glory of the moon, and another glory of the stars: for one star differeth from another star in glory. So also is the resurrection of the dead...
> *1 Corinthians 15:40-43*

The missionaries said, "Did you get that?" "Get what?" I was a little slow to catch on. "So also is the resurrection of the dead." There are three different types of glory in the resurrection: the sun, the moon, and the stars. I said, "Are you guys saying that we can have three different types of bodies in the resurrection?" And they said (as all good missionaries say), "We are not telling you that there are three degrees of glory in the resurrection, the Bible is telling you that there are three degrees of glory in the resurrection." "Oh, yeah. Right, I just read it directly from the Bible, got it!"

This is the method of teaching they used and I really enjoyed it. It was fun and I looked forward to our discussions each week as I learned about Christ and His gospel. They explained that this scripture in First Corinthians is talking about bodies and how, in the resurrection, some bodies will have a heavenly glory as bright as the sun, others will have a glory or a light as soft as the moon, while still others will twinkle like a star. Even the brightness of a star is a small glory, it still has some brightness.

Right then and there, I knew that I wanted a glory like the sun; whatever that is, or whatever it means, it sounds a lot better than the brightness of the stars. However, the most important point in this scripture is that it makes three distinctions of the magnitude of light that is possible for resurrected bodies to have. I had always wondered about heavenly messengers, those angels or beings described in the Bible and where their light came from. For example:

<u>Revelation 19:17</u> describes an angel who stood in the sun.

<u>Revelation 1:16</u> refers to one whose countenance was as the sun.

<u>Matthew 17:2</u> says that an angel's face shone like the sun.

<u>Revelation 12:1</u> states that a woman was clothed with the sun.

<u>Revelation 22:5</u> says that the people needed no light because God and Christ giveth light.

When I grasped the concept from First Corinthians that resurrected bodies could have glory likened to the sun, the images finally synced together, and the other scriptures now made perfect sense.

The missionaries then said: "Ok, that is a glimpse of the ending of the story. Now let's define what or where heaven is: heaven is where God the Father is, or where God the Father resides. Can we agree on that point?" "Yes," I nodded, because that definition to me was fundamental to the core.

They continued and recounted the story of the thief on the cross. They explained that when Jesus was crucified, two men were crucified along with him, both convicted of theft. While Jesus was on the cross at Calvary He spoke with one of the dying thieves, who accepted Him as Christ.

> And Jesus said unto him, Verily I say unto thee, To day shalt thou be with me in paradise. *Luke 23:43*

Perhaps this is why some people believe in deathbed repentance, or the belief that someone can be a thief their whole life and then the moment before they die they can say that they believe in Jesus as Christ and then go to heaven. They think that's all there is to it. This scripture does assure us that the thief did go to paradise with Jesus that day. Yet, the scripture also indicates that paradise and heaven are not the same place. Your spirit exists, even without a body. Once you die, while the body awaits resurrection, your spirit will go to "paradise" or to "spirit prison."

> For Christ also hath once suffered for sins, the just for the unjust, that he might bring us to God, being put to death in the flesh, but quickened by the Spirit: By which also he went and preached unto the **spirits in prison**;
> *1 Peter 3:18-19*

Christ went and preached to the spirits in prison. The Apostle, St. Peter tells us that the gospel was preached to the dead.

> For for *[sic]* this cause was the **gospel preached also to them that are dead**, that they might be judged according to men in the flesh, but live according to God in the spirit. *1 Peter 4:6*

If the boy in China dies without hearing about the gospel, St. Peter says that he will hear the gospel while he is dead and while his spirit is waiting in spirit prison. Prior to resurrection, he will learn about Christ, the plan of salvation and the commandments. This scripture quickened my spirit! God is fair! Hence the boy in China who had never heard the name Jesus Christ in his entire lifetime will learn about Christ in spirit prison. St. Peter says that Christ went there and taught, but it begs the question of when? When did Christ do this?

Here is why I think paradise, spirit prison and heaven are three distinct places: on the morning of the resurrection, the first person to see the resurrected Christ was Mary. When she realized it was her Lord, she reached to embrace Him, and Jesus said,
> Touch me not; for I am not yet ascended to my Father:
> *John 20:17*

We learn from these scriptures that before Jesus Christ died, He told the thief that they were going to paradise that day. Jesus can't tell a lie, so they did go to paradise that very day. However, three days later Jesus said that He had not been to His Father yet. Jesus went somewhere in the spirit called paradise, where His Father was not. Then on the third day, when He was resurrected, Jesus told Mary that He had to go to His Father before she could touch Him. This is a logical sequence of events and it feels right to my soul. Therefore, heaven is where God is, while paradise and spirit prison are where spirits go, prior to their resurrection. Later that day, Jesus appeared to the apostles and they touched His wounded hands and feet. Therefore, Jesus had to have seen His Father prior to this event.

It is worth noting that Jesus instructed Mary, the first person to see Him alive again, to go and tell the apostles about His impending resurrection. Therefore, the first missionary of the resurrected Jesus Christ was a woman!

Grace, Faith and Good Works

One issue in the plan of salvation is the question of faith versus works. Another is that people read the Bible and conclude that everyone is saved by grace. But others add that you must have good works, in addition to grace and faith. It has been a big debate for thousands of years and, lo and behold, I am about to answer it for you. Yes, I am going to solve the debate once and for all. The answer is that all three; grace, faith and good works, are true doctrines. The problem is that students of the Bible continue to confuse three distinct events as they read the scriptures regarding grace, faith and good works. If you will use these three things as described in multiple scriptures and correlate them directly to three events, it is easier to understand.

- The first event is— being resurrected:
(relate this event to **grace**).
- The second event is— getting into heaven:
(relate this event to **faith**).
- The third event is— receiving a body like unto the sun after a person is in heaven:
(relate this event to **good works**).

The Book of Ephesians says that you are saved by grace.

> Even when we were dead in sins, hath quickened us together with Christ, (by grace ye are saved;) And hath raised us up together, and made us sit together in heavenly places in Christ Jesus: That in the ages to come he might shew the exceeding riches of his grace in his kindness toward us through Christ Jesus. For by grace are ye saved through faith; and that not of yourselves: it is the gift of God: Not of works, lest any man should boast. For we are his workmanship, created in Christ Jesus unto good works, which God hath before ordained that we should walk in them. *Ephesians 2:5-10*

Good works cannot save you; otherwise, a person could claim that he had saved himself and did not need Jesus Christ. Ephesians is crystal clear in stating that none of your personal efforts can save you. It's not about works, period. Yet, Second Corinthians says that you will be judged for your works.

> For we must all appear before the judgment seat of Christ; that every one may receive the things done in his

> body, according to that he hath done, whether it be good or bad. *2 Corinthians 5:10*

One scripture says that all you have to do is believe and you will be saved by the grace of God. The other one says you will be judged for your works. Let's read another.

> And I saw the dead, small and great, stand before God; and the books were opened: and another book was opened, which is the book of life: and the dead were judged out of those things which were written in the books, according to their works. And the sea gave up the dead which were in it; and death and hell delivered up the dead which were in them: and they were judged every man according to their works.
> *Revelation 20:12-13*

Grace, faith and good works are all true principles of Jesus, but how do they fit together? The principles appear to compete against one another on the surface, and this apparent competition seems to be a paradox. This plan was all laid out way, way back in the beginning. God and Jesus have it all handled and it makes perfect sense when you think it through and remember the three distinct, separate stages. Grace means that no matter what you do, you will receive a gift.

> Marvel not at this: for the hour is coming, in the which all that are in the graves shall hear his voice, And shall come forth; they that have done good, unto the resurrection of life; and they that have done evil, unto the resurrection of damnation. *John 5:28-29*

> And have hope toward God, which they themselves also allow, that there shall be a resurrection of the dead, both of the just and unjust. *Acts 24:15*

Every person—the evil ones, the good ones, those who have done evil and those who have done good, those who are just and those who are unjust—all will receive the gift of resurrection. We cannot refuse to be resurrected even if we do not want to be. It is a gift for the unjust and the just, and exemplifies the word "grace." Everyone will be saved from the bonds of death through grace. It is a gift from Jesus and by His grace He gives an incredible afterlife. The scriptures say that the resurrection is for both the just and the unjust. Saints are resurrected, but it has nothing to do with their good works. By this reasoning, even Adolf Hitler will be resurrected, even though he ordered the killing of many people. Christ has an incredible love for each person on the earth. I do not fully understand how He can love some of the most evil people on this planet, but He does. That is why He is the Christ. Grace saves every single person from death. It is a true gift and therefore, it is true grace. This is a true definition of grace.

I said to the missionaries, "Wait a minute! Wait one minute! Are you saying everyone who is resurrected gets to go to heaven?" "No," they said, "but you are helping us make our point. Remember, the resurrection and going to heaven are not the same event. Some of us who read the Bible have used the word <u>saved</u> loosely. The writers of the Books of Acts and of John have described the resurrection as a gift; therefore being saved from death is a gift." Being saved from death is one thing and going to heaven is another. These are two separate events. Once you are saved from death in the resurrection by grace, then you get the chance to go to heaven. Going to heaven is also by grace, but you must have one other thing; faith to be born again. You must be born again of the water and the spirit. You must have faith in Christ and show that faith by being baptized. The rebirth from baptism is in recognition of what Jesus has done for you, and it is a plea to be cleansed by Him so that you can be in the presence of the Most High God, your Father in Heaven, the Father of your spirit. It is your promise to try to do your best and be your best.

No matter what obstacles you face, or joys you experience, you are promising to recognize God and Christ in all things. You do not have to actually complete any good works to get into heaven. You just have to keep trying. This is God's grace along with your faith that saves you and allows you to be admitted into heaven. To go to heaven, you must receive the grace of God and have faith in His Son, Jesus Christ. If we wish to go to heaven, we must accept Jesus as our Savior, be baptized, and then just try and try and try again. Everyone knows that we will fail repeatedly. Nothing we can actually complete on this earth can get us into heaven. All Christ wants to know is: will you keep trying? Will you? No matter what is placed before you in this life, will you continue to try to follow Christ? Even after you sin? The fact that you keep trying, this fact alone, shows and proves that you have faith in Jesus and you will never give up trying. That is the faith that saves you enough to enter heaven.

The next step is to recognize what Jesus has done for you and ask Him to cleanse you so that you can be in the presence of the Most High God, your Father in Heaven, the Father of your spirit. All Jesus Christ wants to know is that you are going to try. When you are baptized, you are NOT saying you are perfect, but by being born again, you will strive to keep the commandments and have your faith indicate that your commitment to Christ is solid. As long as you continue to try, Christ will keep cleansing you, because His love for you is infinite. This is how you get into heaven. Using God's grace and your faith.

In the Book of John we learn of a man named Nicodemus, a Pharisee and a high-ranking religious official, who sneaks away one night to see Jesus and ask Him what he must do to go to heaven. The Savior told Nicodemus that he must be born again to see the kingdom of God.

"What do you mean be born again?" Nicodemus asked. "Do I have to go back inside my mother's womb a second time?" And Jesus answered;

> Verily, verily, I say unto thee, Except a man be born of water and of the Spirit, he cannot enter into the kingdom of God.　　　　　　　　　　*John 3:5*

Baptism is essential to entering the kingdom of God. What about that boy in China? He will not know of Jesus Christ. He will not be baptized. How can he possibly enter the kingdom of God? I believe that baptism is a specific, physical ordinance that one must complete to enter the kingdom of God. I realize that this appears to be a paradox, and further begs the question: if you must be baptized, then what about the billions of people who didn't even have a chance to be baptized? That doesn't seem fair, and I can't believe in a God that's not fair. The Apostle Paul answered this question in writing to the Corinthians who for some reason had stopped believing in the resurrection.

> Else what shall they do which are baptized for the dead, if the dead rise not at all? why *[sic]* are they then **baptized for the dead**?　　　　　　*1 Corinthians 15:29*

Baptisms for the dead? In the Bible? We just read it. The people of Corinth were baptizing, by proxy, for their deceased ancestors. If no person is ever going to rise in the resurrection, then why are you doing baptisms for the dead? The Apostle Paul is using logic, and the actions of the people of Corinth, to show them that they would not be doing baptisms for the dead unless the resurrection was real. St. Paul is not asking the people of Corinth *why* they are baptizing for the dead, he's asking why they have stopped believing in the resurrection. Let's read it one more time:

> Else what shall they do which are baptized for the dead, if the dead rise not at all? why [sic] are they then baptized for the dead?　　　　　　　*1 Corinthians 15:29*

Clearly, the dead are going to rise in the resurrection. The boy in China, after being taught about Christ in spirit prison, will have the opportunity to either accept his baptism by proxy, or reject it. It is his decision, but the baptism will be provided for him even if he does not want it. Performing baptisms for those who never had the chance to be baptized is pure loving charity and a demonstration of the true love of Jesus Christ. Whenever you do something for someone that they cannot do for themselves, you are being charitable. The Church of Jesus Christ of Latter-day Saints performs baptisms for those who have passed on and who are having the chance to learn about Christ in either paradise or spirit prison. They can receive the proxy baptism and accept Christ before the day of judgment.

Let us review:

- The first event: Resurrection is given to us by God's grace, no matter what. It is a gift, and we are saved from death by grace.

- The second event: Getting into heaven is a gift from Jesus, also by His grace; plus we need faith, accept Him as our Savior, be baptized, and acknowledge that we will try to follow His teachings, even though we will always come up short.

- The third event: Once you are in heaven, then you are judged for your works, and could possibly get a glory like unto the sun.

This is where the good works come into play. Completing good works does not get you into heaven, but once you are in, they give you certain privileges.

Let me clear something up that many people forget. God will NOT be your judge. God the Father, the Most High God, the Father of your spirit, will not judge you for any of your works.

> For the Father judgeth no man, but hath committed all judgment unto the Son: *John 5:22*

If we keep trying, and are born again, and find ourselves in heaven, then for what purpose are we judged?

The Book of Matthew, Chapter 25 starting in Verse 14 describes a lord who gave one of his servants five talents; another of his servants two talents and one talent to the last servant. When the lord returned after being away, the servant who had turned his five talents into ten talents, the lord made him a ruler over many things. Likewise, the servant who doubled his two talents was promoted to a ruler over many things. However, the last servant was cast aside by his angry lord, for he had hidden his lone talent and returned it to his lord, unused and un-grown. In this parable, we learn that completing good works with your talents will enable you to grow and become something more than you were when you started. As you grow in good works, you naturally earn greater dominion and become a ruler of sorts. The more your talents increase, the more things you control and rule. When you start to play the piano, you are not the ruler of the piano. But after years of practice, you become the ruler of the piano and control the quality of the sound it can and will produce. In this same manner, good works will allow you to receive a body like the brightness of the sun and the Lord will make you a ruler in His kingdom. He will be pleased with what you did with your talents here on earth. This is one way that you are judged for your works, but it occurs after you get into heaven. Works are not a prerequisite for admission.

> In my Father's house are many mansions: if it were not so, I would have told you. I go to prepare a place for you.   *John 14:2*

Sometimes Mormons draw the three heavens on a chalkboard and make the mistake of saying that there is a "top" part of heaven, as if it is in a different physical location. This is not correct and is an easy mistake to make, as I have made this mistake many times in the past. Here is an analogy that makes sense of this.

Heaven is like a football field and God is like the head coach. There is the quarterback, the linemen and the second-string players. The quarterback has more responsibilities and therefore spends much more time with the coach than do the linemen or the second-string players. The second-string players can walk over to the coach and receive instruction from him at any time. They are all on the same playing field. But the quarterback is going to spend more time with the coach because he has proven he can handle the most responsibility. He was not given the job as quarterback, but he earned it by throwing a hundred passes each day all summer long. He was lifting weights and running three miles in the hot sun when other potential players were watching TV at home or on their summer vacation.

For example, Mother Teresa completed many good works on earth that will enable her to have a greater glory like the sun after she arrives in heaven. Therefore, there is no "top" part of a football field, only different levels of occupations or jobs. In like manner, there is no "top" part of heaven. Each person in heaven lives with God on the same field. Only some people in heaven have more responsibilities and therefore rule over many things. They received this status because they were the ones who actually proved that they can take five talents and turn them into ten by completing good works. The great thing about the parable of the talents is that even the servant with two talents, who turned them into four, received the same status as the servant who ended up with ten talents. God does not care what you are right now, He only wants to know what you can become. Can you double what you have right now? If you can, you will be a ruler over many things. Therefore, your "mansion" in heaven, once you are in heaven, is determined by your good completed works.

After studying the scriptures with the Mormon missionaries, this all made sense, and all of these references came from the

Bible. Before I knew much about the Latter-day Saints, I thought that Mormons did not really believe in the Bible, yet I learned things from the Bible and from the elders, that no one had ever even come close to teaching me before. I learned that:

- There is a third heaven.

- There are three different kinds of glory in the resurrection.

- Paradise and heaven are not the same place.

- The Apostle Peter told of a spirit world where Christ taught those who were dead.

- Baptism for the dead was practiced by the people of Corinth.

- I will be judged for my works here on earth.

- A woman was the first missionary of the resurrected Jesus Christ.

Finally after years of searching, I understood how a boy in China could accept Christ before judgment day and then become saved with grace by resurrection. He can then enter into heaven, with God's grace and faith in Jesus and even, perhaps, have a glory like the sun. The message was sweet music to my soul and it was right out of the Bible. I had just never put it together. This plan of salvation is for all men, women, children and almost all spirit children of the Most High God. It answered my question to the fullest, and I was very grateful.

Many years later, after I had committed my life to Jesus Christ, my oldest son was called to serve a mission and learn Mandarin Chinese so that he could spend two years teaching the Gospel of Jesus Christ to the Chinese in their native tongue. Near the end of his mission, I flew to see him. His name is John Stephen Pennington; the sixth John Pennington in my lineage. This trip allowed me to visit some of the Chinese people to whom he had taught the gospel and who had been baptized. One man in particular said something that really brought this whole subject home. We sat with this Chinese man and his family as he and my son conversed in Mandarin. Then the man turned and looked straight at me and in terribly broken English, with a heavy Chinese accent he said, "Mr. Pennington, your son is a very, very good man, and before I found the gospel I was nothing. I was not Christian, I was not Buddhist. I was nothing. And now that I am a follower of Jesus Christ, I am something." This sentence took a minute or two to utter as my son coached him with the correct English words to use, but I finally understood. My concern about the boy in China, which I had posed to my pastor so many years before, was finally, completely, satisfyingly answered. My answer was that you, me, everyone, and especially my sons, are going to teach all of China, and everyone else in the world, and also in the world of spirits, about Jesus Christ. WOW. It took thirty-seven years, but God answered my question and my prayer to the fullest. The Chinese man, who was close to my age and a boy living in China at the time when I first asked my pastor, "What about the boy in China?" was eventually taught the gospel of Jesus Christ and baptized by my son.

The Mormons showed me the answer to my question.

Had this plan of salvation ended there, I believe that I would have been content my whole life. However, the story became deeper and more interesting as I continued my study with the missionaries over the next few months. The concept from the Apostle Peter that your spirit and your body are two separate things, and that just because your body is in the grave does not mean that your spirit is also dead was an eye-opening scripture that resonated in my mind for weeks. But as I learned later, God's plan was much, much bigger and more complete than I had ever imagined.

CHAPTER 2
WHY WAS THERE A WAR IN HEAVEN?

The Mormon elders told me about several things supported by biblical scripture: a third heaven in 2 Corinthians 12:2; the three glories of the resurrection in 1 Corinthians 15:40-43; about baptisms for the dead in 1 Corinthians 15:29 and the spirit world supported by 1 Peter 4:6. I read those scriptures over and over to know for myself that I was reading them correctly. A few weeks later, the missionaries came back and finished the story. True to form, they finally told me the beginning of the story, but they told it last. They said that my spirit is a creation of God and had been organized and existed long before I was born. As you can imagine, this was a new concept that I had not considered before in my prior studies of the Bible.

We had a pre-earth existence.

They also told me that Jesus' spirit existed before He was born on this earth, which I already believed. However, the concept that our spirits exist prior to birth caused me to view myself, Jesus and the plan of salvation, from a new perspective. Before I was born, I was a spirit-child of our Heavenly Father. Here are some scriptures to verify this point. In the first one, God speaks directly to Jeremiah.

> Before I formed thee in the belly I knew thee; and before thou camest forth out of the womb I sanctified thee, and I ordained thee a prophet unto the nations.
> *Jeremiah 1:5*

The Book of Acts goes further:

> Forasmuch then as we are the offspring of God, we ought not to think that the Godhead is like unto gold, or silver, or stone, graven by art and man's device.
> *Acts 17:29*

If we are God's offspring, then God is our Father. He's not made of gold or silver or of stone. He's probably going to have the same image as you and me, not exactly alike, but close. That is why the Bible uses the word "image" to relay a concept. The Book of Hebrews tells us that God is the Father of our spirits;

> Furthermore we have had fathers of our flesh which corrected us, and we gave them reverence: shall we not much rather be in subjection unto the Father of spirits, and live?
> *Hebrews 12:9*

In the next verse Jesus Christ is talking directly to His Father;

> And now, O Father, glorify thou me with thine own self with the glory which I had with thee before the world was.
> *John 17:5*

Jesus Christ says here that before the world was, He had glory with the Father. He is acknowledging that He existed before the world was created!

This next verse is a key scripture, talking about when the disciples met a blind man.

> And his disciples asked him, saying, Master, who did sin, this man, or his parents, that he was born blind?
>
> *John 9:2*

The key point here is that the disciples are asking Jesus if this man sinned before he was born, assuming it was a punishment and implying that the sin would have occurred before birth. The Master didn't correct them by asking what they meant, nor did He correct their assumption or implication; thus, the blind man must have existed in some fashion before he was born.

Jesus created everything under God's plan

The missionaries also told me that God the Father did not actually create the world, but gave Jesus the plan and allowed Jesus to create the world. What? As you can imagine, this concept was foreign to my mind. Here are two scriptures to clarify the statement.

> And to make all men see what is the fellowship of the mystery, which from the beginning of the world hath been hid in God, **who created all things by Jesus Christ**:
>
> *Ephesians 3:9*

Jesus had to have been with God, in the beginning, before the world was made.

> God, who at sundry times and in divers manners spake in time past unto the fathers by the prophets, Hath in these last days spoken unto us by his Son, whom he hath appointed heir of all things, by **whom also he made the worlds**; *Hebrews 1:1-2*

Who is it that made the worlds? The Son. Who is the heir of all things? Jesus Christ. Who made the world under the direction of the Father? The Son of the Most High God. The Bible says that the Son made the worlds, not the Father. Wow! God created all things, but He did it through His Son Jesus Christ.

The Book of Genesis talks about the body of Adam, and how God placed cherubim and a flaming sword in front of the Tree of Life, because if Adam ate of the Tree of Life he'd live forever in his body. This raises another presumption, that it is possible for Adam's body to last forever. How can that be? How can Adam's body have the power to be eternal with his spirit? The answer is, because his body was made in the image of "us." What, or who, is "us?"

> And the Lord God said, Behold, the man is become as one of **us**, to know good and evil: and now, lest he put forth his hand, and take also of the tree of life, and eat, and live for ever: *Genesis 3:22*

It appears that other beings are present with God when He created Adam's body.

> And God said, Let **us** make man in **our** image, after **our** likeness... *Genesis 1:26*

Who is God talking to? If God is in the beginning of creation and no one is there with Him, then why does He use the terms "us" and "our?" From John 17:5 we learned that Jesus had glory before the world was; therefore, He is probably included within the term "us." I assume the Holy Ghost was also there and is part of the "us" referred to in Genesis. The point is, if God is using the words "us" and "our," God is not talking to Himself.

We know that Adam is made in the image of God. Some Bible-based faiths do not believe this even though it is written in the very first chapters of the Bible. God was not alone when the creation of this earth began, and He, along with "us" (including Jesus) created a man who looked something like Himself, in His own image. The missionaries said that before the earth was created, God the Father was there, along with Jesus. All of our spirits were there too. God, the Father of our spirits, basically said that we were His spirit children and we had progressed as much as possible as spirits. To further our knowledge and understanding, He had a plan to create and populate an earth so that each spirit could grow, progress and have experiences in a body. All of His spirit children would have an existence that heretofore had been impossible. The Father laid out the plan of this earth, but His Son, Jesus Christ, fulfills that plan by building, governing, and eventually living on this earth Himself and by taking on a body of flesh-and-blood. The Son would cleanse the earth in the Garden of Gethsemane and on the cross. He would break the bonds of death and be resurrected. He would provide a learning opportunity to each spirit child of God, about the plan, before the great judgment day, at which Christ would be the judge.

Lucifer - First Estate - War in Heaven

God's plan had risks, but God knew it was the only way for His spirit children to gain valuable experience and learn to have dominion over their bodies. This plan was embraced by most of God's spirit children, but an angel named Lucifer, "a son of the morning", did not like the Father's plan. He presented a competing plan and was expelled, along with his followers, a third part of the hosts of heaven, from heaven, by a mighty angel named Michael. This pre-earth existence is called the first estate and the war in heaven.

> And the angels which kept not their **first estate**, but left their own habitation, he hath reserved in everlasting chains under darkness unto the judgment of the great day. *Jude 1:6*
>
> Raging waves of the sea, foaming out their own shame; **wandering stars**, to whom is reserved the blackness of darkness for ever. *Jude 1:13*

In Verse 6 of St. Jude, there are angels that kept not their first estate, and in Verse 13, wandering stars will have, "everlasting chains under darkness unto the judgment of the great day." The wandering stars are the spirits who were in that third part of heaven who aligned themselves with Lucifer. Who are these wandering stars or wandering angels and why did they not keep their first estate? The Book of Revelation talks about a war in heaven, and about Satan.

> And his tail drew the **third part** of the stars of heaven, and did cast them to the earth... *Revelation 12:4*

> And there was war in heaven: Michael and his angels fought against the dragon; and the dragon fought and his angels. *Revelation 12:7*

> And the great dragon was cast out, that old serpent, called the Devil, and Satan, which deceiveth the whole world: he was cast out into the earth, and his angels were cast out with him. *Revelation 12:9*

These wandering stars were the third part of heaven cast out with Satan (the Dragon) and they fought against Michael and his angels. Satan and his angels lost the war in heaven and were cast out into the earth.

When was this war? If we use the logical sequence of events, the first time we ever hear about Satan is in Genesis, when he is in the Garden of Eden tempting Adam and Eve. Thus, the war must have happened before the Garden of Eden because the Bible says that Satan was cast unto the earth with his angels. So, he is on earth, in the Garden of Eden, and how many angels were there with Satan? A third part! There were a bunch of them, and they each wanted a body but they did not keep their first estate.

Our pre-earth life or pre-mortal existence is referred to as the first estate. That first estate is, in essence, the initial spirit state of being. It is not physical. In His divine wisdom, God saw that the spirits had grown as much as possible. His plan was to create an earth where our spirits could live in a physical form; to walk the earth in a human body; to experience life as we know it and to grow in capacity and dominion.

Satan didn't like that plan for some reason; he proposed an alternative that would not allow people to choose for themselves and not allow them to sin. He promised that all people would go to heaven and that he, Satan, would retain all the glory for doing it and not give any glory to the Father. In contrast, Jesus Christ committed to fulfilling the Father's plan and would give all glory to the Father.

Lucifer's followers rebelled, and were kicked out of heaven and those followers did not receive physical bodies. Surely they felt cheated, for physicality is a privilege on the earth.

The Third Part of Heaven Who Lost the War (The Losers)

This next story illustrates the desperation of the fallen angel spirits and how badly they wanted their own bodies. In the Book of Mark there is a man who had been bound with chains and no one could tame him. He wandered among the tombs and mountains, cut himself with stones and wailed. However, something interesting happened when he saw Jesus from "afar off." The man ran to Jesus and began to worship him, crying with a loud voice;

> What have I to do with thee, Jesus, thou Son of the most high God?   *Mark 5:7*

The first question that comes to mind is: how could the man identify Jesus from "afar off?" The second question is: why did he so quickly capitulate to Jesus' will, by asking, "What have I to do with thee?"
Think about what is happening here. The Book of Mark wants to explain that this man is a wild person, who is crazy and cannot be bound or tamed, but as soon as he sees Jesus, suddenly now he can focus, ask coherent questions and refer to the person he is talking to by their name. He not only knows Jesus's name but also His proper title as the Son of the most

High God (The Book of Mark is certainly making a point). In addition, the wild man also knows that Jesus is going to deal with him (them) and there is very little he (they) can do to resist the commands of Jesus. Thus, the question; "What have I to do with the?" Or another way of saying it is; What are you going to do with me? Maybe they knew what Jesus was going to do to them, just like a small child knows when he is going to be punished, after he has done something wrong.

Because this man knows so much about Jesus, then Jesus would have logically wanted to know when they had met before. To try to identify who Jesus is talking to, the first thing Jesus did was ask him a question. Jesus asked him;

> What is thy name? And he answered, saying, My name is Legion: for we are many. *Mark 5:9*

The man was unable to produce a proper name for himself. There were many unclean spirits lurking within him.

A good shepherd knows each of his sheep. However, Jesus's sheep are not the third part of heaven who lost the war. When Jesus ascertains that these spirits were not his sheep he then has to deal with them in a swift and absolute manner. Jesus understood that He could not allow these fallen, first-estate spirits to reside in the man's physical body. Thus, He commanded all of those spirits, named Legion, to exit the man's body.

How did those spirits know who Jesus was from far away? The answer is simple if you just think in a logical sequence of events. They knew Jesus from the first estate. They were the losers of the war in heaven, the **wandering fallen angels**, who, through their own rebellion, had been denied a life inside of a human body.

How do we know they wanted bodies? Because Legion, (many spirits), asked Jesus to allow them, after they leave the human

man's body, to inhabit a herd of swine that were over on the hillside. Their longing and desperation for a physical form was so fierce that they were willing to live inside the bodies of pigs. Jesus must have laughed to Himself, for He surely knew what was going to happen. He knew the physical body of a pig couldn't handle a spirit designed to occupy a human body built in the image of God. So, Jesus granted their request, and all of the Legion spirits came out and entered the pigs, causing the pigs to go into a crazed rage. In the Book of Mark, we read that approximately two thousand pigs ran violently down the mountain and into the sea, drowning in the water. Therefore, we learn that the Legion of spirits must, again, vacate these physical forms also. I can just imagine Jesus walking away, shaking His head, and chuckling. It probably was a very humorous event.

Enmity between the seed of Satan and the seed of Eve.

We can therefore assume from this story that Satan was desperate to obtain physical bodies for his spirit followers; an action that would place himself on an even level with God in the eyes of his followers. In the Garden of Eden Satan was trying to get physical bodies for his followers. This could be why God, in the Garden of Eden, had to put enmity between the seed of Satan and the seed of Eve.

> And I will put enmity between thee and the woman, and between thy seed and her seed... *Genesis 3:15*

This enmity was put in place to thwart Satan's attempts to circumvent God's original plan of salvation. Satan wanted physical bodies for his followers.

Winners of the War in Heaven Receive Physical Bodies.

Jesus Christ is fulfilling God's righteous plan to make sure that all the spirits who had the faith to follow Him will not only get human bodies, Christ also assures all mankind that they will receive a resurrected body, with a glory likened to the sun, or the moon, or the stars. The followers of God's plan are not lost and wandering stars. Instead, they are executing a grand plan of salvation which will enable them to receive an eternal, resurrected body. Why? And how? Especially, when some humans turn out to be evil and do very bad things? Why are evil people rewarded with a resurrected body by the grace of God? Why are they saved from the bonds of death with such a great reward?

Answer: Every person on this earth is a spirit child of the Most High God. When God presented His plan with Jesus to fulfill the plan, we all chose to follow Jesus, while believing and having faith that Jesus would complete the plan from start-to-finish. That means that Jesus would; (i) create a world using God the Father's blueprint, (ii) suffer for the world in the Garden of Gethsemane and on the cross, (iii) provide a resurrection for the world and (iv) also be the judge of the world.

> For the Father judgeth no man, but hath committed all judgment unto the Son: *John 5:22*

> For I came down from heaven, not to do mine own will, but the will of him that sent me. *John 6:38*

> I go unto the Father: for my Father is greater than I. *John 14:28*

The Most High God

Jesus says that His Father is greater than He is. This is why the Bible refers to God the Father, as the Most High God.

Genesis 14:18 says that Melchizedek, King of Salem was the priest of the Most High God.

Genesis 14:22 says Abraham lifts up his hand to the Most High God because He possesses the heaven and the earth.

Daniel 3:26 declares that Shadrach, Meshach and Abednego were servants of the Most High God.

Acts 16:17 states that the Apostle Paul was a servant of the Most High God who showed us the way of salvation.

This next scripture is very interesting to me:

> I have said, Ye are gods; and all of you are children of the most High. *Psalm 82:6*

This is why Acts 17:28-29 says that we are the offspring of God, and Romans 8:17 says that we are heirs of God and joint-heirs of Christ. Thus, we pray to the same being that Jesus Christ was praying to in the Garden of Gethsemane. We pray to God because all glory is unto Him. In the Garden of Gethsemane, Jesus prays to the Father:

> And he went a little further, and fell on his face, and prayed, saying, O my Father, if it be possible, let this cup pass from me: nevertheless not as I will, but as thou wilt. *Matthew 26:39*

As you can see, God answers "No" to the prayer of Jesus. Many of us sometimes feel sorry for ourselves when God says "no." This is why Jesus of Nazareth is the Savior of all mankind. He was not doing it for Himself. Doing things for others that they cannot do for themselves is the true love of Christ.

The Plan of Salvation is for the Winners of the War in Heaven.

The plan of salvation allows us to progress and grow our talents. We are given dominion over our bodies here on this earth, and what we do with them is going to determine what kind of resurrected body we will receive. Do you want to go to the third heaven like it says in 2 Corinthians 12:2? Do you want a body like the brightness of the sun? Then you must accept Christ and seek to grow your talents through good works.

Even the boy in China will, before the resurrection, have an opportunity to learn about Jesus Christ, the Garden of Gethsemane, the cross and the resurrection. He will be able to be born again through baptism. The entire world, with all the people who ever lived, have this chance to learn about Christ and have their baptism written in the Book of Life. Then Jesus will present the completed Book of Life to His Father for the record of all of His children who kept their first estate, and also kept their second estate, which is earth. Christ's program is called the commandments. If we continue to try to keep the commandments over a lifetime, they will teach us to learn to be in control, versus being out of control, and a slave to passions, which is an important lesson in our progression to become more Christ-like.

God gives us the chance on this earth to find out who we truly are and what we can become, by overcoming all obstacles in this life using our faith in Jesus Christ. God has helped me understand that <u>I need to continually pray to increase my love and understanding for those people who sin in a different manner than I do.</u> Thus, allowing me to become a brother instead of a judge.

Now, think about this; I am just a regular guy reading the Bible and trying to figure out the Creator of the entire universe. It seems like an impossible task; trying to understand the God who created the entire universe from a book that I can hold in my hand.

What I can tell you is that understanding this plan of salvation has, time and time again, given me peace. When I am down in life; when things aren't going well, I need only remember His plan, because it brings me joy and purpose. I don't think of—or dwell on—the bad things for long, because I know it is all part of God's plan. He put me in a body on this planet to do His work, to try and try again. I know Jesus is the Christ. I know God lives.

CHAPTER 3
THE SOLAR SYSTEM & THE SCRIPTURES

Many of my friends have fallen away from God, or their belief in God, because of science. I have Catholic friends, Protestant friends and Mormon friends who have allowed science to place a wedge between them and their belief in a deity. I have wondered; how can this be? Because in contrast, the more I learn about science and this incredible universe and how physical science applies to it, the more science amplifies my knowledge of the Master Architect who carefully laid out this exquisite place for us to inhabit. As my scientific understanding grows, so does my love for God. For me, science is God and God is science. This chapter is devoted to my friends who haven't yet seen God's hand in science.

Science attempts to answer how things happen, while religion tells us why things happen. When the two cross over and try to answer each other's questions, we become confused. However, I believe religion and science will align one day. I use analogies and philosophical comparisons to illuminate my points, and it may be a stretch, for some, to see the parallels. But I assure you that the focal point is always Jesus Christ and that everything in this universe can be used as a testament of Him.

Let's begin by comparing the stories of Christ, Adam, Eve and

Satan with the sun, earth, moon and Jupiter. I will compare Jesus Christ to the story of our sun; Adam to the planet earth, Eve to our moon, and Satan to the planet Jupiter.

Mormons believe that God the Father planned our entire existence and the creation of an earth, but that it was Jesus Christ who implemented the plan. This is an important distinction in the beliefs of Mormons and most other faiths.

> God, who at sundry times and in divers manners spake in time past unto the fathers by the prophets, Hath in these last days spoken unto us by his Son, whom he hath appointed heir of all things, by **whom also he made the worlds**; *Hebrews 1:1-2*

> And to make all men see what is the fellowship of the mystery, which from the beginning of the world hath been hid in God, **who created all things by Jesus Christ**. *Ephesians 3:9*

In the Book of Genesis, we learn that the plants, fowl, and beasts were all derived from the ground, and Adam was formed from the dust of the ground. Eve, in contrast, stemmed from a rib taken from the side of Adam. Eve's creation is the odd part of the story, for she doesn't come from the same substance. She is the anomaly, as her story is unique from the other creations in Genesis. Thus, Adam says in Genesis 2:23, that she is the "bone of my bones, flesh of my flesh."

Throughout history, all great storytellers and teachers use a pattern. Then once the pattern is established, they break from the pattern to direct our attention to a key principle. Consider the story of the Good Samaritan, in which an injured man on the side of the road is passed over first by a priest and then a Levite; neither of whom stop to help. Then a Samaritan comes upon him and stops to aid the injured man. This is the break from the pattern and the part where the storyteller refocuses our attention, enabling a resonation within our memory cells.

Using a pattern is also evident in the story of the talents in the Book of Mark, in which the master gave coins, or talents, to three men, then went away. When the master returned, he saw that two of the men doubled their talents, and the master was glad and made them rulers; thus, the pattern is set. But the third man had hidden his talent and did nothing with it, so the master became angry. When something is odd or out of place within a story, that is where you should focus your attention.

The Moon and Eve

Let's compare the story of Eve coming from the side of Adam to the early story of our solar system and the formation of our moon. The center of our solar system hosts the sun, which is made up of mostly hydrogen and helium. Circling the sun are ten orbiting celestial bodies, eight planets and two dwarf planets. The planets, starting closest to the sun are: Mercury, Venus, Earth, Mars, Jupiter, Saturn, Uranus, and Neptune. Beyond those are the two dwarf planets named Pluto and Eris. Eris is actually larger than Pluto and much more distant. This is easy to remember because everyone has ten fingers and ten toes.

> Note: Almost everyone has ten digits, however the giant Goliath in the Old Testament had a brother, also a giant, who had six fingers and six toes. That family just knew how to grow extra stuff, like height and even extra digits on their hands and feet. (*2 Samuel 21:20*)

Slip off your socks and shoes and look at your feet, beginning with your little toe on your left foot. Consider it the planet Mercury, then the toe a little bigger next to it is Venus, and the middle one is Earth. Mars is next, and then the big toe on your left foot is Jupiter. The big toe on your right foot is Saturn, then Uranus which is a little smaller and then Neptune, (smaller yet) Pluto and finally Eris represents your little toe on your right foot. The two largest planets in the solar system are Jupiter and Saturn correlating to your two big toes. The sizes of the ten orbiting bodies are almost in the correct order, relative to size, except that Mars is smaller than Earth and Pluto is smaller than Eris. God gave us all a map of the solar system right on our feet. These planets and dwarf planets all have moons. In fact, as the date of this writing, they have a total of 170 moons orbiting them and astronomers keep finding more. The only two planets that do not have a moon are the two closer to the sun than the earth. Mercury is a bachelor and Venus is a bachelorette, neither having a moon. Earth is the only planet that has just one moon, so the earth is the only planet with a monogamous relationship. All of the other planets have no moon at all, or have two or more moons. Our moon seems to have formed differently than all of the other celestial bodies in the solar system. Our moon is an anomaly defined as; anything that is two standard deviations away from the mean; something that is odd or not normal.

The predominate scientific theory is that our moon was formed from—or came from—the side of the earth. Our moon is too big, with too much mass, for the earth's gravitational pull to have captured it as it was floating by; it is simply too large relative to the size of the earth. Scientists believe that something very large crashed into the earth about 4.65 billion years ago and the energy from that crash turned everything into molten rock, a portion of which separated from the earth and started the earth spinning. Then the broken off part began to spin itself, cooling and rotating into a sphere to ultimately become our moon. That is the only way an earth-sized planet could have such a large moon and this is different from all other celestial bodies in the solar system. Remember what Adam said about Eve in Genesis 2:23: "bone of my bones, and flesh of my flesh." Genesis says that life on earth was made from the ground, or the dust of the ground, except for Eve; she is not created from the same material. Instead, Eve is created from the side of Adam. Genesis emphasizes the change in the pattern of the creation story by focusing on how Eve's creation is different from all of the others. In like manner, our moon came from the side of the earth and therefore, the moon was not created the same as the other celestial bodies in the solar system. The pattern changes with both stories for Eve and the moon. There is always something to learn from any shift in any story.

1. Both are made from the side of something else.

2. Both are not created like all other creations in their respective class.

Almost every scientist believes that our moon is essential to life on earth. The moon provides balance as the earth spins, pulling the tides to provide energy for the oceans and causing water to run over shallow lands. The moon protects the earth by attracting asteroids rather than allowing those asteroids to hit the earth. It is a protector of the earth and many scientific theories suppose that earthly life would not be possible if we did not have such a large moon in relative size to the earth. Compare this theory to Genesis, when Adam gives the woman the name of Eve:

> And Adam called his wife's name Eve; because she was the mother of all living.   *Genesis 3:20*

Sun, Earth, Moon Compared to Christ, Adam, Eve

Also, in the Garden of Eden, Eve eats the forbidden fruit first and then Adam eats the fruit so that both are punished by God. However, Eve's punishment is greater than Adam's.

In Genesis 3:16 we learn that Eve is subject unto Adam as he is a ruler over her, then Adam is punished by having to leave the presence of God in the Garden of Eden and must look for the Christ that is to come to redeem him and his posterity. Summary: Eve is subject to Adam and Adam is subject to Christ. Now compare that story with this: the moon's center of orbit is the earth and the earth's center of orbit is the sun. So the moon is subject to the earth and the earth is subject to the sun. These two companions, Adam and Eve, leave the Garden of Eden together and foster all human life throughout the world: just as the earth and moon, as companions, dance together through the cosmos, depending upon each other and working together to produce / maintain an environment that is teeming with life.

To do their work, the earth and moon must have the sun. There is no life on the sun, but the earth and its moon require the sun to foster life. These three spherical objects all work together by using their combined power permitting life to flourish. Without all three, we could not be here. In comparison, Adam and Eve need the Son of God for eternal life. These three combine their energies to generate humans with souls who will receive resurrected bodies. The story of the solar system parallels and points to Jesus Christ as the Savior of all mankind.

Jupiter Compared to Satan

We know that in the solar system there is one sun, eight planets, two dwarf planets and 170 known moons that total 181 celestial bodies (as of the date of this writing). But the largest orbiting body by far is Jupiter. Let us compare the story of Satan to the story of Jupiter. Satan wanted to be the Son of God; the Christ. He didn't want any other entity to be closer to God than he himself could get.

> And I, the Lord God, spake unto Moses, saying: That Satan, whom thou hast commanded in the name of mine Only Begotten, is the same which was from the beginning, and he came before me, saying—Behold, here am I, send me, I will be thy son, and I will redeem all mankind, that one soul shall not be lost, and surely I will do it; wherefore give me thine honor.   *Moses 4:1*

Satan wanted to be like the Son of God, or really, he wanted to be the Son of God. Now let us read where Satan came from:

> And this we saw also, and bear record, that an angel of God who was in authority in the presence of God, who rebelled against the Only Begotten Son whom the Father loved and who was in the bosom of the Father, was thrust down from the presence of God and the Son, And was called Perdition, for the heavens wept over him—he was Lucifer, a son of the morning. And we beheld, and lo, he is fallen! is [sic] fallen, even a son of the morning!   Doctrine and Covenants 76:25-27

Let's contrast the fall of Satan to the story of Jupiter, a gas giant that is the most dominate member of the solar system. Our sun is comprised of mostly hydrogen and some helium and Jupiter is mostly hydrogen with a bit more helium. Both have a very close element base. While similar to the sun, Jupiter is unique in that it has sixty-three moons! If Jupiter had gotten bigger and accumulated more mass, we would have a solar system inside of our solar system, a two-sun solar system. There are other solar systems in the Milky Way galaxy that have binary sun systems, but not ours, as we only have one sun. Jupiter had the same potential to become a sun, but just did not have enough stuff to get there. If Jupiter had been bigger, we would have two very bright objects in the sky that emit light; however Jupiter only reflects light from the sun.

The following is quoted from the National Aeronautics and Space Administration, or NASA website: "Jupiter is the most massive planet in our solar system; with four large moons and many smaller moons it forms a kind of miniature solar system. In fact, Jupiter resembles a star in composition, and if it had been about 80 times more massive, it would have become a star rather than a planet."

NASA is stating that Jupiter was on its way to becoming a sun with its own solar system. If you have ever tried to look directly at the sun, you know you can't. You can take a small glance and then you must look away, for the sun is so bright that you just cannot look at it straight on. However, Jupiter is bright in the sky, but not too much to gaze upon with the human eye. Contrast that fact with these verses in the Book of Moses. Moses is talking with Satan because Satan wants Moses to worship him.

> And it came to pass that Moses looked upon Satan and said: Who art thou? For behold, I am a son of God, in the similitude of his Only Begotten; and where is thy glory, that I should worship thee? For behold, I could not look upon God, except his glory should come upon me, and I were transfigured before him. But I can look upon thee in the natural man... *Moses 1:13-14*

1. God has too much glory to be looked upon with a human eye.
2. The sun is too bright in the sky to look at without some type of filter.

Here is where these two parallel stories get really interesting. Not counting the millions of asteroids, there are 181 celestial bodies in the solar system. Of those, Jupiter has sixty-three moons, the most moons of any planet. So, if Jupiter could have gotten a little bit larger and amassed more hydrogen, then Jupiter could have become a sun and had its own little solar system with sixty-three orbiting bodies. Let's do some math: 181 divided by 63 equals about one third of all the celestial bodies in the solar system are around Jupiter. When the solar system was forming, Jupiter's gravitational pull drew about one third of all of the celestial bodies in the solar system and tried to create a solar system of its own. WOW!

Compare this to the Book of Revelation, which refers to Satan when he was banished from heaven:

> And his tail drew the third part of the stars of heaven...
> *Revelation 12:4*

Satan drew a third part of the stars from heaven. Satan, when he was kicked out of heaven, took with him a third part of the hosts of heaven. To summarize the parallel stories:

1a. Satan had been an angel in authority.
1b. Jupiter is the predominate member of the solar system.

2a. Satan tried to be like the Son of God and failed.
2b. Jupiter came close to becoming a sun but couldn't.

3a. Satan drew with his tail a third part of the heavens when he was banished from heaven.
3b. Jupiter drew with its gravity one third of all of the celestial bodies in the solar system.

4a. Satan tries to mimic the Son of God.
4b. Jupiter mimics the sun by having a mini-solar system with 63 moons.

5a. Christ is the center of our existence.
5b. The sun is the center of our solar system.

Oh my heavens! Talk about similar stories. God is everywhere in science.

Meridian of Time

Let's move on to another concept: the word "meridian" is not found in the King James Version of the Bible, or in the Book of Mormon, but it is in the Doctrine and Covenants and also in the Joseph Smith Translation. Almost every time it is used by Joseph Smith in the Doctrine and Covenants and in the Joseph Smith Translation, it is referring to Christ, who shall come in the meridian of time. This doctrine is unique to the Latter-day Saints, but when you think about the seven distinct time frames, or the seven thousand years of the earth in the Bible, it does not really add up. If Adam walked out of the Garden about

4000BC, then Christ was born in 1AD. There have been two thousand years since Christ. Then there will be one thousand years of the millennium, during which time Christ reins on earth. This would total to seven thousand years. Using simple math, Christ really doesn't seem to come in the meridian of time. However, maybe we are not looking at the big picture.

Let's compare the meridian of time to the life span of our sun. Physicists tell us that our sun has about five billion more years of fuel left before it burns out. Science also tells us that our earth is at least 4.65 billion years old and that the sun must have been around before that time frame. Therefore, scientists estimate that the sun is perhaps five billion years old and the earth is, right now, in the middle of the sun's life. So, when Joseph Smith says that Christ will come in the meridian of time, maybe he is not talking about the lifespan of the earth. Maybe he is referring to the life of our sun. Based on this timeline, Christ was born exactly in the meridian of time for this solar system. Studying science helps me figure out the scriptures and studying the scriptures help me understand God.

Perfect Eclipse

What I'm about to tell you next is such an enormous statistical anomaly, it is almost nonexistent. From our perspective here on earth, the moon and the sun appear to be the exact same size. How is that possible, when we know the sun is much larger than the moon? How can they appear to be the same size in the sky? The width of the sun is four hundred times larger than the moon, but the moon is exactly four hundred times closer to the earth than the sun. This is how the moon forms a perfect eclipse. When the moon blocks the sun for a short period of time, this becomes a rare scientific anomaly. Then the odds of having an intelligent species on their home planet, at the exact time, to view a perfect eclipse, are astronomical (pun intended). Eve, by eating the forbidden fruit first, is the one who blocked out the light of life from Christ for a small period of time. This perfect eclipse might be a reminder from God of the story in Genesis. Recognizing the odd part of any story is where learning is amplified. A perfect eclipse is very, very, very odd in our universe.

December 25th

Another solar system story that testifies of Jesus Christ is the date December 25th. Many people do not know this, but each and every year on December 21st, at noontime, the sun drops to the lowest degree in the sky and for the next three days the sun stays at that same low degree in the sky. Then on December 25th, the sun rises one degree in the sky, which marks the return of the sun. Ancient Romans and Egyptians claimed that the sun was reborn on December 25th after being dead for three days. Does this sound familiar? God gave the ancient people of the earth signs and evidence that Jesus is the Christ. He made everything in the solar system testify that Jesus is the Christ. Everything points to Jesus Christ. This is not by coincidence.

> Note: The date of December 25th will be discussed in greater depth in Chapter 7: "Why Do Christians Celebrate Halloween?"

The Element of Iron

Now, let's move on to how elements of the solar system are formed. One element important to our story is iron. Every person has iron in their blood coursing through their veins. Humans need iron to exist, but where did iron come from? Science tells us that iron is created by a sun. It is a heavy element with twenty-six protons and twenty-six electrons.

However, before we can proceed with the creation of elements, let's first talk about the relationship of Christ to God and also compare Christ to the Holy Ghost, cited in two scriptures. The first scripture is found in the Book of John:

> For the Father judgeth no man, but hath committed all judgment unto the Son: *John 5:22*

The Apostle John teaches us that God is neutral and Christ is the proponent. Christ is the one who built the earth; suffered for the earth; died for the earth; will be the judge of the earth and the proponent that enables us to live in heaven with God. Even though this is all God's plan, He leaves the judgment to His Son.

The second scripture refers to the relationship between Christ and the Holy Ghost. The Book of John says that Jesus and the Holy Ghost will not be in the same place at the same time. This is Christ talking to His apostles after He has been resurrected:

> Nevertheless I tell you the truth; It is expedient for you that I go away: for if I go not away, the Comforter will not come unto you; but if I depart, I will send him unto you. *John 16:7*

Jesus and the Holy Ghost cannot be in the same place at the same time. When Jesus was baptized, the Holy Ghost was with Him in the form of a dove, but once Christ was resurrected, the Holy Ghost and Christ do not share the same place at the same time. This scripture is extremely important as we learn about Jesus Christ's relationship with the Holy Ghost. Let's read that one more time:

> If I go not away, the Comforter will not come unto you... *John 16:7*

However, these three; God the Father, the Son and the Holy Ghost make up the "Godhead" and basically rule, regulate and control everything in the universe. They bring order to chaos. God is neutral when compared to Christ as our judge and Christ will not take up the same space as the Holy Ghost.

Neutrons, Protons and Electrons

Now compare the Father, the Son and the Holy Ghost to the known elements of the solar system. All elements on the periodic table have three components: a neutron, a proton and an electron. Essentially, if you arrange these three components in different quantities or configurations, you can make anything in the universe. These are the three building blocks, and when combined, they use their collective power to regulate and create all that we can see, touch and feel. They also bring order to chaos and their characteristics are similar to God, Jesus and the Holy Ghost. For instance, the neutron and the proton are always in the center of an element. The neutron has a neutral electrical charge and the proton has a positive electrical charge. They are both central, giving an element its stability and mass. However, the electron is very small compared to the mass of the neutron and the proton, but the electron has a negative electrical charge. Thus, the proton, with a positive electric charge and the electron, with a negative electric charge, cannot touch. Basically, they cannot be in the same place at the same time. They serve different functions, and each has a different electrical charge. God the Father is akin to the neutron, Christ is similar to the proton and the electron is comparable to the Holy Ghost. Just as the Godhead is the maker of everything described in the scriptures, in like manner and function, a neutron, proton and electron, in a myriad of combinations, make up everything in the knowable and material universe.

On the periodic table, the first element is assigned the number one, which is hydrogen, having one proton and one electron. Helium is next, assigned the atomic number of two, because it has two protons and two electrons. Carbon has six protons and six electrons, therefore, has the atomic number of six. Iron, which is important to our discussion, has the number of twenty-six with, yes, twenty-six protons and twenty-six electrons. Gold has the atomic number of seventy-nine with seventy-nine protons and seventy-nine electrons, and so on.

Along with these combined protons and electrons, every element has a neutron, in varying quantities, except one. There is one element that <u>does not</u> have any neutrons at all. It is the anomaly, or odd part of the story, of the periodic table. This element is also the most dominate element by far in the entire universe, and that element is hydrogen, the first element. To create any higher order of element you need a neutron. You cannot make any heavier or more complicated or more sophisticated element without it. To make the element helium, which has the atomic number of two, you must first fuse together a few hydrogen elements. Also, in like manner, to generate anything sophisticated in the universe you need God the Father.

OK, let us go back to the beginning of this chapter and review the mystery in heaven that God had hidden. The mystery in Hebrews 1:1-2 and also in Ephesians 3:9 is that God had a plan to make a world, place people on it, and Jesus would fulfill the plan. By doing everything under the direction of the Father, Jesus satisfies and achieves the completion of the plan. Jesus creates everything. However, there is an exception to the story. Jesus created all things except for one thing. What? What is the one thing that God the Father steps in and assists Jesus to create? Genesis 1:26 says that when it came to the creation of man, God used the term "us," and only used it when He is speaking about the creation of a man. This is the first time in the scriptures that this term is ever used. The term "us" is important and distinct, enabling the reader to differentiate this part of the creation story. The mystery in Hebrews 1:1-2 and Ephesians 3:9 is that Jesus created everything. However the exception is the creation of man. Because when it came to producing a man, (a being much more sophisticated and complex than the other creations), the term "us" gives the reader a clue that Jesus was not acting alone. This creation is different than the previous creations. It is most eloquently written in the Book of Moses:

> And I, God, said unto mine Only Begotten, which was with me from the beginning: Let us make man in our image...
> *Moses 2:26*

This scripture is <u>not</u> cohesive to Hebrews 1:1-2 and Ephesians 3:9, just like a hydrogen element is not cohesive to all the other elements on the periodic table. Complex and sophisticated creations need a neutron in science and in like manner the most complex creation in Genesis needs God the Father. God the Father was essential to the complex fabrication of man, referring to His "Only Begotten" and I assume the Holy Ghost was also there, as He made Adam's body. This was a cooperative effort enabling the formation of higher and more complex forms of life. With this logical sequence, I can only conclude that Jesus and the Holy Ghost did not make man without the help of God the Father; <u>unlike</u> Hebrews 1:1-2 and Ephesians 3:9 state. The creation of man was an exception to the story. It was in collaboration with God the Father. Just like if you want to fashion anything more sophisticated or complex than basic hydrogen, the neutron is essential with protons and electrons. They collaborate. The three of them, working together and relying upon each other, formed every other element in the universe.

In like manner, three celestial bodies (the sun, earth and moon) in concert, enabled a world that uses three particles (neutrons, protons and electrons) to foster life. Without all three, there could be no life.

The question is, where is the factory, or the heart of creation, from which the elements on the periodic table spring? Where can we find so much energy that two hydrogen elements can fuse to make helium and then helium elements can fuse together to form heavier elements and those elements can fuse together to make even heavier elements? Where is there enough heat and energy to manufacture these elements? These factories are abundant in the universe. They are located in the center of each and every sun. A sun, at its core, has enough heat (approx. 27 million degrees Fahrenheit) to fuse elements. The size of the particular sun determines what elements will, or will not, be produced. There are many different sizes of suns in the universe. Our sun is able to fuse elements as heavy as iron. Our sun is also long-burning, about 10 billion years and this type of long-lasting sun allows an earth-type orbiting planet the time and regularity to nurture life. However, our sun will not produce much iron. The second type of sun is much larger than ours and at the end of its life will begin to produce more massive amounts of iron. Suns of this size do not last very long; they burn through their energy quickly, so their short life span probably does not allow the regularity of an orbiting planet to create life. Once a sun starts to produce iron, then its life will be over very soon through an explosion. Such an explosion, a supernova, allows the fusing and creation of all elements that are heavier than iron. For instance, gold, at atomic number seventy-nine, is much heavier than iron. Therefore, gold and heavier elements are only created when a sun sacrifices itself and makes these heavier elements. Scientists believe that our solar system was created by at least two previous larger suns that exploded prior to the existence of our current sun. The gold on earth was not generated by this earth, nor by our sun, but by a previous supernova, and the iron in our blood is the result of a previous sun. Science indicates that our human bodies are actually made of stardust: because the elements are made in the core of and by a supernova exploding sun, hence, the dust of a star.

Just as a large ball of hydrogen and helium had to sacrifice itself to spawn elements that can ultimately support life here on earth, so did Christ sacrifice Himself so we could have eternal life. Christ suffered for us in the Garden of Gethsemane and on the cross and did so freely for us to have eternal life after death.

You might wonder; how will the story of our sun end? Unlike the larger suns that explode into their own supernova, our sun is not massive enough to do that; instead, it will one day expand until it engulfs and consumes Mercury, Venus and the earth. The sun will not consume Mars, Jupiter and the outer planets. Once again I reference NASA's web site: "After a low mass star like the sun exhausts the supply of hydrogen in its core, there is no longer any source of heat to support the core against gravity. Hydrogen burning continues in a shell around the core and the star evolves into a red giant. When the sun becomes a red giant, its atmosphere will envelope the earth and our planet will be consumed in a fiery death."

The sun will consume the earth. There are prophecies relevant to this event from both Joseph Smith and St. John the Revelator, each attempting to describe something so majestic and fantastic that words seem inadequate:

> This earth, in its sanctified and immortal state, will be made like unto crystal and will be a Urim and Thummim to the inhabitants who dwell thereon, whereby all things pertaining to an inferior kingdom, or all kingdoms of a lower order, will be manifest to those who dwell on it; and this earth will be Christ's.
> *Doctrine and Covenants 130:9*

Here Joseph Smith said that our earth will be like a crystal and this earth will be Christ's earth. Also, the Apostle John in the Book of Revelation attempts to describe an incredible vision of the New Jerusalem and the place where our earth ends up and where we live with God.

> And he shewed me a pure river of water of life, clear as crystal, proceeding out of the throne of God and of the Lamb.
> *Revelation 22:1*

> And before the throne there was a sea of glass like unto crystal...
> *Revelation 4:6*

Then Joseph Smith gives us clarity:

Question: "What is the sea of glass spoken of by John, 4th Chapter, and 6th verse of the Revelation?" Answer: "It is the earth, in its sanctified, immortal, and eternal state."   *Doctrine and Covenants 77:1*

But they reside in the presence of God, on a globe like a sea of glass and fire, where all things for their glory are manifest, past, present, and future, and are continually before the Lord.   *Doctrine and Covenants 130:7*

And I saw as it were a sea of glass mingled with fire: and them that had gotten the victory over the beast, and over his image, and over his mark, and over the number of his name, stand on the sea of glass, having the harps of God.   *Revelation 15:2*

And the building of the wall of it was of jasper: and the city was pure gold, like unto clear glass.
Revelation 21:18

And the twelve gates were twelve pearls; every several gate was of one pearl: and the street of the city was pure gold, as it were transparent glass.
Revelation 21:21

The Apostle John and Joseph Smith are describing the place where we will all live after this life ends. Both St. John the Revelator and Joseph Smith use the terms; crystal, sea of glass, transparent glass, clear glass, and like unto crystal. They are doing their best to describe something difficult to articulate. In affirmation, I found this description on the website (www.cfa.harvard.edu) of the Harvard Smithsonian Center for Astrophysics regarding what will happen when our sun runs out of fuel: "Our sun will become a white dwarf when it dies five billion years from now. Some two billion years after that, the sun's ember core will crystallize as well, leaving a giant diamond in the center of our solar system... Our sun will become a diamond that truly is forever."

WOW. The Apostle John and Joseph Smith are, once again, right on the mark. The sun consumes our earth and becomes a sea of glass or crystal, the only words these men had to describe what they were seeing. Who could have predicted that, except two prophets of God? Astronomers have found a similar burned-out sun, called a white dwarf star and they estimate that this very hot carbon-based core is now one huge diamond. They speculate that it is the size of 10 billion-trillion-trillion karats. It is the crystallized carbon core of a sun that has finished burning hydrogen. Comparing the likeness of the Son of God to the sun in the sky is not difficult at all.

1 John 1:5	God is Light.
1 John 4:8	God is Love.
Revelation 1:16	His countenance was as the sun.
Revelation 19:17	An angel standing in the sun.
Revelation 21:1	There was a new heaven and a new earth, and there was no more sea. (Maybe the water evaporated off due to extreme heat?)
Revelation 21:23	The city had no need of the sun... the Lamb is the light thereof.
D&C 88:7	Christ is in the sun.
D&C 88:13	The power of God is light.

Unlike my friends who have fallen away from God because of science, I am drawn closer to God through science. Here is how my mind works:

1. When I heard about the moon coming from the side of the earth, the first thing that I thought was, "Oh, that is kind of like Eve coming from the side of Adam."
2. Reading that Jupiter could have become a sun, and that Jupiter had a third of the celestial bodies in the solar system around it, I thought of Satan taking a third part of the angels with him when he was kicked out of heaven.
3. Learning that the sun will become a diamond reminded me of Joseph Smith saying that the earth will crystallize like a sea of glass.
4. Learning that our sun's lifespan is about ten billion years and it has existed about five billion years helped me remember how Joseph Smith used the words "meridian of time" to describe when Jesus was born. So Jesus did come in the meridian of time of the sun's life span.
5. When I learned that a perfect eclipse is so rare in the universe, it reminded me of Eve blocking out Christ in the Garden of Eden.
6. When I understood that the combination of three things: neutrons, protons and electrons make up everything, I compared that to three beings and how God, the Son and the Holy Ghost created everything.
7. When I learned that protons and electrons could not be in the same place at the same time, it sent my mind to the Book of John and what Christ said about Himself and the Holy Ghost not being in the same place at the same time.
8. When I learned that a sun must sacrifice itself to create all heavier elements than iron, allowing for building blocks for life to be created, this appeared to be exactly like Christ sacrificing His body so we could have everlasting life.

Iron is the element that defines the end of a sun's life, for when a sun introduces the production of iron into its spherical body, the life of the sun will soon be over. Therefore, when the scriptures say that Christ will rule with a rod of iron (Revelation 2:27 and Revelation 19:15) well, this might be more than just a casual phrase or comment. And as you know, once the Roman soldiers put iron nails into the body of Christ then His life on earth was soon to end also. Two similar stories.

This is what I think happens when my friends believe that science proves that God does not exist. My friends who have drifted away from religion are influenced by science every day of the year. In contrast, they study about God two hours a year; one hour on Easter Sunday and one hour at Christmas. We call them "Chrieasters." Is there any wonder they don't find God in science? They are not looking in the right place. They have great knowledge of science, but are ignorant in the teachings of God.

The scientific theory of the Big Bang, which I don't necessarily believe a hundred percent, says that there was nothing, and then there was something the size of a pin head that had such an incredible burst of energy and heat, that this energy transferred itself into mass and therefore created everything in the universe. It basically says that $E=MC^2$, or energy can transform into mass. That theory describes the creation in the Bible and it seems to go perfectly with the evidence that there is a God. Therefore, if you believe in the Big Bang then you should believe in God. The story of the Big Bang seems to testify that there is a God. Everything was created from nothing!

Read your scriptures, go to the temple, study the universe, and you will find that God is the Master Architect. He has laid out this magnificent paradise on earth for us to discover evidence of Him and Christ everywhere we look. Isn't He great!

John S. Pennington Jr.

CHAPTER 4
WHY WAS THE PRIESTHOOD RESTRICTED?

My friend Bill is a mountain of a man, big and tall. He's well over six and a half feet tall, with the heart of an artist in the body of an athlete, sporting a shaved head, a broad smile, and eyes that display keen awareness and intelligence. Curious about nearly everything, he's an avid student of the world's religions.

A few years ago Bill—who is not a member of my church—asked, "How can you believe in a God who would discriminate His priesthood?" I was puzzled. "What do you mean when you say discriminate?" Bill replied, "Well, before 1978, your church had a discrimination policy when it came to the priesthood, and women are still not allowed to hold the priesthood." I told him that I like to use the word "restriction" as opposed to "discrimination" and asked if I could explain it to him. Bill's tone was antagonistic, so I settled in for a lengthy discussion. I told him that it was a long answer but I thought I could answer his question. First, I needed to provide some background and context on the subject.

I asked Bill if he realized that the priesthood did not have any restriction when Joseph Smith was alive. Men of all nationalities, German, Scottish, American Indian, and African-

Americans, all received the priesthood before Joseph Smith was killed. In fact, the first African-American man in The Church of Jesus Christ of Latter-day Saints received the priesthood in 1836. Bill paused for a moment, because he had not realized this little-known fact. Before the year 1848, other than for women, there was no restriction of the priesthood. The nationality or bloodline did not matter. However, for some reason no one quite understands (including current church leaders), Brigham Young restricted the priesthood in approximately the year 1848 but made it official in 1852. And from that time going forward, no other church president reversed the restriction until the year 1978. Therefore, the restriction lasted about 130 years, from 1848 to 1978.

Then I asked Bill if he understood the difference between the Aaronic Priesthood and the Melchizedek Priesthood. He said no, so I continued. A man named Melchizedek lived in Salem about 2000BC. I then asked Bill if he knew how to spell Melchizedek. He said that he could not, and then I chuckled and told him that it doesn't matter, because back then they probably just called him "Mel." Bill did not laugh, he remained serious, but my point was that the King James Bible spells the name two different ways (Melchizedek and also Melchisedec). One order of priesthood was named after him and a sub-order was named the Aaronic Priesthood. The Melchizedek Priesthood is the greater and the Aaronic, sometimes referred to as the Levitical Priesthood, is the lesser priesthood. Melchizedek lived in a city named Salem.

There was another man named Abram, whose name was changed by God to Abraham. Abraham paid his tithes to—and was granted his priesthood from—Melchizedek, rather than from his father who was named Terah. Abraham's father was not a follower of God. In fact, Terah had tried to sacrifice Abraham to the Gods of Egypt, (Abraham, Chapter 1), which probably put some animosity between the two. "Ya think?" I said to Bill. "If your father's intent is to sacrifice your body on some Egyptian altar, you'd probably want to find a good realtor and relocate right away." I was trying to soften up Bill by making jokes along the way. It was not working.

After Abraham received the Melchizedek priesthood, he then had a son named Isaac by his first wife, Sarah. Then Isaac had a son named Jacob. Abraham, Isaac, and Jacob: by bloodline they are the grandfather, father, and son. Like Abraham, his grandson also had his name changed from Jacob to Israel by a messenger from God. The Bible says that Jacob was wrestling with a "man," and this man blessed Jacob and changed Jacob's name to Israel. Most scholars of the Bible believe the man was either a messenger from God or an angel, because when this story is over, Jacob says that he had seen God "face to face" (Genesis 32:30). Jacob realized that this wasn't just a man, but an angel of the Lord.

When I first learned about Jacob wrestling with an angel, I thought Jacob was wrestling in a dream or in his mind. However, it says that Jacob was wrestling so hard that his thigh or knee was thrown out of joint. It also says that Jacob would not let the angel leave until the angel blessed him. The angel eventually conceded, and changed Jacob's name to Israel.

Israel had twelve sons, and those sons had so many children that each family became a tribe; a "tribe of Israel," or the "Twelve Tribes of Israel." Three of those sons of Israel are key players in this story. One is Levi, who led the tribe of the Levites. Another is Judah, sometimes spelled "Juda," whose family became the Jewish tribe or the tribe of Judah. Then there is Joseph, who had two sons that we will discuss later. What many people don't know is that Israel had one daughter named Dinah. In Genesis Chapter 34, Levi kills a man named Shechem, because he believed he was in defense of his sister Dinah's honor. The slaughter of Shechem and his brothers, by Levi, angered Israel, mainly because Israel feared that his family wasn't large enough to defend itself against Shechem's people. Due to his brash action, Levi lost his inheritance and did not receive his twelfth part of Israel's possessions when Israel died. When Israel gave his blessing to Levi in Genesis 49:5-7, he told Levi that because he had killed Shechem and his brethren many years ago, Levi's share would be divided among the other tribes of Israel, with nothing left for the Levites.

In most large families there is usually a rebel child and a prized child. Levi was the rebel and Joseph was the favorite. Everyone knows the story of Joseph. He was the boy who wore the coat of many colors and was sold into Egypt as a slave. Then he was thrown into prison, interpreted some dreams and ultimately became second in command to Pharaoh. Joseph helped Pharaoh store all the food and grain, so when they had a seven-year famine, the people from all around could come to Egypt to buy food. Israel and the tribes moved to Egypt and lived under the protection of Joseph, as Joseph had a lot of food and they were hungry. Joseph married and had two sons named Manasseh and Ephraim. On his deathbed, Israel was giving blessings to his sons. We know that Levi received nothing and in contrast, instead of giving Joseph a share, he asked for Joseph's two sons to be brought before him with intent to make Joseph's two sons just as his own. Israel wanted to bless Joseph's lineage with an extra part of the inheritance. Joseph's sons, Manasseh and Ephraim, stood before Israel who crossed his hands to put his right hand on the younger of the two and the left hand on the eldest. Then Joseph, noticing where his father's hands rested, says; hold on Dad, you're doing it wrong. You have your right hand on the younger son. The old man, who was close to death but still clearly in control, knew exactly what he was doing. As he blessed the young boys, Israel stated that the grandsons were as his own sons, each to receive a twelfth part of Israel. This is why you never hear about the tribe of Joseph, except once in the Book of Revelation. Instead, there was a tribe called Manasseh and another called Ephraim. Thus, there were actually thirteen tribes, with Levi's tribe not being counted.

Many years went by and Israel, with all of his sons, eventually passed away. All the tribes of Israel were still living in Egypt, having a great time eating and basking in the popularity of their ancestor Joseph. But then it says in Exodus 1:8 that there was a new pharaoh who "knew not Joseph." He had no loyalty to Joseph and perhaps thought all of these tribes were freeloading, so he decided to make them his slaves. The tribes of Israel were held in captivity for centuries.

Among them was a man named Moses, a Levite. However, an Egyptian Princess raised Moses as her own, keeping his lineage a secret. As a prominent member of Egyptian royalty, Moses killed a man and fled in fear of being found out. While in the wilderness, Moses met a man named Jethro and eventually married one of his daughters. But more important, Moses realized that Jethro had the priesthood of God and was further surprised that he traced his priesthood back to Abraham and Melchizedek. Many people don't realize that Abraham had two wives: Sarah and then Keturah. Keturah had a son named Midian. Jethro, a priest of Midian, was a Midianite. Thus, Jethro traces his priesthood back to Abraham and Melchizedek. Doctrine and Covenants 84:7-14 gives a long list of the lineage of Jethro's priesthood, tracing it back to the "hand of God" through the blessing of Abraham, who had received the priesthood from Melchizedek.

After many years had passed away, Moses returned to Egypt and led the children of Israel out of slavery and into the wilderness. He climbed a mountain to receive tablets from God, on which were written the Ten Commandments, or the "The Big Ten," as I like to call them. When he came down the mountain, Moses saw that the children of Israel were worshiping an idol that they had created by melting their gold to construct a golden calf. Then Moses soared into a rage, hurling down the stones tablets, which crumbled into pieces and destroyed the golden calf. Moses demanded that everyone who believed him to be a prophet of God take one step forward. Only the Levites, those of Moses' own tribe, stepped forward and confirmed that they still believed in him. He told the Levites that because they believed, they would be given some special privileges that others would not receive.

Another interesting part to this story is that the Levites were not counted as they came out of Egypt. When we read the Book of Numbers, we see that everything was counted before the tribes left Egypt. There is a record of every person in the tribe of Reuben, everyone in the tribe of Simeon, of Issachar, Judah and so on, but there is no mention of anyone from the tribe of Levi. They even counted the animals. It is as if the Levites did not exist, becoming the uncounted tribe. However, out in the wilderness, the Levites received a special blessing. The writer of the Book of Numbers says in Chapter 8 that an atonement was made for the Levites. "Atonement" is the actual word used to describe the Levite transformation. From that time forth, the Levities were the only tribe that could hold the priesthood. And inside the Levite tribe, only the descendants of Aaron (the Aaronic Priesthood) could hold the office of a priest. The point here is that both brothers, Moses and Aaron, are of the tribe of Levi and central to restrictions of the priesthood.

Aaron became the head of the Levitical Priesthood and by God's commandment, Moses instructed Aaron and the Levites, to build a tabernacle made of cloth in the desert, which would be a precursor to the Temple of Solomon, made of stone. The purpose for the tabernacle was two-fold: (i) to house the ark of the covenant, and (ii) to establish a holy place to make sacrifices to the Lord. The ark of the covenant held the crushed pieces of tablets from the "Big Ten," a bowl of manna, and the staff of Aaron. This staff was most notably used to strike a rock, from which sprang a stream of water. Manna was a food source that fell in the night. It was gathered in early morning before the sun rose. It was their life bread. Truly a blessing from God, because so many in the desert were starving. On the sixth day of the week, the Israelites would collect a double portion of manna, for the seventh day was their Sabbath when they did not work. The Hebrews observed their Sabbath on Saturday, which is the seventh day of the week. Christians adopted Sunday, the first day of the week, as their Sabbath, for that is the day Jesus Christ was resurrected from the tomb. So the Israelites placed a bowl of manna, the crushed tablets, and the staff of Aaron inside the ark of the covenant. Then the Levites, who were the only ones who could hold the priesthood, built the tent tabernacle to house the sacred items.

I asked my friend Bill if he had ever been to a doctor's office and noticed a picture of a staff or pole with a snake wrapped around it, either as art, or a lapel pin sometimes worn by a physician. This symbol of healing comes from the Old Testament as venomous snakes were biting the children of Israel. To solve the problem, Moses constructed a staff with a bronze snake wrapped around it, which he stuck in the ground outside of the village. He told the followers that all they had to do was look upon this staff and they would be healed. That was it; pure faith was all it took to be healed. The strange thing is that many Israelites would not do it, because they did not have faith, or it was too simple. Bill agreed that if he got bit by a snake and I told him to just walk down the street to look at a flagpole, he would think I was crazy, ignore me and hurry to the nearest hospital for treatment.

Wielding the power of God, Moses made a lot of unusual things happen. The tabernacle alone was an oddity; it had a ball of fire, or ball of light, that hovered directly over it at night. When a person stepped out of his tent at night and looked toward the tabernacle, this ball of light implied that God was with them and they should look to the tabernacle for light and enlightenment, evidence of God's presence. During the day there was a cloud over the center of the tabernacle. And when the cloud started to move, guess what happened. The Levites, who were the only ones allowed to touch and move the tabernacle, would collapse it and then walk and walk and walk, following the cloud until it stopped. And when the cloud stopped, they would erect the tabernacle anew beneath the cloud, where it remained until the cloud moved again. For forty years this tabernacle and the children of Israel roamed the desert following a cloud.

I remember Bill looking at me and saying, "Are you making all of this stuff up?" I laughed. "No, no, Bill. It's all in the Bible, right there in the Old Testament."

Aaron's sons and grandsons were the only ones allowed to officiate inside the tabernacle—thus, they were the only ones who could hold the office of "priest." The key here is that to be a Levite you had to have a direct bloodline back to Levi. In order to be a priest inside of the Levite tribe, you had to be a direct descendent from Aaron, the older brother of Moses. All of the Aaronic Priesthood holders are Levites, but not all Levites are descendants of Aaron.

In the time of Moses, if you were from the tribe of Judah and wanted to make a sacrifice, you could not do the sacrifice yourself. Whether of the tribe of Judah, Dan, Ruben, Manasseh, or any of the others, except the tribe of Levi, you could not make a sacrifice to God on your own. You needed a Levite, or even better, a descendent of Aaron who was a priest, to perform the ritual on your behalf. A person from the tribe of Judah would have to take an unblemished dove or lamb and give it to the priest, who would then make the offering for him. Those Levites were tabernacle workers, doing sacred work, for and on behalf of others.

The timeline for Moses and Aaron is approximately 1300BC to 1200BC and the priests of Aaron had specific things that they had to wear inside the tabernacle.

It says in Ezekiel 44:16-18 and in Exodus 28:42 that they could not wear anything that was wool or that made them sweat. They wore linen breeches that reached down to their thigh. The term "thigh" in the Old Testament is more properly translated as the knee or knee area. These were long linen shorts or short pants that reached to the knee. They also wore bonnets on their heads with certain colors, which is outlined in detail in the Book of Exodus. Without these special garments, the tabernacle workers were unable to perform their duties.

Now, let's fast-forward to about 1000BC, during the time of David. He is the little boy who killed Goliath with a stone and sling. David eventually became King of Israel and he had a plan. He aimed to replace the tent tabernacle with a stone temple. However, the Lord God did not allow David to build the temple, but he was allowed to gather all of the materials for it. The actual assembly of the temple was left to David's son, Solomon. That is how the temple in Jerusalem became known as King Solomon's Temple.

I then asked Bill, "Can you tell me at this point in time, 1000BC, why David, who is the King of Israel, could not hold the priesthood? He is King, he's Jewish, God loves him very much, but why is he restricted from holding the priesthood? As a young man, David killed Goliath, used the prophets and their counsel to conquer the Philistines and was definitely blessed and loved by God. David became King of Israel but couldn't go inside the tabernacle because he was descended from Judah. Why couldn't David hold the priesthood, can you tell me why?" I then sat there and waited for an answer.

Bill didn't respond. My friend had no idea. He said very slowly, "I don't know." At that point our conversation changed. Bill had been antagonistic all along until this moment.

Then he began to process truths in the Old Testament that he had never learned before. He had never considered, in this context, who could—and could not—hold the priesthood, and why. My statement to him was this: "When you can tell me why a good Jewish boy, named David, could not hold the priesthood and could not go inside of the temple or tabernacle in approximately 1000BC, then I can tell you why certain men could not hold the priesthood for 130 years before the year 1978 and why women cannot hold the priesthood today."

Bill paused for a moment and I said to him; "You told me earlier that you could never believe in a God who would restrict His priesthood based on bloodline. You said you could never believe in a God who would do something like that based on lineage, or who a person's father or grandfather was. Well, Bill, I have just shown you that this did happen in the Old Testament. And the most perplexing thing is that this restriction came directly from God through His prophet Moses. So is what you are saying to me is that you will not believe Moses, or will you not believe in the God of the Old Testament?"

"Surely," I continued, "In a one thousand three hundred-year period of time, do you ever think that there was an eighteen-year-old from the tribe of Dan or of the Tribe of Judah who prayed to God and said, Father in Heaven, I am a good Jewish boy. I have a cousin over there who is a Levite. I pay my tithes and I keep all the commandments, so I'm just as good as my cousin. Why can't I go inside the temple or hold the priesthood? I am just as good as my cousin! The only difference is my great-great-great-grandfather was Judah, and his great-great-great-grandfather was Aaron. Father in Heaven, just because my cousin has a different great-grandfather than I have, why does that alone qualify him to go inside the temple and leaves me outside of the priesthood? That does not seem fair, Heavenly Father." Bill, do you think that this basic prayer ever happened in that one thousand three hundred-year span? For one thousand three hundred years, the priesthood was restricted to all of the other tribes. Before there was a tabernacle, there was no restriction on the priesthood. In modern times (and I'm not sure exactly why; in fact, no one is sure why, including current church leaders) Brigham Young placed a restriction on the priesthood at about the time the Nauvoo Temple was completed. Both restrictions started about the time each group had a new tabernacle or temple and each group started to wear special tabernacle or temple clothing. This is a parallel story of two groups of people following the God of Israel, when a new temple or tabernacle was constructed. The priesthood was restricted, once for one thousand three hundred years and then for one hundred and thirty years.

One group had a new tabernacle ordinance in 1300BC, and the other group had a new temple ordinance in the year 1845AD.

King Solomon built the temple from solid stone. Rumor has it that Solomon chose stone because the previous temple had been built out of sticks and the one before that had been built out of straw and a big bad wolf destroyed both as he huffed and he puffed and blew them down. This is probably just a rumor, (Bill finally laughed at this joke) but we all know that a stone building is more solid than one of sticks or straw. Again, this is probably just a rumor and I am not saying the wolf story is doctrinal fact. I just wanted to see if you were still paying attention. Ha!"

The parallel is that King Solomon's Temple was constructed close to a sea of salt, the Dead Sea. He built it in a city called Jeru-Salem. This city was once called Salem, where Melchizedek lived, but now it's called Jerusalem. It took King David about thirty-three years to gather all of the materials. Once Solomon was King, it took him approximately seven years to assemble the temple, thus about forty years from start to finish. Just like King Solomon, Brigham Young built a temple of stone close to a sea of salt, the Great Salt Lake located in Utah. King Solomon fulfilled King David's dream of a stone temple, and Brigham Young did the same for Joseph Smith's vision. Both temples took about forty years to assemble and construct.

Yet another parallel in the two stories is that when Moses was in the wilderness, the children of Israel wanted to eat meat because they grew tired of eating manna every day. The Bible says in Exodus Chapter 16, that Moses prayed to solve the problem and a flock of quail flew in over the mountains into the valley. The quail were so exhausted that they fell upon the ground enabling the Israelites to eat meat. Numbers 11:31 says that there were so many quail in some places that it was piled two cubits high. A cubit being measured from the tip of a man's elbow to the tip of his longest finger.

This likewise happened when Brigham Young was forced to travel west, at that time, out of the United States. The second wagon train to leave came upon a river and stopped because they were starving to death. On October 9, 1846 flocks of quail flew into the camp, and were so exhausted that children could walk around and pick them up. These quail were like manna from God and kept them from starving in the wilderness. (Ensign Magazine June 1997 edition "Pioneer Trek")

These are the only two times in history that I've heard of this happening: (i) Moses and his Exodus with the children of Israel from Egypt and (ii) Brigham Young when he and his people were making their exodus from the United States because of religious persecution. It might, or might not be a coincidence, but the only two recorded restrictions of the priesthood both coincide with the building of a new temple, or new tabernacle and the wearing of special linen garments. As soon as Moses had a tabernacle, the priesthood was restricted. Conversely, before the Nauvoo Temple was completed, all worthy male members from any country or bloodline could hold the priesthood if they were baptized members of The Church of Jesus Christ of Latter-day Saints. However, as the Nauvoo Temple was nearing completion in 1845, it appears that Brigham Young placed a restriction on the priesthood and made it official by 1848 and that restriction lasted until 1978. Both restrictions began with a new dispensation, with the construction of a tabernacle or temple, the wearing of special linen clothing and both began with a new prophet, to whom God gave new scripture. Also, both new prophets were assisted by their older brother, Aaron for Moses and Hyrum Smith for Joseph Smith.

Bill was fascinated at these stories from the Old Testament and his mind open to the possibility that God works in unexpected and unexplained ways; even that God could restrict His holy priesthood.

There is more to consider before we end this chapter. King David had a son named Solomon and Solomon had a son, then his son had a son and eventually, a thousand years later, there was a great-great-grandson named Joseph. King David had a lot of sons, one of whom was named Nathan. Nathan had a son, who had a son, who had a son until eventually a thousand years had passed, and a daughter was born whose name was Mary. These two, Mary and Joseph, were engaged to be married and both had direct bloodlines back to King David. Therefore, when the scriptures say that Jesus was the "King of the Jews" it may be more than just a casual wording or phrase, because King David himself was a Jew. King Solomon was from the tribe of Judah, and both Mary and Joseph had direct royal lines back to King David. Therefore, if the land of Israel and Jerusalem had not been conquered by the Roman Empire when Jesus was born, then Jesus might actually have been the King of the Jews.

Still, all this time, from 1300BC until the time of Christ, there was only one tribe who could hold the priesthood; that of Levi. Therefore, when John the Baptist baptized Jesus, using the priesthood, he must have been a Levite. John the Baptist is the same man, in his resurrected body, who gave Joseph Smith his priesthood. Who is John, and how do we know that he had the priesthood? Here is a clue to the answer. Do you recall how John the Baptist received his name when he was a baby? His father Zacharias was inside the temple when the Angel Gabriel came to him and told him to name his son John.

Wait. Wait. Did you catch that?

Zacharias was inside the temple, so he would have to have been a Levite and probably a direct descendent of Aaron. John, therefore, was surely a Levite, a cousin of Jesus and would've been in the right tribe to have the priesthood. This all makes perfect sense once you understand the history of the restriction of the priesthood among the tribes.

The gospel all fits together once you understand the big picture. The most logical person to give Joseph Smith the Aaronic priesthood would be John the Baptist. That would be a direct line or lineage of priesthood.

I said to Bill; "This reminds me of a scripture in the Book of Hebrews. If we would have read this when we began, we would not have had the knowledge to understand it. But now that we have studied the history of the priesthood, we can comprehend the greater depth of this scripture."

> If therefore perfection were by the Levitical priesthood, (for under it the people received the law,) what further need was there that another priest should rise after the order of Melchisedec, and not be called after the order of Aaron? For the priesthood being changed, there is made of necessity a change also of the law. For he of whom these things are spoken pertaineth to another tribe, of which no man gave attendance at the altar. For it is evident that our Lord sprang out of Juda; of which tribe Moses spake nothing concerning priesthood.
>
> *Hebrews 7:11-14*

The Book of Hebrews says that the Lord Jesus Christ is from Judah, not Levi. But we know that Jesus had the Melchizedek priesthood and was a priest. Therefore, the law must have been changed, allowing other tribes to have the priesthood. Jesus changed it, for His apostles were not all from the tribe of Levi, yet they baptized and performed priesthood functions, such as healings, etc. St. Peter, St. James, and St. John got their Melchizedek priesthood from Jesus, who was from Judah. Joseph Smith received his Melchizedek priesthood from the resurrected St. Peter, St. James and St. John.

There is one other story that will be easier to understand now that we understand the priesthood history. It is about the Samaritans. In approximately 600BC, King Nebuchadnezzar raided Israel and took captives back to Babylon. However, there was a small band of Israelites around the area of Samaria who managed to escape the enslavement. These Israelites in Samaria intermarried with non-Israelite spouses, crossing and polluting their bloodlines.

When Cyrus the Great of Persia conquered Babylon, he freed the Israelites and let them return to Jerusalem. This enslavement was only about seventy years, but the damage was done. From then on, the Jews labeled the Samaritans as unclean half-breeds.

The parable of the Good Samaritan tells us that there was a man lying on the side of the road, half-dead and having been robbed. A priest walked by, saw the man and didn't help him. Then a Levite passed and did nothing to help the wounded man. Finally, a Samaritan came upon him and stopped to give aid. The priest has a pedigree going back one thousand, three hundred years, and the Levite knew that he had a bloodline that other men wished to have. But the Samaritan was a half-breed with a convoluted bloodline, and was dirty in the eyes of the Levites, priests, and Jews. Yet he was the only one to stop and help.

Jesus is making the point that a priest and a Levite, with perfect bloodlines, can be blinded by their pedigree and not live by the commandments of God. The Samaritan was the only one truly keeping one of the great commandments to; "love thy neighbour [sic] as thyself" (Matthew 22:39). The priest and the Levite were depending on their pedigree chart to get them into heaven instead of living the commandments. In these last days, before the second coming of the Lord Jesus Christ, we need to honor our priesthood and serve others just as Jesus Christ has taught us to do.

This was my point to my friend Bill. I'm not exactly sure why Brigham Young decided to place a hundred and thirty-year restriction of the priesthood before 1978. I'm uncertain why women cannot hold the priesthood today and I don't know why the sons of Judah, the Jews, the sons of Joseph and even the sons of Ruben could not hold the priesthood. But the tribes of Israel were restricted from the priesthood; it did happen! It was restricted for some reason that only God understands.

I think it is a problem for anyone to dare say that, "God could never do this or that," because usually I can find a story in the Old Testament where God did do something like this or that. If your reason for not wanting to believe and live the gospel is because of God restricting His priesthood, then I encourage you to study the Old Testament and accept that God works in mysterious ways. Our tiny human brains have a difficult time comprehending the Creator of the universe.

Last, I want to say that I know Jesus Christ lives. His gospel has changed my life and has made me a better husband, a better father and a better Christian. It has blessed my life, my children's lives and it has helped me become more like Jesus Christ. I know that the priesthood is one of God's tools to help people reach their potential as children of God. The priesthood is for all men who want to accept the responsibility that goes along with it. I implore you to honor it and sustain it. It is rewarding to be a valuable member of God's team. If you follow the gospel's teachings you will eventually be numbered in what is known in the Bible as the "sons of God." By being a doer of the word, not a hearer only, the priesthood has helped me understand Christ and his teaching.

CHAPTER 5
WHAT HAPPENED TO THE APOSTLES?

In order to fully understand what happened to the apostles, we must start from a common point of reference, like a particular date in time. Let's start with the year Jesus was born. What year, on our calendar, did Jesus take on a body of flesh and blood? The year "zero" does not exist. Tradition says that Jesus was born in 1AD. "AD" is an abbreviation for *Anno Domini*, which translates to "the year of our Lord." Our starting point of reference for Jesus' birth is the year 1AD, although the date is disputed among scholars and faiths.

Some modern Christian apologists claim that Jesus was born on December 25th in 1BC and then six days later, the year starts as 1AD. Therefore, if Jesus died at the age of thirty-three in the months of March or April, then He would have died in the year 34AD, at the age of 33 years old.

Referring to the years before the birth of Jesus, we use BC, which simply means "Before Christ," or, a new term utilized by scholars, BCE for "Before the Christian Era."

A few years ago I had the opportunity to travel to Israel. It was one of the best trips I have ever taken, and I would strongly encourage everyone to make that trip. In Israel, I went on a tour with a Jewish guide who repeatedly stressed that King Herod, who ordered the killing of all of the baby boys in Bethlehem, died in 4BC. The following day, I went on another tour with an Islamic guide who yielded the same information that King Herod died in 4BC. Both of these very knowledgeable men, from different non-Christian backgrounds, emphasized that the king who ordered the death of the baby Jesus actually died four years before Jesus was born. Two men of different religions, Jewish and Islam, tried to discredit Christians by exclaiming that there is a problem with the Bible story of the birth of Jesus. No doubt there is room for error in our calendar, as it dates back thousands of years, long before there was a computer database to keep up with details. Some students of the Bible believe that Jesus was born in 5BC because of an error in calculations by a medieval monk while tabulating the calendar. (We will go into an in-depth explanation of this subject, in Chapter 8).

Another item that I learned is that the name "Jesus" is a Greek word and it was translated from the Hebrew name of Joshua. However, middle-east dialect would pronounce the "J" in Joshua with a "H" sound. They would say Hoshua the Christ, not Joshua the Christ. The correct pronunciation is a "Hach" or a kind of gravel in the throat like sound with emphasis on the "H." When the Bible was translated into English, the translator (William Tyndale) retained the Greek word "Jesus" and now everyone refers to Him by that name even though He never was referred to by that name while He was on earth.

Having two new bits of information about the Savior, His real name and His date of birth, will help me understand His story and the story of the apostles. It also helps me understand the fact that I should prepare to accept new truths, no matter how irregular they might be.

However, for this chapter we will use the year 1AD as the date of His birth.

When Jesus was thirty years old, He began His ministry in 31AD, the year He was baptized by John the Baptist, who was then imprisoned and killed by King Herod. This is a different King Herod than the one that died in 4BC. Then at the age of 33, in the year 34AD, Jesus died and was resurrected.

That same year, the Apostle Judas Iscariot killed himself. There are two accounts of his death. One says that he hung himself from a tree and the other says that he jumped off a cliff and fell on some rocks. Joseph Smith said both accounts are true; that Judas hung himself from a tree and the tree branch broke, sending Judas onto rocks below.

After this event, the remaining eleven apostles met, knowing they needed to have twelve to complete their quorum. The Book of Acts explains that they had narrowed their choice to two candidates, named Matthias and Barsabas. This was an important event. Jesus had died, He'd been resurrected and the apostles had been instructed to go and preach the gospel throughout the world. But for some reason they paused, feeling compelled to fill the twelfth vacancy before they continued on their assignment. This vacancy caused a conference of the apostles and forced them to pursue these two men to join them as an apostle of the Lord Jesus Christ.

> And they appointed two, Joseph called Barsabas, who was surnamed Justus, and Matthias. And they prayed, and said, Thou, Lord, which knowest the hearts of all men, shew whether of these two thou hast chosen, That he may take part of this ministry and apostleship, from which Judas by transgression fell, that he might go to his own place. And they gave forth their lots; and the lot fell upon Matthias; and he was numbered with the eleven apostles. *Acts 1:23-26*

The casting of lots! Do you think this is strange? The apostles knew one of these men was supposed to join them, but they weren't sure which one. So, they let God direct them by casting lots, or tossing sticks. Whichever name the lot **fell** upon would be God's will; thus, their selection for the twelfth apostle. The first time I had ever heard about the casting of lots was when I read about Nephi and his brothers outside of Jerusalem, trying to decide on something by casting lots. I thought that I needed a deeper understanding of this practice, especially since one of the apostles had been chosen to His office using this form of selection. This just didn't sound right to me until I found this:

> The lot is cast into the lap; but the whole disposing thereof is of the Lord.   *Proverbs 16:33*

I take from this scripture that followers of God, in the Old Testament, and early Christians would basically say something like; "Heavenly Father, we are confused and You know everything. We don't know exactly what to do, and we need Your help. We're going to cast these lots and we have faith that You will make the lot fall upon the person who is supposed to be the next apostle." This practice is surprising to a modern student of the Bible, but Proverbs tells us that the Lord's hand was at work, making perfect sense for the brothers of Nephi outside of Jerusalem and also it evidently was a common practice enabling the apostles to use this method to make decisions for the next apostle.

Matthias was chosen, and the twelve apostles began to travel and preach. They went to Corinth and taught the Corinthians about Christ. They would baptize new Christians and before they left they would call and ordain a bishop, giving him charge over the congregation, promising to send further instruction by writing letters and sending messages. The apostles traveled to Ephesus and taught the Ephesians; they would baptize; grow a congregation; ordain a bishop and they would go to the city of Rome, to the city of Byzantium and so forth. We know of these places and the congregations by the letters written by St. Paul to the Corinthians, the Ephesians etc., giving instructions to keep on the correct track of Christ, preserved for future generations in the New Testament. This went on for years, with the apostles teaching, baptizing, ordaining and sending letters.

The Apostle Peter died in 64AD, by being crucified upside down. St. Peter was killed for teaching truth about his belief in Jesus Christ. St. Peter did not feel worthy to be executed the same way as his Lord had been. So, tradition says that he asked to be crucified upside down. As you can see, truth was not surviving very well in this time period.

Let's say, hypothetically, that in 67AD the Bishop of Corinth dies. What is the first step to getting a new bishop? The people of Corinth would simply send an email or fax down to church headquarters. Not really. They would have sent a letter by a mule, then a boat, and another mule, no doubt the fastest way to get messages delivered in those days. Once the apostles received the personally-delivered message, they would travel, by mule and boat, to the congregation of that city and then offer prayers, along with some fasting, and find a man there to serve as a bishop to lead the people. Then they would ordain that righteous man as a bishop with keys to oversee the congregation. Then let us say in 80AD the Bishop of Ephesus died. Again, the apostles traveled to the city and prayed, fasted and then ordained a new bishop. That is how all the original bishops were called and set in place. What about when any of the apostles died?

They knew they needed to maintain a quorum of twelve, but they were being persecuted, growing old and dying off faster than they could get back together. The Disciple Stephen was stoned to death. St. Peter was crucified upside down. They didn't have planes and automobiles like we have today. They couldn't travel faster than their persecutors, who were determined to extinguish the existence of Christianity. What was their crime? They were preaching the truth, and truth was not surviving very well in this time period.

To combat this, the resurrected Christ called a new apostle by choosing a man named Saul, who is believed to have been present at the stoning of Stephen. Saul was on a trek to hunt down and execute the additional disciples and apostles. The Lord spoke to Saul in the desert and converted him to Christianity. His name was then changed to Paul. This is the same St. Paul who wrote a large part of the New Testament. The power of Christ is amazing when it can take a hunter of the apostles and turn that same man into an apostle himself. Though no one knows exactly when, but even St. Paul was eventually killed by the influences of the Christian-haters in the mid-60s AD. Why was St. Paul killed, and what was St. Paul's crime? It was because he too, was teaching truth. Truth is not surviving very well.

The last apostle that we hear about is St. John, also called John the Revelator. He wrote the Book of Revelation in around 96AD. So let's just round it up and say 100AD is the last time we hear from him.

Therefore, if the Bishop of Ephesus died in the year 125AD then how did the Ephesians re-fill his office? How about in 132AD if the bishop of Corinth died; how was he replaced? There were no apostles remaining, and they couldn't send an email or a fax down to church headquarters to send someone up and ordain a new bishop.

At that point, the system changed, because they had no alternative. So, they held an election and voted. There would be candidates, and an election would determine who the next bishop would be over the community.

To understand this, we must first grasp the severity of the persecution of Christians living in an empire so hostile to their beliefs. The Romans believed that Christians were enemies of the state. Today, we pay big money to go to a large stadium to watch a game of football. Back in Roman times, they went to the Colosseum to watch the spectacle of Christians vs. Lions. I believe that the lions were undefeated. This was a gory time for Christians, who would be thrown into the Colosseum for lions to maul and eat.

In approximately 312AD, the Emperor of Rome converted to Christianity after winning a military battle where he saw a vision of a cross that he attributed to Jesus. By this time, despite the persecution, Christianity had grown throughout the Roman Empire. For hundreds of years, Roman citizens had watched Christians willingly die in the Colosseum, rather than deny their belief in Christ. They had been repeatedly told that Jesus Christ was a fraud, and if they would agree with this statement their lives would be spared. Time and time again, Christians chose death and sealed their testimony with blood. This stalwart conviction for Christ must have caused many average Roman citizens to consider the beliefs of those Christian saints, who died so willingly for their God.

The Emperor Constantine had accepted Christ as the Messiah. However, some believe that Constantine really cared more about a very large piece of real estate called the Roman Empire. Many scholars believe converting to Christianity was a well-thought-out attempt to unite a fragmented empire. Constantine understood the powerful effects a religious movement can have, so to unify the people, he led his empire to the acceptance of Jesus the Christ. Constantine needed all of the factions to have one single doctrine.

<u>The following is a hypothetical example to illustrate a point.</u>

In order to investigate this new religion, Constantine asked each bishop about baptism.

The Bishop of Rome answered that we baptize by sprinkling a few drops of water on the forehead; that is how baptisms are properly performed.

The Bishop of Ephesus disagreed and said that the physical ordinance of, and act of baptism, doesn't really matter to God. If you truly believe in your heart, you then can consider yourself baptized.

The Bishop of the Corinthians said that he baptized people by dipping them all the way under the water, because that is the way he believed Jesus was baptized.

The Bishop of Byzantium poured water on the forehead.

The point is, Constantine worried that the Christian world was drifting apart regarding the most basic ordinances, doctrines and practices. He knew that a division could lead to different factions and could result in unrest or worse, dissension. Constantine invited, or more likely ordered, some 318 major bishops to congregate in Nicaea, mandating they remain until they agreed on a set of beliefs and practices, or a common doctrine. The holy men met day after day for about <u>two years</u>, to no avail. One bishop didn't think that a particular doctrine was important, while another one believed it was essential. They debated and argued until they realized that they would never agree on everything. It was a no-win battle.

Ultimately, the bishops drafted and published a statement in 325AD that became known as the Nicene Creed. It affirmed that there is one God, but God is also a trinity: the Father, the Son and the Holy Ghost or the Holy Spirit, three-in-one and one-in-three. The bishops were surely pleased with themselves, because it was ambiguous. It allowed them to return to their parishes and interpret the Godhead as a mystery; that God is so big that He can fill the universe but so small that He can dwell in a man's heart. Their work satisfied Constantine and allowed them to teach their own version and interpretation of the Nicene Creed, the agreement which has fostered centuries of conjecture. It is ambiguous!

Over the years, the Bishop of Rome came to think of himself as the senior bishop, the "big kahuna," naturally, since the Roman Empire was founded in Rome. He would write letters to the other bishops telling them what they should and shouldn't do. However, when Constantine became emperor, he moved the capitol of the Roman Empire from the city of Rome to the city of Byzantium, and changed the name of the city to Constantinople. Naturally, the Bishop of Constantinople felt that he was the most important, the senior bishop, as he was closest to the emperor. Today, the city is named Istanbul which was named Constantinople, which was previously named Byzantium. It is the same city, just three different name changes.

This—who is the senior bishop or most important bishop—issue went on for years and years. Both bishops tried to wield their influence, seeking alliances from the lesser bishops, vying for the emperor's favor and rebuffing subordination to each other. Finally, there was a division and this is where the religion split into two factions. Those devoted to the Bishop of Rome formed the Roman Catholic Church and the ones who allied themselves with the bishop of Constantinople became the Greek Orthodox Church, developing into a major split in the religion.

Christianity was formed in 31AD, when Jesus was baptized. If God wanted His religion to grow, then He certainly knew where to begin. It began within the most powerful country on earth, the superpower of the time, with broad-spread influence, the best roads and largest navy for fast and swift communication. Rome was a country with the greatest wealth per capita of any country on earth and with the largest and most powerful armies. If you were to go back in time to the tenth century AD, which church would you want to be involved with? I am not saying that any of them were bad churches. I personally believe that the Pope of the Catholic Church in the 21st century is a really great and righteous man who has Christ-like charity in his heart. Likewise, the Archbishop of the Greek Orthodox Church is a really great and righteous man who has a Christ-like charity in his heart. Both are dedicated men, trying to lead as many people as possible to the teachings of Jesus Christ. Also, I think they do not believe that the Latter-day Saints have the correct doctrine of Jesus Christ and I, as a member of the LDS church, do not believe they have the fullness of the gospel. But what is beautiful about this scenario is that we are all trying to lead people to Jesus Christ, and I think that is fantastic. However, if I went back in time, to 1000AD, I don't know which church I would join. Both the Roman Catholic and the Greek Orthodox, in my opinion, would be just as great and good as the other. Both would do their best to teach me the gospel of Jesus Christ. However, I believe that by the time 1000AD rolled around, there was a sort of "falling away" of the original doctrine of Jesus the Christ.

Mormons believe that in the early nineteenth century, Joseph Smith restored the fullness of the gospel of Jesus Christ. Logically, if there was a restoration of doctrine, it would be preceded by a falling away of doctrine. The New Testament Book of 2 Thessalonians predicts this falling away:

> Now we beseech you, brethren, by the coming of our Lord Jesus Christ, and by our gathering together unto him, That ye be not soon shaken in mind, or be troubled, neither by spirit, nor by word, nor by letter as from us, as that the day of Christ is at hand. Let no man deceive you by any means: for that day shall not come, except there come a falling away first...
> *2 Thessalonians 2:1-3*

It is ebb and flow, when something fades, another thing builds to take its place. Say you go through a time of craving chocolate, then... well, that's not a good example, because no one gives up on chocolate. OK, what about fruit smoothies for breakfast during the summer, then as cool weather comes, you shift toward oatmeal. It's not that you don't like smoothies anymore it is just that you drifted away from the original. What I want to emphasize is that it was <u>not</u> a turning away, but a falling away:

that's why we needed a restoration. The 2nd Book of Timothy concurs:

> For the time will come when they will not endure sound doctrine; but after their own lusts shall they heap to themselves teachers, having itching ears; And they shall turn away their ears from the truth, and shall be turned unto fables. *2 Timothy 4:3-4*

Let's review how baptisms are performed. Today, as in the first decades after Christ, some faiths baptize with sprinkling, and others say that you need only to believe in your heart for you to be baptized. Some dip, or immerse completely under water. Mormons believe that you must immerse or dip the body completely in water to be baptized correctly. Why? Because we believe this is the way Jesus was baptized.

In the Book of John, it talks about a man named Nicodemus, who was a high-ranking official and came to Jesus in the night asking Him what he needed to do to enter into the kingdom of God. Well, Nicodemus, this is what you need:

> Jesus answered and said unto him, Verily, verily, I say unto thee, Except a man be born again, he cannot see the kingdom of God. Nicodemus saith unto him, How can a man be born when he is old? can [sic] he enter the second time into his mother's womb, and be born? Jesus answered, Verily, verily, I say unto thee, Except a man be born of water and of the Spirit, he cannot enter into the kingdom of God. *John 3:3-5*

Jesus Himself said that we all must be baptized to <u>enter</u> into the kingdom of God. But what is the proper way to be baptized? The Apostle John speaking about John the Baptist, in the Book of John explains:

> And John also was baptizing in Aenon near to Salim, because there was much water there: and they came, and were baptized.
> *John 3:23*

"Because there was much water there." If John were pouring a little water on the forehead, this statement would not have to been written into the Bible. The original word for baptize was *Baptismo*. *Baptismos* was the Greek word for baptism, originating from "bapto" which meant to "dip" or "immerse." By the fifteenth century, the word "baptism" was being used figuratively to include sprinkling, or what today is also called "christening." Mormons adhere to the original definition and spirit of the word, rather than the more modern dilutions. Mormons believe that baptism is a symbolic death and rebirth that requires complete submersion underwater. Therefore, if the word actually means to dip or immerse and John needed "much water" to baptize, then how did so many faiths fall away from this literal translation of the Bible?

Furthermore, being immersed completely in water has some interesting representations that relate to the teachings of Christ when He told Nicodemus that he needed to be born again. Think about this, you are standing there in an element called H_2O (water) and you are allowing yourself to be immersed into an element that can take your life away. That is, if you linger under water for very long, you will die. But once you are raised out of that element, you have a new life and are born again as Christ instructed Nicodemus.

I have friends of other Christian denominations who tell me that if I do not believe in the Nicene Creed, then I am not a true Christian. This is not logical to me. I believe that there are three essential things you need to be considered a Christian. I believe that you must have a conviction that:

1. Jesus Christ suffered in the Garden of Gethsemane and on the cross for all mankind.
2. Jesus Christ gave His life for the entire world.

3. Jesus Christ is resurrected and alive today.

If you truly and wholeheartedly believe these three things, whether you are baptized or not, I think you are a Christian. How could anyone in the world label you anything but a Christian if you wholeheartedly affirm those three things? However, Jesus Himself said that if you want to <u>enter</u> the kingdom of heaven, you must be born of water and of the spirit. These are the words of Christ Himself, and are incontestable. If you stand in the waters of baptism and say to yourself, "When I come up out of this water, I'm going to be clean from my previous life. I'm taking on the life of a disciple of Jesus. I'm going to emulate Him. I'm going to seek to follow His commandments, and try to direct my life path in His teachings." Your thoughts and commitment would be akin to laying your life down in the ground and coming up to live again, just as Christ did on that Sunday morning more than two millennia ago.

St. Paul answers the question for those people who never had a chance to be baptized. St. Paul writes in 1 Corinthians 15:29 that there were Christians baptizing in proxy for people who had died. Mormons are one of the only denominations that I know of that practice this ordinance rite called "baptisms for the dead." Don't get all excited; they don't dig up people's bones and baptize them. A proxy is an agent or substitute. In this case, a person is baptized for someone else in a proxy baptism. The people of Corinth, for some reason, had stopped believing in the resurrection. So, St. Paul wrote a letter (which became the Book of 1 Corinthians) to convince them that the resurrection is a real event. In the following scripture, the Apostle Paul uses logic to convince them that the resurrection is real, when he says:

> Else what shall they do which are baptized for the dead, if the dead rise not at all? why *[sic]* are they then baptized for the dead?   *1 Corinthians 15:29*

St. Paul is not asking why they are performing baptisms for dead people. St. Paul is saying to them, "Listen guys, if you have stopped believing in the resurrection, then why are you still doing baptisms for the dead?" He is using logic to show them their faulty thinking. That is, the resurrection is real; if not, there would be no reason for them to go on performing baptisms for people who have died. This scripture makes sense when you realize that the letter to the Corinthians was sent from St. Paul to convince them that the resurrection is a true principle. And as we can see, even some of the Corinthians were falling away from basic doctrines and principles. If the resurrection were not real, then you would not be doing baptisms for the dead, but since you are doing baptisms for the dead, then the resurrection must be real. Let's read it again;

> Else what shall they do which are baptized for the dead, if the dead rise not at all? why *[sic]* are they then baptized for the dead?   *1 Corinthians 15:29*

The point is that the dead are going to rise. Therefore, that is why they are conducting baptisms for the dead. St. Paul is logically making the conclusion that the people of Corinth already know that in their hearts.

Let's fast-forward in time and talk about the mid-1500s. How is truth surviving during this time period? Is it flourishing? Is it being accepted? No. Truth is still not faring well in the 1500s.

During the mid-1500s, there was a brilliant man named Copernicus. He discovered that the earth was not the center of the universe and that the sun didn't go around the earth. Instead, the earth revolved around the sun. Copernicus was teaching truth, but it didn't matter. He was called a liar. He was told that if he believed this, then he could not believe the Bible and that made him a heretic. They, therefore, threatened to excommunicate him from his church if he did not retract his theory. Copernicus was threatened and persecuted for telling falsehoods, or, in reality, for telling the truth.

The great reformer Martin Luther did not believe that the correct and original doctrines of Christ were being taught. Martin Luther protested the proliferating false teachings of his time and era, and that's how Protestant denominations came into existence, by breaking away from their church.

A friend of mine commented to me once that he thought that there was no need for Joseph Smith to restore the fullness of the gospel on earth. The doctrines and truths were surviving very well; therefore, there was no need for a restoration. I replied to my friend that the book of Timothy in the New Testament did not agree. Nor did the great Martin Luther agree, and a man named William Tyndale, who died in the year 1536, would not have agreed either. My friend had never heard of William Tyndale. I told him that Mr. Tyndale was imprisoned for over a year, tried in a court of law, and sentenced to burn at the stake. My friend then asked me, what horrible thing did William Tyndale do to receive such a severe punishment? The answer is, because he translated the Bible from Hebrew and Greek into the English language and then published it. That's all he did and as we can see, the laws of Western Europe in 1536 emulated those of the Romans in the third century. Clearly there was a need for a restoration.

This is how the United States began; in protest of religious persecution in European countries. Europeans were not allowed to practice their faith, but if they sailed across the Atlantic Ocean, they could worship the way they wanted. They started coming to America in the 1500s, and finally, in 1776, a country was founded on the basis that each individual has the right to believe and worship the way they choose, as long as it doesn't hurt anyone else. What a concept: freedom of religion! No persecution of a man for his beliefs. No killing of Christians with lions. No burning people at the stake for translating Bibles. No excommunications for suggesting that the sun does not go around the earth / the earth is not in the center of the universe.

The United States of America was founded in the year 1776, but it took the Revolutionary War, which concluded about seven years later, to finally secure and establish the premise of freedom and freedom of religion for all. Once our country was secure, God didn't waste any time, because it only took about twenty-five years for God to place Joseph Smith on the planet in this newly-founded country.

Joseph was born in 1805, and by 1829 the priesthood was restored to the earth by heavenly visitations from some of the original apostles. The resurrected St. Peter, St. James, and St. John gave the Melchizedek Priesthood to Joseph Smith. In the decade prior to 1829, God the Father and His Son Jesus Christ taught and restored other gospel truths through Joseph Smith. These divine beings gave instructions for twelve new modern-day apostles to be called, set apart and given a mandate to spread the message of Jesus Christ. The new quorum of the twelve accepted the mandate and sent the few missionaries they had to as many parts of the world as soon as they could. However, Joseph Smith was killed in 1844, and in 1847, Brigham Young, one of the modern apostles, led the Latter-day Saint Christians out of the United States to flee religious persecution. These new Christian followers had to leave a country that was founded on freedom of religion because that country could not, at the time, guarantee that same, hard-won freedom to the Latter-day Saint Christians.

It is notable here to say that they didn't go all the way to California, where the land was rich and fertile. Instead, Brigham Young moved them from the borders of the United States of America to a high western mountain location next to a lake that was filled with salt water. The Latter-day Saints were out in the wilderness and were settling throughout the mountains of the west. They made a life for themselves and became "a people." Even with their meager means, these new-age apostles sent missionaries throughout the world to tell of and preach of the atonement/resurrection of Jesus Christ and of the restoration.

After many years of living in this high mountain place, these Latter-day Saints applied for their settlements to become a state of the Union in the United States of America. They wanted their new state to be called Deseret, after a word in the Book of Mormon that meant honeybee and industry. However, when they petitioned the U.S. Congress, twice, to become a state, they were denied both times. Eventually, Congress granted them statehood, but denied their petition for the naming of their state to be Deseret. Instead, Congress named it Utah. By naming this new State of the Union, the United States Congress may have fulfilled a prophesy from the Old Testament.

> And it shall come to pass in the last days, that the mountain of the Lord's house shall be established in the top of the mountains, and shall be exalted above the hills; and all nations shall flow unto it. *Isaiah 2:2*

The word Utah is a Native American word from the Ute Indian tribe, meaning "tops of the mountains" or "peaks of the mountains." Therefore, if we were translating the Bible into the Ute Indian language, then Isaiah 2:2 could read, "And it shall come to pass in the last days, that the mountain of the Lord's house shall be established in <u>Utah</u>, and shall be exalted above the hills; and all nations shall flow unto it." I believe what happened here is that the U.S. Congress fulfilled a prophecy from Isaiah, written thousands of years ago.

In the Roman era, God planted Christianity inside one of the most powerful nations on earth and it took about three hundred years to go mainstream under Emperor Constantine. In modern times, God also restored the gospel inside of a country that was to become the only world superpower.

The Church of Jesus Christ of Latter-day Saints was placed inside of the United States of America by a divine plan. The influence of the USA on the world stage is unprecedented, and it enhances the abilities of the Latter-day Saints to proclaim the message of the atonement of Jesus Christ and the plan of salvation to the world. Just like it took three hundred years for a Roman emperor to become Christian, it only took the USA a little over two hundred years for a Latter-day Saint to become a viable candidate for president. Mormonism, in the United States, has become mainstreamed or accepted, similar to the Christians being accepted inside of the Roman Empire.

The Church of Jesus Christ of Latter-day Saints currently is the fourth-largest and fastest growing faith in the USA and it is based in the most powerful nation on earth. A few years ago, *Time Magazine* did a feature story on the Mormons, referring to them as a "booming religion" when most other faiths were shrinking in numbers. The Mormons are unique in that they did not break away or divide from a previous church. They are not Protestants. They originated their faith in the USA with a new set of revelations from God. At any given time, there are approximately 70,000 to 90,000 dedicated full-time missionaries worldwide, teaching about Jesus Christ. Each one is under the direction of a mission president for a particular region of the world, and that mission president, along with the missionaries, is under the direction of one of the twelve modern-day apostles of The Church of Jesus Christ of Latter-day Saints.

So, what happened to the apostles?

They are alive and well, operating their missionary effort to the world from the tops of the mountains and doing what apostles do best; spreading the message of Jesus Christ, who is the Savior of all mankind. He is the Son of God, the Only Begotten, who broke the bonds of death to become resurrected.

The Nicene Creed diluted the truth of Jesus and the apostles, creating reason for conjecture and ambiguity. This caused the world to wait for hundreds of years until the restoration of the gospel and the inarguable power of the word of Christ.

These modern-day apostles sent missionaries to my home many years ago to teach me about Jesus Christ. Since then, I have committed my life to help spread His message. Following the teachings of Jesus Christ is rewarding, and when you have the strength of the apostles helping you, charity springs from your heart. Once you find Christ, it becomes impossible to contain. Jesus is the Christ! If you have doubts you might want to read some of the books that the apostles wrote. They are best-sellers. The books of Saint Mathew, Saint Mark, Saint John and Saint Peter could change your life, just as they have for millions and millions of people. And they can do it for you too! You will not regret it. It was the best decision of my life and could be the best decision you will ever make.

John S. Pennington Jr.

CHAPTER 6
SECRET NAMES OF ANGELS

One Sunday night at about 6:00pm, I answered a knock on my door to find a young man with scriptures in hand. This teenager, a friend of my sons who had been to my home many times before, said that he had some gospel questions that he would like to discuss. Once settled at my kitchen table, he pulled from his pocket a wrinkled paper with a list of about forty questions. The young man's name is Kasey, and he was seventeen years old at the time; in search not only of spiritual enlightenment, but also scriptural clarity. He was seeking a foundation to give him roots for his basic beliefs. Most people need this type of scriptural expedition at some time in their life. In his mere seventeen years, he could only study so much material on his own. I, on the other hand, had grey hair and was nowhere close to being a young man, but vividly remembered my own list of questions when I was his age.

Kasey's scriptures had highlighter marks and penciled-in cross-references. He was full of the conviction of Jesus Christ, but was looking for substance, hungry for the meat of the scriptures, not just the milk. I could tell from the wording of his questions that Kasey had been conversing with a friend of a Protestant denomination, and that their theological banter had been going on for quite some time, as most of his questions pointed to the beliefs and oddities of the Mormons.

Most important, the questions were sincere and easily answered with just a few moments of referencing. However, there were two questions that stuck out and required in-depth explanations and study.

The New Name

The first was one that many other Mormons have wondered about, as I had in my youth; "Why does anyone need a new name?" Many people in the Bible are given a new name from heavenly messengers or by God. Kasey was referring to a book used by Mormons known as the Doctrine and Covenants:

> Then the white stone mentioned in Revelation 2:17, will become a Urim and Thummim to each individual who receives one, whereby things pertaining to a higher order of kingdoms will be made known; And a white stone is given to each of those who come into the celestial kingdom, whereon is a new name written, which no man knoweth save he that receiveth it. The new name is the key word.
> *Doctrine and Covenants 130:10-11*

St. John the Revelator, an original apostle of the Lord Jesus Christ, in the Book of Revelation, introduced the original concept.

> He that hath an ear, let him hear what the Spirit saith unto the churches; To him that overcometh will I give to eat of the hidden manna, and will give him a white stone, and in the stone a new name written, which no man knoweth saving he that receiveth it.
> *Revelation 2:17*

This is not an original Mormon doctrine, but from one of the original twelve apostles who walked in the shadows and footsteps of the Lord Jesus Christ. To fully grasp this practice, we need to understand how significant and important it is and under what circumstances the children of God receive a new name. In fact, even Jesus received a new name. In Hebrews 1:4, it says Christ will obtain a "more excellent name," and also the Apostle John foretells the same.

> Him that overcometh will I make a pillar in the temple of my God, and he shall go no more out: and I will write upon him the name of my God, and the name of the city of my God, which is new Jerusalem, which cometh down out of heaven from my God: and I will write upon him my new name. *Revelation 3:12*

Therefore, Jesus Himself obtained a new name. Both the Doctrine and Covenants and the Book of Revelation stress that no man knows the new name except for the one who has received it. It is private and should be kept by the person who receives this blessing.

Names have a great importance in the Bible, especially to those individuals who pray to and worship the Most High God of Israel. Remember that Saul became Paul (Acts 13:9), after he had conversed with Jesus while crossing a desert. The part of the story I want to emphasize is that his name change occurred after he spoke to the resurrected Jesus Christ.

Likewise, after Abram walked before the Almighty God, he had his name changed to Abraham (Genesis 17:3-5) and Abraham's wife also had her name changed by God from Sarai to Sarah (Genesis 17:15). Abraham's grandson's name was changed from Jacob to Israel. This is the same Jacob whose father was Isaac, and Isaac's father was Abraham.

In Genesis Chapter 32, Jacob is directed by an angel to return to his homeland. On his journey home, Jacob sees many angels and then wrestles with a man (he thinks) until the break of day. When I first read this story, I thought that Jacob was wrestling with this messenger in his mind, or in a dream-like state. But then I read that Jacob's thigh, or knee, was thrown out of joint (Genesis 32:25). This is when I realized it had been a physical wrestling match. It is so vividly real that all the story is missing is a referee with a black-and-white-striped shirt and a whistle.

These two physical beings wrestled through the night until dawn. It says that the messenger had to leave because the "day breaketh" (Genesis 32:26) and asked Jacob to let him go. Perhaps the messenger worried that someone would see them in the daylight, or maybe messengers from God have curfews, just like teenagers. Whatever the reason, the messenger pleaded with Jacob to let him go. But Jacob, being a tough guy, still scrapping to the end, with his thigh or knee joint out of joint, said;

> I will not let thee go, except thou bless me.
> Genesis 32:26

Jacob's defiance begs the question as to who, or what, this messenger really must have been. What kind of a being is this that Jacob would demand a blessing from him? If this were just an ordinary man, then why would Jacob seek a blessing? Or why was Jacob so willing to let him go in exchange for a blessing? It does not sound as if Jacob's opponent was a normal man.

Many biblical scholars believe that angels visited Jacob. If you read the full story, you will know that Jacob was seeing and being visited by angels throughout his journey. You can also safely assume that this wrestling partner must have been an angel and messenger from God. In asking for a blessing, Jacob implies that his competitor is of a heavenly origin and to make this point even more relevant, right after this experience, Jacob claimed that he had "seen God face-to-face" (Genesis 32:30).

> Note: Some Bible enthusiasts claim that the angel could not have been a physical being because this is the Old Testament and the resurrection had not happened yet. My reply is that the whole city of Enoch was taken up to heaven very early in the Old Testament and all those people had bodies. (See the Book of Moses Chapter 7:23-69). Therefore, the angel could have had a physical body before the resurrection.

As Kasey and I continued to talk, I said to him, "Let me ask you, if a messenger of God was about to bless you, what would you ask for? What would you think or believe would be a good blessing for you that a messenger of God could give you? Would you ask for a blessing of health and strength? Or increased knowledge? Maybe you would ask for wealth and financial success?" All of these blessings would come to my mind if I wrestled with an angel. If I was given any one of these blessings, then wrestling to the point to where my thigh or knee being thrown out of joint, would have been worth it, and I would have let the heavenly messenger go. But not Jacob! No. He didn't get a blessing of health and strength. He did not even ask for wealth or knowledge. Jacob didn't ask for any of these things. He got something that is perplexing to a reader of the Bible in the 21st century. To satisfy Jacob and his request for a blessing sufficient enough to let the messenger go, all Jacob gets is a new name. That's it. The messenger says: "Thy name shall be called no more Jacob, but Israel..." (Genesis 32:28).

I don't know about you, but it seems to me that if you wrestle an angel all night, and he is begging you to let him go, you are probably going to get a pretty good blessing. Why would Jacob be satisfied enough with a new name to let the messenger go? Does this conclusion to the story sound odd to anyone else? Do you think that Jacob should've gotten a bigger or better blessing? Would anybody have predicted that this story would end like that? That is, the angel gives him a new name and Jacob says, "Ok... The End." Huh?

However, if you consider what the Apostle John was talking about in the Book of Revelation, as to how important a new name is, then the story has substance and meaning. Jacob is grateful for the blessing of a new name and likely also for having seen God face-to-face. Here is where the story gets really interesting; before Jacob lets the messenger leave, he asked the messenger to reveal his name.

> And Jacob asked him, and said, Tell me, I pray thee, thy name. And he said, Wherefore is it that thou dost ask after my name? *Genesis 32:29*

What is out of the ordinary here is that the messenger was offended because Jacob wanted to know his name. This messenger of God will wrestle with you all night, throw your thigh or knee out of joint, and give you a new name, but don't even think about asking him to identify himself. That is, apparently, a no-no? The messenger resists and does not answer, but reverses the conversation with an aggressive posture by inquiring why Jacob wants to know his name. In the end, Jacob is left wanting. Why is the angel's name so sacred, or secret, that he cannot tell it to just anyone?

This story becomes more meaningful when we consider the next Old Testament story from the Book of Judges. Manoah, a Danite from the tribe of Dan, lived in the town of Zorah, with his wife who was barren. One day an angel of the Lord appeared to her and told her that she would bear a son.

This angel gave her instructions to never let her son drink wine, strong drink, or eat anything unclean, and also said that; "no razor shall come on his head: for the child shall be a Nazarite unto God..." (Judges 13:5)

A Nazarene was someone born in Nazareth, like Jesus. But a Nazarite was a person who performed disciplined actions, such as never cutting his hair, and being on a strict diet. This baby boy, Samson, grew up to be a Nazarite and an Old Testament muscle-man and hero.

The angel proclaims that Samson would help deliver the tribes of Israel out of the hands of the Philistines. To Samson's mother, this prophecy, delivered by an angel of God, must have been very exciting. Not just that she would bear a son, but that this son would be placed on earth with a specific mission from God. This was a great honor and responsibility placed upon her. As you can imagine, she ran and told her husband the marvelous news.

> A man of God came unto me, and his countenance was like the countenance of an angel of God, very terrible: but I asked him not whence he was, neither told he me his name: *Judges 13:6*

The writer of the Book of Judges emphasizes that the angel did not reveal his name. This emphasis is for a reason and will be illuminated later in the story.

After Manoah heard this fantastic tale, he sought the Lord in prayer, asking that He send this man of God once again to teach them of what they should do for the child that was to be born. The story says that God listened to the voice of Manoah and sent His angel back to the woman as she was sitting alone in the field. She quickly ran for her husband, who asked of the visitor, "Art thou the man that spakest unto the woman? And he said, I am" (Judges 13:11). Manoah asks his questions about how the child was to be reared, then the angel gives a warning to the woman to "not eat of any thing that cometh of the vine, neither let her drink wine or strong drink, nor eat any unclean thing:" (Judges 13:14). Like a good host, when the angel was finished, Manoah beseeched the angel to stay with them for a while so they could prepare a feast. My advice to Kasey was that if he ever, ever, ever had an angel telling him about his future, that he should at least invite him for dinner and some light entertainment. That would be proper, polite and advantageous, because the longer he stays the more information you might get out of him. In the Book of Hebrews it says we might have angels around us and we don't even know it.

> Let brotherly love continue. Be not forgetful to entertain strangers: for thereby some have entertained angels unawares. *Hebrews 13:1-2*

Manoah was definitely entertaining an angel unawares, and the angel was onto Manoah's plan to detain him. The angel tells him that he would not eat of his bread or his burnt offering, stating that all of Manoah's offerings must be to the Lord and he is not going to be accepting any credit for the prophecy, but wants all glory to be given to the Lord (Judges 13:16). I told Kasey that this sounded to me like an extremely good angel! However, Manoah had not realized that the messenger was an angel until his dinner invitation was declined. Then Manoah asks a very pointed question: "What is thy name, that when thy sayings come to pass we may do thee honour?" (Judges 13:17) The angel does not tell, but sternly fires back a question;

> Why askest thou thus after my name, seeing it is secret? *Judges 13:18*

The angel actually says that his name is a SECRET! When we take this story and reference it with what the Apostle John said in the Book of Revelation, that no one would know the new name except the person who receives it, this dialogue becomes astonishingly clear. The angel adamantly refuses to deliver his name to Manoah. Why would this be so important? This question is not answered as to why, but from the story we glean that an angel of the Lord will not reveal his name to a human and is offended when asked to do so.

The messenger who appeared to Jacob wouldn't reveal his name either, but the angel who appeared to Manoah goes further to say that his name is secret. Therefore, these stories fit perfectly into what St. John was writing about;

> To him that overcometh will I give to eat of the hidden manna, and will give him a white stone, and in the stone a new name written, which no man knoweth saving he that receiveth it.　　　　　　　　　　*Revelation 2:17*

After their experiences, Jacob, Manoah, and Manoah's wife all claim they have seen God, "face-to- face." Also, Israel and St. Paul's stories are similar in that after they spoke with heavenly beings, their names were changed. The point is that those who receive a new name have talked to a heavenly messenger first, or in some cases, with Jesus Christ and/or God.

Kasey sat across the kitchen table from me that night, enlightened through scriptures written thousands of years ago by prophets who documented the words of God. Do you think that the prophets of old knew that these particular words would make a difference to a young seventeen-year-old boy in the 21st century? Maybe—and maybe not--but this is why the scriptures are so compelling, for they usually answer questions when—and only when—the reader is ready for the answer. It is uncanny how they help each of us so personally at different times in our lives.

Special White Clothing

After discussing this subject for quite some time, Kasey turned to the second big question on his wrinkled paper. He asked, "Why are Mormons required to wear special white clothing to go into the temple?" My answer was straightforward, but initially it confused the young man because not all Mormons wear special white clothing. The only Latter-day Saints who wear them are those who have taken on temple covenants.

Only worthy, temple-attending Latter-day Saints are privileged to wear the sacred garments. If you belong to a faith that does not have temples, then there would be no reason for you to wear such apparel. Please let me explain. In approximately 1300BC to 1200BC there lived a prophet named Moses, who led the twelve tribes of Israel out of Egypt after hundreds of years of slavery. Out in the desert, the Lord God instructed Moses to build a tabernacle out of cloth, basically a tent, with walls made of fabric and poles. This tabernacle was to house the ark of the covenant and provide a place for sacrifices to be offered and performed. The people could not perform the sacrifice themselves. They were required to bring their unblemished animal to the tabernacle and give it to a tabernacle worker, who would perform the sacrifice for them. For approximately one thousand three hundred years, God would only allow the Levites, one of the twelve tribes of Israel, to perform this sacrifice. Therefore, for those one thousand three hundred years, only the Levites could work in or around the tabernacle. Of the descendants of Levi, only a few of them, the descendants of Aaron, were allowed to perform the actual sacrifices. In about 1000BC Solomon's Temple was completed, replacing the tabernacle made of cloth. Before a Levite was allowed to be a tabernacle worker, or later a temple worker, he had to be dressed in certain types of clothing. The style, material and length of the garments are described in detail from the Book of Exodus:

> And thou shalt make them linen breeches to cover their nakedness; from the loins even unto the thighs they shall reach: *Exodus 28:42*

Tabernacle or temple workers were commanded to make long linen shorts that reached to the "thigh." Here you have the Bible dictating the style of clothing, the length of the short pants and the type of material that the workers were required to wear. This entire chapter in Exodus discusses the dress code. Only a few of the Israelite descendants were privileged to wear special clothing, because only a few were temple workers. All of the other tribes of Israel could wear whatever they wanted. In the Old Testament they usually referred to the knee or knee area as the "thigh," and therefore, these linen shorts needed to reach down to the knee.

These biblical stories should help you see that the Latter-day Saints are being directed in the proper dress and clothing requirements as is taught in the Bible. They have the same dress code mandated by God and taught by Moses since the first tabernacle was erected. Rather than ask why Mormons wear special white temple clothing, you must reverse the question. Why would any person who reads and understands the Bible not realize that all temple-going people must have special clothing? It is required by the dictates of the Bible itself. If the Latter-day Saints did not build temples to the God of Israel, then there would be no use or reason to wear temple clothing. But that is the point: they do build temples, work in temples and worship in temples. They are following the Bible's direction as outlined in the Book of Exodus, which was written by Moses, one of the greatest prophets who ever lived.

Here are a few scriptures that illuminate the importance of these garments. Of those who have not defiled their white clothing;

> They shall walk with me in white: for they are worthy.
> *Revelation 3:4*

> Blessed is he that watcheth, and keepeth his garments, lest he walk naked, and they see his shame.
> *Revelation 16:15*

This is, of course, opposed to those who lose the privilege of entering the temple; who have not watched and kept their garments. Some people will defile the covenants they made to be temple-going people. However, the beautiful thing about the gospel of Jesus Christ is forgiveness. Forgiveness is universal and awaiting all those who seek it and who (hopefully) keep it. The scriptures solidify blessings for those people who reverently and stalwartly retain their temple-worthiness; retaining the admiration of Jesus Christ to become known as the sons and daughters of God.

That Sunday evening, Kasey and I were learning what it is to be referred to or called the sons of God. We had learned some valuable scriptures, and as the discussion continued, his young countenance was glowing. We were both growing. We weren't learning a subject of trivial pursuit, but a grand plan that was cast by the Word of God long before He, Jesus Christ, came to earth in the flesh.

In one of the last chapters of the Bible, the Apostle John brings a summation of the new name and the special white clothing to an incredible vision and clarity for those seeking answers on this subject. Because Kasey and I had built a foundation of scriptures over several hours, we had a better basis to understand what we were about to read:

> And he had a name written, that no man knew, but he himself. And he was clothed with a vesture dipped in blood: and his name is called The Word of God. And the armies which were in heaven followed him upon white horses, clothed in fine linen, white and clean. And out of his mouth goeth a sharp sword, that with it he should smite the nations: and he shall rule them with a rod of iron: and he treadeth the winepress of the fierceness and wrath of Almighty God. And he hath on his vesture and on his thigh a name written, KING OF KINGS, AND LORD OF LORDS. *Revelation 19:12-16*

His name is written on His vesture (*or vest*), and on His thigh (*or knee*), and no man knew His name but He Himself, and with that name, which is the Word of God, He called upon His most faithful followers of heaven. These faithful stalwarts had on fine

linen, white and clean, evidence that they are righteous and saintly;
> For the fine linen is the righteousness of saints.
> *Revelation 19:8*

Therefore, we learn that saints can lose their privilege to wear fine linen if they decide they no longer want to try to be righteous. That is why the Mormons refer to themselves as the Latter-day Saints. They are constantly seeking to follow the commandments of God in righteousness. This is not by coincidence, but a design from the Master Designer.

Another scripture we studied that night was in the Book of Mormon:

> And I would that ye should remember also, that this is the name that I said I should give unto you that never should be blotted out, except it be through transgression; therefore, take heed that ye do not transgress, that the name be not blotted out of your hearts. I say unto you, I would that ye should remember to retain the name written always in your hearts, that ye are not found on the left hand of God, but that ye hear and know the voice by which ye shall be called, and also, the name by which he shall call you.
> *Mosiah 5:11-12*

In these passages, it seems very important that Mosiah relayed this message to his audience; that a name by which you were called needs to be remembered. So that when you are called, you will recognize the caller as your Savior calling from the bonds of death unto the life of resurrection.

In the Book of Mark Chapter 5, it talks about a crazy man continually crying in the mountains and cutting himself. They had tried to bind him with chains and fetters, but each time he would break free. The Apostle Mark emphasizes that the man was "far off" when he saw Jesus and ran up to Jesus to worship

Him, and calls Him, "Jesus thou son of the most high God." The crazy man, even from far off, recognized Jesus. When Jesus realized the wild man knew His name, naturally, Jesus wondered where they had met. The first thing Jesus says to him is, "What is thy name?" (Mark 5:9). The wild man cannot give him a proper name because he was filled with many devils or spirits and just says, "My name is Legion: for we are many." Here, the wild man failed the first test, just like Mosiah had outlined. He needed to produce a name that, "never should be blotted out." The devils crammed inside this man's body were the same spirits who had followed Satan when they lost the war in heaven. Therefore, their names had been blotted out from the Book of Life. That is how they knew who Jesus was from "far off;" they remembered Jesus from the war in heaven and now they do not have a proper name.

The significance of a new name is hidden within the Apostle John's writings. The subject is thin, frail, anemic in volume, and St. John really never provides a great deal of detail on the meaning, stature, responsibility, or authority that a new name might bestow on the recipient. What we do know from the stories in the scriptures is that a new name is personal and individual, and can be a life-changing experience. One's name often determines identity and personality. We witnessed Saul do a 180-degree turn in heart and spirit when he became St. Paul. It is no trivial matter to be picked for Christ's team. Rather, it is a high honor and privilege, but those very words, "honor and privilege", seem to fall short of the magnitude. As the author of this book, I am at a loss for words to describe how great the blessing of being renamed by God really is.

A few years ago, I was on a tour in Israel, and while in Jerusalem I visited the Dome of the Rock and the West Wall. While my friend and I were standing next to the West Wall of the old temple, an elderly Jewish man, dressed like a rabbi in black-and-white clothing and a black hat, approached us, asking for a donation for the children of Israel. My friend, standing next to me, gave him a few dollars and returned to observing the wall that dates back thousands of years. The aged man came back and asked my friend, for twenty dollars, if he wanted a new name. He said that for twenty dollars, he would give my friend a new name. We were just standing there in a small crowd of people and this was transpiring unbeknownst to the rest of the group. So my friend gave him a twenty-dollar bill and the old Jewish man tied a dark piece of thread around my friend's finger in a knot, and then drew close and whispered in his ear a new name. Now that I think about this experience, I realize that the Jewish people, especially an old Jewish rabbi, would have an extreme interest in Old Testament stories regarding new names. It was an experience that I will never forget.

The wearing of fine white linen and the old Jewish rabbi giving a new name to my friend are both biblically-based doctrines. For people or faiths not interested in temples or new names, these references in the Bible may be confusing. Naturally, they would question their meaning and not understand the significance. These subjects would simply have no relevance to them. Temples are for those who wish to be the elect of God and who hope to be called up by Jesus, on the last day, with their "linen white and clean."

Repeatedly reading the scriptures helps us learn in one way, but performing unselfish acts shows the pure love of Christ.

When we obtain a state of charity, where our love for someone is greater than the love we have for ourselves, then that is when we are ready to receive the greatest of all the gifts of God. The act of doing for others and not considering ourselves allows us to become true followers of Christ. That is what temple workers do. They do ordinances for people who cannot do them for themselves. In the Garden of Gethsemane and on the cross, Jesus did something for us that we could not do for ourselves. In a like manner, when we attend the temple and sacrifice our time for those people who cannot do their own temple ordinances, we then learn, by repetition, a very small part of what Christ did for us. We do things for other people that they cannot do for themselves, just as Jesus did something for us that we cannot do for ourselves, and in the process, we learn a little more about how to become like Jesus. The Apostle James told us to be; "doers of the word, and not hearers only, deceiving your own selves" (James 1:22).

That night, Kasey and I spent more than three hours at the kitchen table. Kasey learned about three thousand year-old dress codes for temple workers, and that if he ever wrestles with a messenger from God, he should use the rising sun as a bargaining chip for a really cool blessing. And when you talk to an angel, you must wait for him to offer his name freely; asking for his name will get you nowhere and may offend him.

One of the amazing things about the gospel of Jesus Christ is that you can put all the time and effort you want into it and it always pays you back more than you deposit. During that discussion with Kasey, I learned and received much more enlightenment than he did. No matter how much I give to Christ, He returns much more than I ever put in. Isn't it great!

CHAPTER 7
WHY DO CHRISTIANS CELEBRATE HALLOWEEN?

The practices of Halloween, Christmas and Easter stem from origins that you might not realize. The reason we celebrate Halloween might be similar to why we celebrate the birthday of Christ on December 25th. But I am getting ahead of myself.

Have you noticed that Easter falls on a different date every year? Christmas is always on the same date, December 25th. In contrast, Easter is not the first Sunday of any certain month, and it moves from March to April and then back again. It is on a different date each year. Why? It is because Easter is based on the movements of the moon, specifically, the preceding full moon, known as the Paschal Full Moon. Easter is observed on the first Sunday after the first full moon after the spring equinox. Easter is based on the phases of the moon.

I was teaching this in one of my Sunday school classes once and I remember this fifteen-year-old girl saying, "No it is not! You have got to be kidding!" "Yes, it is true." I said.

Spring equinox is approximately on the 21st day of March. Equinox occurs in spring and autumn, twice each year, when there are exactly twelve hours of sunlight and twelve hours of darkness. Winter solstice occurs on, or near, the 21st day of December, which, in the northern hemisphere, is the shortest day of the year with the longest night. Summer solstice is the opposite; on about the 21st day of June, when the sun shines for the longest. Solstices are reversed in the Southern Hemisphere, but the spring and autumnal equinox are the same everywhere on the globe. To determine what day Easter will be on, you must wait for the spring equinox (March 21st), then wait for the next full moon; and when that happens, the very next Sunday is Easter Sunday. By definition, there must be a full moon between Palm Sunday and Easter Sunday. Palm Sunday was when people waved palm leaves in front of Jesus as He entered Jerusalem, and Easter Sunday is the day we celebrate Jesus' resurrection. Therefore, Easter Sunday could arrive anywhere between March 22nd and the third week in April. Easter is also closely related to the Jewish Passover, not just due to the similarities in symbolism, but because of the lunar cycle.

Why do Christians celebrate Halloween? I have friends who are Christian and non-Christian, and they both question why Christians have Halloween parties in their church buildings, or even why we allow Santa Claus to attend church Christmas parties. I personally had this same question years ago when I was a Protestant and our church had Halloween parties. Mormons have them too, but it just did not make sense to me until I learned about Easter, Christmas, Santa Claus, Christmas trees and yes, Halloween. My original thought was that we should abolish Halloween because it is evil. I didn't understand why we allow Santa Claus at church Christmas parties or even where Christmas trees came from.

Then I learned why we have Christmas trees. In search of answers to what seemed like simple questions, I realized that the question was much deeper than I had imagined.

I used to think that if something--anything--can or is being used for evil, then we must shun it and the problem would be solved. Me and my simple mind! As if the world's problems were just an easy little math problem to be solved. If this same logic applies, then no one should use sharp knives, and the plug should be pulled on that nasty internet. Clearly, this "simply shun it" solution is not a good answer. To understand this, we must accept the premise that we act upon things, instead of allowing things to act upon us. Wielding our surroundings rather than blaming them is the deeper side to the issue. This concept is simply laid out in my favorite chapter of the Book of Mormon:

> Both the heavens and the earth, and all things that in them are, both things to act and things to be acted upon. *2 Nephi 2:14*

Then it says that Adam and Eve are;

> Free forever, knowing good from evil; to act for themselves and not to be acted upon... *2 Nephi 2:26*

I want to be one who acts instead of being acted upon. I want to be proactive, and responsible for my thoughts and deeds. When the angel Lucifer became "Satan," it meant that he was against God and His plan. Therefore, anything designed to thwart God's plan is a "satan," or from Satan.

Almost any tool in this world can be used for good or for evil and that is only determined by the person who is wielding the tool, or (in the case here) holiday. It is not a result of the tool, but by the hand and heart of the operator. If you place a computer on one man's desk, he will work with that computer and use it to fly three men to the moon and return them to the earth safely. He uses that tool for good. You can place that same computer on another man's desk, and all he can figure out to use it for is to view nude pictures on the Internet. He uses the tool in an adverse way. Both men have the same tool; but while one used it for a marvelous outcome, the other used it for self-gratification. Which kind of man/person are you?

Give one man a sharp knife and he will use it to carve beautiful wood furniture, make fantastic meals for his family, or protect the women and children of the village. Another man can use that same sharp knife to threaten people and rob them. Different users utilize the same tool for different purposes.

Some people believe that computers are evil and should be banned. If that logic were true, then we would also have to abolish sharp knives. Any righteous man can take anything, even a holiday, and use it for good. Conversely, an evil man will do the opposite. It is not the tool's fault; it is the man's choice.

If you use this type of thinking then you believe that all humans can only be acted upon, but I don't believe that. That is why I joined the priesthood of God. I joined an order of the priesthood referred to within the Bible as the Priesthood of Melchisedec (which is spelled two ways in the Bible), the same priesthood that Jesus held.

> If therefore perfection were by the Levitical priesthood, (for under it the people received the law,) what further need was there that another priest should rise after the order of Melchisedec, and not be called after the order of Aaron? For the priesthood being changed, there is made of necessity a change also of the law. For he of whom these things are spoken pertaineth to another tribe, of which no man gave attendance at the altar. For it is evident that our Lord sprang out of Juda; of which tribe Moses spake nothing concerning priesthood.
> *Hebrews 7:11-14*

I try to use the disciplines of this priesthood order to learn to act upon things, rather than to allow things to act upon me. Some religions believe that women should be covered from head to toe in cloth so that a man cannot see any feature, even the eyes, of a woman. They believe men cannot control themselves, sexually or mentally, if they gaze upon a woman. I think this is an example of a man allowing his surroundings to act upon him and therefore has not learned how to be in control of himself.

Learning to control our thoughts and actions is one reason we are here on earth; to become the masters of our own bodies, not slaves to them. The commandments are a guide for people to step into dominion; where the mind is in control instead of physical hungers, passions, or will. This is one way to become like Christ. Over a lifetime of trying to keep the commandments, we slowly become masters of our minds. Self-control is part of what we strive to learn. Jesus taught about this in the Garden of Gethsemane when, even though He was in tremendous pain, He maintained control and did not allow His surroundings to control Him. Jesus asked the Father to take the "cup," or task, from Him because it was very difficult to do. However, as the master of His body and mind, He obeyed the will of the Father and did not yield, but completed the Father's plan.

Another example is in the fourth chapter of the Book of Matthew when Jesus, having fasted for forty days, was being tempted by Satan. First, Satan suggested that Jesus turn a stone into a loaf of bread to calm His hunger. If I had not eaten for forty days, I can see how this would be enticing, but Jesus refused, maintaining control of Himself and the situation.

Then Satan taunted Jesus to prove that God's angels were actually with Him, suggesting that Jesus jump from the top of the temple and see if the angels would keep Him from harm. Jesus refused and maintained control.

Third, Satan showed Jesus all of the kingdoms of the world and said, "fall down and worship me" and I will give you all of this and more. Usually, in a story of three wishes, choices, or temptations, the last one is the most alluring and difficult. When I first read this story in the Bible, I didn't get it, because at the end of days, the world and all of the kingdoms of the world would belong to Jesus anyway, so how could that entice Him? It just did not make sense. This just didn't seem like a big third temptation.

After further study of the plan of salvation, I believe that Satan was not offering Jesus the kingdoms of the world, but the people inside of those kingdoms. I think Satan was saying, "Worship me and I will stop tempting everyone." Therefore, the sins of the world will be greatly reduced. That would allow Christ to bring many more people back to the presence of God. Satan knew that Jesus has so much pure love for mankind that this may have been a huge temptation. If Satan stopped working against God's plan, think about how many would come unto God! If we imagine this dialogue, it makes sense that Jesus surely might have been tempted by the offer from Satan. Notice that all three temptations <u>would require Jesus to do something</u>. We learn, therefore, that Satan cannot force us to do anything. He only makes suggestions and we must make the choice to act, or not to act. It is up to us. Satan was trying to act upon Christ. He has no power over us until we allow him the power.

The Book of 2nd Nephi tells us that Satan does not force us to give up our liberty, but that we give up our liberty if we yield to Satan's influence. The moment we cave to a temptation is when we concede our liberty. There are many types of temptations; cheating on a test, stealing, lusting in your heart, using drugs or alcohol. These are all evidence of a man who is not in control and one who is allowing himself to be acted upon, which causes him to slowly lose his liberty. He is not mastering himself, but instead becoming a slave.

The priesthood reminds, helps, and directs me in the teachings of Christ. As a priesthood holder, I am committed to a lifelong course to take any tool, holiday, or concept that is placed in my path and direct it to Christ. Even though initially it may appear evil, I will seek a way to use it for good.

Now, about those Christmas trees. Some of you are wondering, what does Brother Pennington have against a cute little Christmas tree? Many of the secular traditions, holidays, and rites have heathen or pagan origins. However, some have been adapted to be used for good purposes. The Christmas tree is described way back in the Old Testament as a heathen tradition. You may say it isn't so, but:

> Learn not the way of the heathen... For the customs of the people are vain: for one cutteth a tree out of the forest, the work of the hands of the workman, with the axe. They deck it with silver and with gold; they fasten it with nails and with hammers, that it move not. They are upright as the palm tree... *Jeremiah 10:2-5*

Did you catch that? It was the heathens who began this tradition of cutting a tree, standing it upright with nails, and decorating it with gold and silver, but the followers of God took that same tradition and changed it into a symbol of the life and resurrection of Jesus Christ. Christians have transformed heathen actions into a beautiful symbol inside homes and businesses all over the world, to remind everyone that the celebration of Christ's birth is at hand.

Today, people want to know why we have Halloween parties in church buildings, but the Halloween argument and that of Christmas trees is basically the same argument. Both traditions came from heathen traditions and have people saying that because it is evil we should abolish the tradition, like sharp knives or computers. As Christians, we all have the responsibility to try to use everything that is placed in front of us to the service of good. When it comes to how Christians celebrate holidays, it all comes down to how the holiday is used and how the individual uses or implements the activity. It has nothing to do with the event, but how the event is used.

If heathens can create something cool, but they use it for evil, then I can certainly grab that same thing and turn it into something that focuses our thoughts on the Most High God and His Son, giving Satan a little taste of his own medicine. If Satan can take things from us and try to turn them into evil, then I have no reservation about turning the tables on him and I also take real pleasure in doing so.

This brings us to why we celebrate the birth of Christ on December 25th. This holiday date also began as a pagan celebration. In the second century AD, the Romans were using the 25th of December as a huge celebration to honor their sun god. December 21st is winter solstice and the shortest day of the year in the Northern Hemisphere. So every year, three days after the shortest day, when their sundials confirmed that the days were actually getting longer, the Romans celebrated the return of the sun. The solar system testifies of Jesus being the Christ by using the date December 25th. Many people do not know this, but the Romans and Egyptians claimed that the sun was reborn on December 25th after being dead for three days. You see, God has given us signs and evidence that testify that Jesus is the Christ.

He made everything in the solar system to testify that Jesus is the Christ. It is not by coincidence. In fact, their tradition stated that on December 21st the sun would die, by dropping to the lowest point in the sky (at noon) and for the next three days stay at the lowest point (lowest degree) in the sky during December 22, 23 and 24th. Then, after the three days of being at the lowest degree in the sky, on December 25th, the sun would rise one degree in the sky and thus be reborn.

Does this sound familiar? As we have discussed in Chapter 3, the story of the solar system points to and testifies that Jesus is the Christ. It is as if God wrote the date of Jesus' birth in the sky with His finger and therefore Christians would naturally and cosmically conclude this date as the birth date of Jesus Christ. Christians would teach the Romans about the true meaning of December 25th and convey the message that God is trying to teach them about Jesus being the Christ. Therefore, tradition states that Jesus was born on December 25th in 1BC and seven days later, it became the first day of the year 1AD.

> Note: For a more in-depth discovery of Jesus' birth year, please read the last half of Chapter 8, "Atheists, Agnostics and Anti-Mormons" regarding the supernova that was recorded by Chinese astronomers in 5BC.

The point is, Satan had obtained a day of pagan celebration, widely accepted by the Roman Empire, when they worshiped the sun in the sky on December 25th, instead of the Son of God. Satan and his angels had the entire population of the most powerful empire in the world focusing on the sun instead of Christ. Satan had primitively clouded that date. Because Satan knew that if he didn't front run the date and poison the meaning of December 25th before Jesus was born, that this symbolism would have been too powerful of a testimony that Jesus is the Creator of the solar system and everything else.

So Satan focused on that day to make it a day of pagan worship. He had to do it well in advance of the birth of the Savior, with the Egyptians and the Romans. Satan's angels must have reveled in their accomplishment. But look out, here come the Christians and by the third century AD, there were "part Christian" families that were half-Christian and half-Roman sun god worshipers. December 25th became such a huge holiday that most everyone had the day off work. But Christians re-established this date with Christ in the center; with the symbolism perfectly lining up the cosmos, and Jesus being resurrected on the third day.

Satan might have seen this as the Christians trying to muscle in on his day, or perhaps he thought that they would become lax and soon they, too, would be sucked into worshiping the sun in the sky instead of the Son of God. It even sounded similar and could be used to confuse the Christians. Surely, some Christians didn't really want to do it at first—that is, use December 25th as Christ's birthday, I mean. "No, no, no," they would have thought. They would have wanted to abolish the sun god worship day and use a different day for Christ. Just like today, some people, including me a few years ago, wanted to stop all Halloween celebrations.

Well, the Christians took over. They elbowed in on Satan's sun god day, to the extent that today very few people recall one of the biggest holidays in the Roman Empire. Give the Christians a few hundred years and look what they can do. Maybe it will take a few hundred years to change Halloween, but we are going to start. Boycotting is sometimes a useful strategy, but in this example of the 25th of December, introducing an alternative prevails over a boycott. The definition of a leader is the one who takes the lead, and Christians certainly took the lead on that one.

No doubt Satan was not pleased and was probably yelling at his followers. How did this happen? How did Jesus take over my sun god worship day? Surely furious, he had to come up with a new business plan.

Some Christian groups feel that Santa Claus is a diversion from Christ and that Satan is using Santa to get children to think about what they are going to get, rather than what they can give. Doesn't Santa wear the color red, like Satan? And the names Satan and Santa use the same five letters.

Again, this goes back to why I joined the priesthood of the Most High God. I wanted to learn how to take anything or anyone placed before me and try to do what Christ would do, for good. Remember St. Paul in the New Testament, hunting down the original twelve apostles to kill them? He had murder on his mind and in his heart. Then Christ made him an apostle, and St. Paul went on to teach truth and write a large part of the New Testament. How thick is that irony? WOW. Talk about Christ acting rather than being acted upon. That is the kind of priesthood holder I want to be. Christ could have had St. Paul die in the desert of heat stroke, but instead, he turned a murdering heart into a giving heart. At some point in history, I suspect that some Christians wished St. Paul dead, but then he became a saint. Go figure?

The modern day Santa does divert some children's thoughts to getting rather than giving. However, rather than ban Santa, I must teach my children about the man known as St. Nicholas, from whom Santa Claus is derived and has become diluted. He was a great man who understood the mission of giving; one who used action and song to help the poor and the needy; a true saint with saintly actions. This is why Mormons refer to themselves as Latter-day Saints. They seek to be a giving people to all in need, in their actions and deeds.

Anything that takes your focus away from Christ is a "satan." Thus, I use Christmas as an opportunity to teach and model the true message of Saint Nicholas—that is, if we really wish to remember Jesus Christ and become like Christ, then we must give. Santa Claus reminds us to give. I believe we should never surrender and never give Satan a single day, much less let Satan claim a person like Saint Nicholas. We need to take the good saint back and make him our own. We must take everything under our control and turn it to good. We can use each Christmas Eve to teach from the Books of Matthew, Mark, Luke, and John. We invite our family and friends to join us, to celebrate the art of giving, and become the best Christians we can be.

We can use Santa Claus as our alter-ego; to visit old folk's homes or shut-ins, and sing Christmas carols and take gifts and food to less-fortunate neighbors. I am not going to stick my head in the sand just because I think Satan has a grip on Christmas or Halloween. At one time, Satan had a grip on the Christmas tree and December 25th, but then Christians kicked Satan down the street. Just like Michael the archangel and the angels kicked Satan and his angels out of heaven. See, it can be done, and we are the ones to do it. If Santa Claus can help us fight Satan, then we should use him, just as Christ used St. Paul to convert millions of people.

Halloween is celebrated on October 31st. In the last thirty years, I have seen Mormon wards sponsor Halloween parties inside their church buildings. When I first observed this many years ago, I shook my head in disbelief. What are we doing? What kind of message are we sending to our children? I was a boycotter, I wanted to ban this practice because this holiday has origins of evil.

Then I learned about the origins of the Christmas tree and December 25th. I learned about other holidays like Easter. I decided not to stand back and allow Satan the twenty-four hours of October 31st to be king. We should not give him a day in which he can do anything he wants and everyone thinks it's okay. No way. We should not give Satan a single day! Not even a second!

Instead, we must reclaim it by turning this day into a costume party for our children. As always, we begin with a prayer to bless the food and ask for a safe activity, a fun, wholesome party, where people put on Superman suits, dress up like the Three Musketeers, and imitate Sponge Bob Square-Pants. We have a party where there are no evil, grungy, or devilish clothing allowed. We will give awards for the most creative costumes. We may not know exactly how we are going to change it, but we are going to start. It might take us three hundred years, but in the end, Satan will not have a day that he can call his own.

What message will it send if I stay home on October 31st, turn off all of the lights and not answer the door? Some friends tell me that this is exactly what I should do. If everyone did it, then we would stop the Halloween celebration. It would be like banning the internet to eliminate pornography. We need to lead by activity and instigate a more effective strategy. The people who need our help are not those who attend church every Sunday, but the ones we're more likely to encounter at a Halloween party. They may need our help the most. Jesus told us that He did not come into the world for the righteous, but for the sinner. I can do more good in the world by providing a safe place for people who are already going to celebrate this holiday. Just like the Romans, who celebrated Christmas on December 25th, I am going to celebrate Halloween. Ninety-nine people out of every hundred are going to do something on Halloween night. I believe we can change the world through calling them to an active cause.

One day God might want you to do something important; a task that requires a person of great trust with unwavering integrity. You can be that person. Be the one who can act, rather than being acted upon. Learn the disciplines of liberty by being one who embodies righteousness and receive the power of Christ to act for yourself.

John S. Pennington Jr.

CHAPTER 8
ATHEISTS, AGNOSTICS & ANTI-MORMONS

Almost two millennia ago, a humble prophet named Moroni engraved the following words onto golden plates:

> And when ye shall receive these things, I would exhort you that ye would ask God, the Eternal Father, in the name of Christ, if these things are not true; and if ye shall ask with a sincere heart, with real intent, having faith in Christ, he will manifest the truth of it unto you, by the power of the Holy Ghost. And by the power of the Holy Ghost ye may know the truth of all things.
> *Moroni 10:4-5*

Then, almost two centuries ago, another prophet translated these words into English and put the test to the world: the challenge of feeling the power of the Holy Ghost and developing a testimony of the truthfulness of the Book of Mormon.

Who has read the Book of Mormon? Have you read it from cover to cover? Years ago, when I was on my mission for the LDS church, I had a missionary companion who had never read the Book of Mormon. Elder Winegar had only been in the mission field a few weeks when I discovered that he had never read the Book of Mormon from cover to cover. He had been raised in the LDS church his whole life. I had heard him testify of the truthfulness of the Book of Mormon, but what he had was an intellectual testimony.

An intellectual testimony example is; (i) my dad is smart and he believes it, (ii) all my friends believe it's true, and (iii) millions of Mormons can't be wrong. This is what is referred to as an intellectual testimony. Every religion has some members like this; it is normal in all religions of the world, but it was not normal for a full-time Latter-day Saint missionary.

One day, my companion and I knocked on a door and we met a man who was not Mormon, but he owned more Mormon books than we had as missionaries. He referred to himself as an agnostic Christian.

An atheist is someone who does not believe in God. A Christian is someone who believes in Jesus Christ. However, an agnostic Christian says that he wants to believe in Christianity but he does not have enough evidence to prove it to be true. On the other hand, he does not have enough evidence to prove it to be false. So, an agnostic Christian is waiting for enough evidence to prove either that there is no God, or to prove that God does exist.

This is the dilemma that torments agnostics, because it is impossible to prove a negative. For example, someone might want to prove that unicorns do not exist in the entire universe. In order to do that, this person would have to be behind every rock, in every valley, and on every mountaintop in the entire universe at the exact same time to be certain that unicorns do not exist. Therefore, if someone knows for a fact that God does not exist, that person would have to be behind every rock, in every valley, on every mountaintop, and in every dimension of the universe at the exact same time to be sure that God does not exist. However, if that person could be in every valley and on every mountaintop at the exact same time in the whole universe, then who would that person be? That person would have to be God. Like I said, there is no way to prove a negative.

So this agnostic Christian had many questions for two young missionaries from The Church of Jesus Christ of Latter-day Saints. The first question that he wanted to know was, where was Jesus born? Elder Winegar and I answered him by saying that Jesus was born in Bethlehem.

He then proceeded to open his own Book of Mormon and read from Alma, which says; "And behold, he shall be born of Mary, <u>at Jerusalem</u> which is the land of our forefathers..." (Alma 7:10).

His follow-up question was, if everyone knows that Jesus was born in Bethlehem, then why does your Book of Mormon state that He was born at Jerusalem? We did not know the answer to this question and like all good missionaries, rather than answer a question that we do not know, we simply said, "We do not know, but we will get back to you and give you an answer at our next meeting." He then gave us a typed out list of questions on several sheets of paper, which he wanted us to answer. The list was written as if he had already known we were supposed to knock on his door that day.

We took the list of questions and went back to our apartment. What would you do in this situation? My response was, "I am going to find an answer to every question." In contrast, my companion, who had never read the Book of Mormon and therefore had never received a spiritual confirmation of its truthfulness, reacted in the opposite way. He started to question why he was out on a mission for The Church of Jesus Christ of Latter-day Saints. His intellectual testimony was now slightly dented.

When we got back to our apartment that evening I simply asked my companion, "Why don't you just read the book? Why don't you sit down and grab the Book of Mormon right now and read it cover to cover and make your decision whether you believe it is true or not." That is, make your own decision rather than relying upon your intellectual testimony, and to his credit, he did! He sat down right then and there and started to read. He read for three days straight, and within those many hours of reading and praying, the Holy Ghost told him it was true. It was an incredible transformation, and I witnessed it first-hand.

The next week we returned to the Christian agnostic's home in an attempt to answer his questions.

The term "at Jerusalem" means, "in or around." Bethlehem is just five miles south of Jerusalem. Therefore, the term "at" would mean in or around a certain place; the optimal word here being around, or in the same vicinity. But if you really think about it, the simplest answer as to why the writer of the Book of Alma used the term "at Jerusalem," was because the ancestors of the people to whom he was talking had not been in the land of Jerusalem for over four hundred years. Therefore, they would not have known where the city of Bethlehem was. They barely even remembered where Jerusalem was. That is why Alma added the ending phrase, "which is the land of our forefathers" after he said "at Jerusalem." Alma had to add this clarification in order to help his audience remember the place he is talking about. They would have probably replied, "Oh yeah, Jerusalem, which is in the land of our forefathers," because it had been four hundred years since their ancestors had left there. That is a simple answer and probably the most correct as to why he used "at Jerusalem." Most of the time, the simplest answer is the correct one.

Here are a few examples of the other questions he had for us:

"Hey, missionaries... Why did Joseph Smith say that all other churches were an abomination to the Lord?" My answer was that Joseph Smith did not say that.

Then the agnostic Christian opened his Book of Mormon and turned to the Joseph Smith history Chapter 1 Verse 19, where it says that Joseph should join none of them, because all of their creeds were an abomination.

Our answer once again was simple, as we replied to the agnostic's error. Joseph Smith did not say that; Joseph Smith is only writing what God said. So you would need to ask God why God said that because Joseph Smith is only quoting what God said. The simple answer wins.

"Hey, missionaries... Joseph Smith added to the Bible and it says in the last few verses of the Bible that: "If any man shall add unto these things, God shall add unto him the plagues that are written in this book:" (Revelation 22:18)

Most missionaries answer this objection by turning to Deuteronomy 12:32, which says the same thing; "thou shalt not add thereto..."

However, Elder Winegar and I used the simplest answer when we returned the question to the agnostic Christian and said, "Which plagues are you referring to? If Revelation is a true book, which we both believe it to be, and if Joseph Smith did add to the Bible, as you infer, then he should have been hit with a bunch of plagues. Correct? Therefore, which plagues do you claim affected Joseph Smith and the Mormons? Joseph Smith was killed by a man with a gun. Are you saying that a man with a gun with murder on his mind was a plague from God? Or, maybe you are referring to the cricket infestation that happened in Utah in the year 1848? But as everyone knows, the crops were saved by thousands and thousands of seagulls who flew in and ate the crickets. The seagulls ate so many crickets that the seagulls would throw up the contents of their stomachs so they could eat more. The crops were saved by the miracle of the seagulls, and as a result of this miracle, the seagull was named the state bird of Utah, even though it is a land-locked state." Therefore, Mr. Agnostic Christian, is that the plague you are referring to? The conclusion must be that no plague ever happened. Therefore, no Mormon, or Joseph Smith, ever added to the Bible. Because if they had added to the Bible, Revelation 22:18 adamantly states that they surely would have received plagues. But the fact is, they didn't! So, your interpretation of Revelation 22:18 is incorrect, because the Bible is a true book and if anyone ever does add to the Bible then plagues will definitely be placed upon that person.

"Hey, missionaries... If the Book of Mormon was coming, then why didn't any of the past prophets foresee it coming?"

So we had him read from the Bible;

> The word of the Lord came again unto me, saying, Moreover, thou son of man, take thee one stick, and write upon it, For Judah, and for the children of Israel his companions: then take another stick, and write upon it, For Joseph, the stick of Ephraim and for all the house of Israel his companions: And join them one to another into one stick; and they shall become one in thine hand.
> Ezekiel 37:15-17

Books used to be written on scrolls that are wrapped around a stick. Therefore, they referred to books as sticks. The Stick of Judah is the Bible and the Stick of Ephraim is the Book of Mormon and both are joined in one hand as the Word of God. Lehi's family in the Book of Mormon are from the tribe of Ephraim who was a son of Joseph, and also most of the last part of the Old Testament is a story about the tribe of Judah.

Here is another biblical reference to the Book of Mormon:

> And the vision of all is become unto you as the words of a book that is sealed, which men deliver to one that is learned, saying, Read this, I pray thee: and he saith, I cannot; for it is sealed: And the book is delivered to him that is not learned, saying, Read this, I pray thee: and he saith, I am not learned.   *Isaiah 29:11-12*

Martin Harris (one of the three witnesses of the Book of Mormon) took a copy of a hieroglyphic page of the Book of Mormon to a scholar named Mr. Charles Anthon to see if it was real and correctly translated. Mr. Anthon gave Martin Harris a paper saying that it was correct and truly translated correctly. Then Mr. Anthon said that the book should be brought to him for translation. Martin Harris replied that the rest of the book was sealed, and that an angel of the Lord had delivered the book to Joseph Smith. Mr. Anthon asked to see the paper back. When the paper was handed back to Mr. Anthon, he ripped up the paper and said that angels do not do such things and that he could not read a sealed book.

The agnostic Christian replied that he did not believe that this story was accurate. Then we said, "Here is some evidence that it is true. After this meeting with Mr. Anton, Martin Harris went on to mortgage his entire farm for the publishing of the first five thousand copies of the Book of Mormon. Martin Harris eventually lost his farm, but he never denied the truthfulness of the Book of Mormon or the story about Mr. Anton. This is extremely good evidence that the story is real."

You see, the simplest answer is usually the best. However, the questions got more complicated.

"Hey, missionaries... In 1 Nephi 16:18 it says that Nephi had a bow of fine steel and everyone knows that steel had not been invented in 600BC. Therefore, the Book of Mormon is false." We read to him a verse out of the Bible in the Old Testament: "He shall flee from the iron weapon, and the bow of steel shall strike him through" (Job 20:24). The Bible itself in the Book of Job uses the term, "bow of steel."

"Hey, missionaries... It says in the New Testament that; But though we, or an angel from heaven, preach any other gospel unto you than that which we have preached unto you, let him be accursed" (Galatians 1:8). So, we again gave the most simplistic answer. "It sure is a good thing that it was God the Father and Jesus who appeared to Joseph Smith and told him what to do, and not an angel."

"Hey, missionaries... Didn't your Jesus in the Book of Mormon fail?" Meaning, that is, that all the people died and that the church He established did not survive. Our answer; under that same logical sequence, then God must have failed when He had to kill all of the people on the earth in the time of Noah. The only way we know about the killing of the whole planet is that Noah survived to tell the story and the only way we know about Jesus in the land of the Americas is that Moroni survived with the engraved plates containing the Book of Mormon.

"Hey, missionaries... How can you believe that Joseph Smith is a prophet when the Book of Mormon copies scripture word for word? Prophets don't copy scripture, they write new scripture."

The Book of Mormon has one hundred and thirty-four perfectly-quoted verses to the Bible, and one hundred and ninety-nine paraphrased verses to the Bible. I had always wondered about this myself, until I learned how the Dead Sea Scrolls had been translated. In the 1940s while they were translating the Dead Sea Scrolls, if they came to a verse that said the same thing in the scrolls as it did in the King James Version of the Bible, they just used the same quotation as in the King James Version. Therefore, modern-day translators and Joseph Smith use the same method.

As we continued to talk with the Agnostic, we were getting deeper into the more difficult questions. Here was one question that required additional study to answer.

The agnostic Christian reminded us that one of the Ten Commandments says that we should not kill, and in the first few chapters of the Book of Mormon, Nephi killed a man named Laban, and an angel told him to do it. The agonistic Christian said that this proves the Book of Mormon is not from God.

To answer this we found this story from Mr. Hugh Nibley, a renowned professor and author from Brigham Young University. He taught a class on the Book of Mormon studies for only Middle-Eastern students at Brigham Young University ("BYU"). To attend this class, you had to be from the Middle-East. In the classroom, as they started reading the Book of Mormon, there was a grumbling amongst the students. As they read on, one student raised his hand and said, "Mr. Nibley, why did it take Nephi so long to kill Laban? What was his hesitation?" Right then, Hugh Nibley realized that this passage, in the first few pages, was evidence that the Book of Mormon was actually translated from a Middle-Eastern text. The culture of the Middle-East itself is a testament to the authenticity of the Book of Mormon.

In the United States, some people believe that this story is out of place to be considered a scripture. However, the Middle Eastern students didn't understand why Nephi would even waver. This passage highlights a cultural difference between the USA and the Middle Eastern way of thinking. If Joseph Smith sat down one day and decided to fake a religious book, then the last thing that he would have done is put in an angel directing Nephi to kill another man in the first few chapters. That is the last thing you would put in the book if you were trying to fake a scriptural text and sell it to citizens of the United States. That's because the culture within the USA would reject the very notion of the event. However, now in the 21st century, it has become evidence that the Book of Mormon did originate from exactly where Joseph Smith said it did; a Middle Eastern text.

Also, the Ten Commandments, in the original Hebrew text, does not say that thou shall not kill; it says, "thou shalt not commit murder." The Prophet Moses, who was the one to deliver the commandment, killed a man all by himself and also ordered the killing of many people in his life-time.

It did not matter, the agnostic Christian would allow evidence like this to roll right around him, without much respect or credence for what we had just proven to him.

"Hey, missionaries... Joseph Smith claims that he translated the Book of Abraham from Egyptian papyri, but years ago scholars found the papyri in the Metropolitan Museum in Chicago and they said it does not match the Joseph Smith translation."

Eyewitnesses of the original papyri.

Joseph Smith's nephew, Joseph F. Smith (after becoming the President of the LDS-Church in 1901 visited the Nauvoo house in 1906 with Preston Nibley) recounted that when he was a little boy, he saw the Prophet Joseph Smith kneeling on the floor studying the Egyptian manuscript and that he had placed rocks and books on the manuscript as weights to hold it down as the long scroll rolled <u>through two rooms</u> in the Joseph Smith Mansion House, in Nauvoo, Illinois. [H. Nibley, "Phase I," Dialogue: A Journal of Mormon Thought 3.2 (Summer 1968): 101].

Oliver Cowdery said that the scroll was "in perfect preservation" and therefore, we infer that the scroll was intact (Doctrinal History of the Church, Vol. 2, p. 348).

Also, there are multiple eyewitness accounts to say that a portion of the scroll was written in red ink, which is the part that talked about the priesthood. The first part of the Book of Abraham talks all about the priesthood.

Now, contrast these eyewitness accounts with the papyri fragments that were found in the Metropolitan Museum in Chicago. The question is, <u>do the papyri fragments you are looking at resemble anything like the description that Joseph F. Smith, Oliver Cowdery and others recorded</u>? Answer is, NOT EVEN CLOSE. So how can anyone believe that they have the original **long scroll** that is described by eyewitness records? It does not seem logical. Therefore, there are two possible answers to this question;

1. The fragments found in Chicago are not the entire original papyri.

2. If the fragments are the entire original papyri then what you have to believe is that the people who were the scribes for Joseph Smith, who helped translate the Book of Abraham papyri, must have watched Joseph Smith get hundreds of English words from each tiny Egyptian symbol. Because the Book of Abraham translation is very long in length but the papyri which was found at the Metropolitan Museum in Chicago is very short in length (physically and in volume of hieroglyphics). Therefore, the second option is not probable.

"Hey, missionaries... Why did Joseph Smith not write down his vision of the Father and the Son for about fifteen years after the event? Also, when Joseph Smith recounted it, he wrote it seven different times in seven different versions."

The answer is that there are biblical precedents for this kind of time lapse between an event and the recording of it. St. Peter saw Moses and Elijah on the Mount of Transfiguration and he heard the voice of God. Then, St. Peter waited over thirty years to write it down. In fact, we do not have any actual proof that St. Peter ever wrote it at all. St. Peter saw this incredible event, then watched Jesus become resurrected, and he then went back to catching fish with a boat and net. So does that circumstantial evidence lead you to conclude that St. Peter was lying because he did not write it down for thirty years?

If you are going to judge Joseph Smith by a certain criteria to conclude he was lying, then you'd have to use the exact same criteria for St. Peter and that same criteria would come to the same conclusion for St. Peter. Just be fair about it. The answer might be that when someone has such an extraordinary experience, writing it down does not seem very important at the time. Also, St. Matthew, St. Mark and St. John wrote their experience at least three decades after it happened. They also all wrote it in the third person, which seems strange to me.

In their books, St. Matthew, St. Mark, St. John and St. Peter named themselves to the office of "Saint" in the titles of their books, which seems odd to me also. But that does not mean that their testimonies are false! If you are using this type of logic to discredit Joseph Smith, then you are going to have a difficult time believing St. Matthew, St. Mark, St. John and St. Peter on the same criteria. Because once you start digging, you will find that there is no proof of what they say in those great books, and there is very little evidence.

There is evidence that the Book of Mormon is true, but there is no conclusive proof. There is evidence that Moses led millions of people out of Egypt into the desert, but there is no proof. There is evidence that Jesus of Nazareth rose from the dead, but there is no proof. I think that is the way God wants it, He wants us to choose the righteous things in life, the right way to live our lives; not because we have proof, but because we have faith in Christ, as a better way to live and conduct ourselves. Not because we have proof, but because we feel that doing unto others as we would have them do unto us, is just the correct way to live our lives.

However, even after all of this, the agnostic Christian just would not stop. He wanted to know why the Three Witnesses, (i) Martin Harris, (ii) Oliver Cowdery and (iii) David Whitmer had been excommunicated from the Church and estranged from Joseph Smith. We reminded him that the Three Witnesses wrote down and signed a document testifying of the plates; a fact the agnostic Christian discounted.

Our answer was that Oliver Cowdery and Martin Harris were both re-baptized later on in their life, long after Joseph Smith had died. But the agnostic Christian objected to that answer. He said that was just because when they got older, they remembered that they used to be celebrities in the LDS faith, and now that the Church was well-established out in Utah, they were re-baptized because they wanted to be popular and be celebrities once again.

OK, we replied, but what about David Whitmer? He left the church. He despised Joseph Smith for the rest of his life and never said a good thing about him ever again. However, he never denied his witness of the Book of Mormon or the plates. Even when the Encyclopedia Britannica printed that David Whitmer had denied his testimony of the Book of Mormon, David Whitmer wrote a letter to the publisher of the Encyclopedia Britannica and told them of his continued testimony of the Book of Mormon and demanded that they remove the reference. Also, on David Whitmer's deathbed, he gathered his family and told them that the Book of Mormon was a true book of God. So, even when he was dying and had been divided from the Latter-day Saints for decades, he still adamantly testified of the Book of Mormon.

The written and signed testimony of the Three Witnesses is even stronger evidence because they were all excommunicated and left the church, especially so in the case of David Whitmer's story. The evidence is even stronger and more credible from three men who were excommunicated but never denied their testimony of the truthfulness of the Book of Mormon.

Ok... Ok... Let me stop here. I don't want anyone to think that we were able to answer all of the agnostic Christian's questions. There were many that we just did not have the knowledge at the time to answer. But it did not shake our faith in what the Holy Ghost told us was true.

After three days of reading and praying, my companion, Elder Winegar, came out of our apartment with a testimony of Jesus Christ and a testimony of the Book of Mormon. He was born again. He became a great disciple of Christ and has spent the remainder of his life serving others and following the commandments of God. The Book of Mormon did exactly what it was supposed to do. It helped one man come to Christ and gave him a purpose in his life that would outlast any challenges that this earthly experience could throw at him. Elder Winegar is a stalwart member of Jesus Christ's team, and it all started with him taking Moroni's challenge to read the Book of Mormon for himself. It will, just like the New Testament, testify to your soul that you need to accept Christ as your Savior and commit to live your life in the pursuit of His gospel.

The agnostic Christian has used his years on earth to create doubt in his fellow human beings about their convictions to the gospel of Jesus Christ. However, Elder Winegar has used his years on this earth in the service of his fellow man by donating his time, money, and talents in the pursuit of other people's happiness while testifying how Christ has improved his life; and how he aspires to Christ's teachings and commandments. In doing so, Elder Winegar found the peace in life that only Christ can give. You do not thirst once Jesus is in your life.

If Jesus is not in your life, then do something to change that state of existence. Read the Book of Mormon and obtain your own testimony of Christ, rather than living on your parents' beliefs. I promise you, once Christ gives you a purpose on this earth, your life will find complete joy.

You see, I made a huge mistake. I didn't trust the promise. I tried to prove the Book of Mormon to the agnostic Christian instead of letting the Holy Ghost work.

My companion, after reading the Book of Mormon, did challenge the agnostic Christian to read the book and put Moroni's challenge to the test, but I was the senior companion and continued to discuss factual answers. Elder Winegar ended up being the one who taught me, reminding me to trust in the Lord and not man. I thought I was the teacher, but he—the one who was humble—ended up teaching me the power of God. I should have just trusted Moroni's promise and followed my companions lead.

Over thirty years later, I ended up living only a few miles from Elder Winegar. He is a stalwart in the faith of God and Christ. He recently went through a battle with cancer and won.

Sometimes facts do not coincide with the Bible Story, however this should not weaken your belief that Jesus is the Christ.

The agnostic Christian wanted us to doubt our faith; just as an atheist, Jew or a Muslim wants us to doubt our faith, when they point out the fact that King Herod, the king who ordered the killing of all the baby boys in Bethlehem, died in 4BC, four years before Jesus is supposed to have been born. This history book fact sometimes weakens those who have not truly received the full testimony of Christ and His gospel.

King Herod's death was recorded by Josephus, occurring right around the time of a lunar eclipse. Astronomers have told us that there was a lunar eclipse that was visible from Jerusalem in 4BC and that is why everyone believes that Herod died in the spring time of 4BC. But astronomers have told us recently that there was another lunar eclipse visible from Jerusalem in 1BC. Either way, our current calendar is off by one to four years.

But at first glance, this calendar thing might shake the faith of a few Christians. It may seem to be a negative fact that might weaken some person's belief in Jesus Christ, inferring that the Bible is not a real or even a correct story. The truth is that this so-called negative may turn out to be a positive testifier of the truthfulness of the Bible story as we learn how our modern-day calendar evolved. Let me explain.

In the year approximately 1580, Pope Gregory XIII realized the Roman and Julian calendars were not in sync. So, Pope Gregory XIII employed some very smart men to research it. They went back to the 6th century monk Dionysius Exiguus, who had tried to calculate the year of Christ's birth. The facts of what I am about to tell you are not complete and clear, but it appears that he may have made a couple of errors. First, he did not include a year zero in the calculation, because there was no zero in mathematics in the 6th century. The concept of a zero was introduced into European mathematics about two hundred years later by the Islamic culture.

However, every person born does not count their first day they are born as year one. Everyone has a zero starting point when calculating their years on the planet. This is difficult for 21st century students of the Bible to grasp, but mathematics back then just didn't need a zero. Second, he may have not included the first four years of Caesar Augustus' rule, because for the first four years, Augustus went by the name Octavius, and somehow the monk Dionysius didn't put that together. Therefore, Dionysius' dating of the calendar in the 6th century AD may have ended up being off by five years.

If this is true, then the thing that I thought was a negative may actually have become a positive to verify that the Bible story is accurate. Around 1BC there does not seem to be much evidence of many unusual stellar events. But if we stop looking at 1BC and start looking at the years before 4BC, there are a multitude of unusual stellar events.

This following information is taken from Bruce Gerig's paper, in which he quotes the astronomer Mark Kidger's research and data on the Star of Bethlehem (Princeton University Press, 1999). He says that from the perspective of the wise men (who possibly were from the city of Babylon - modern day Iraq, which is east of Jerusalem) this is what they could have observed as astronomers in the night sky:

1. In the month of May, 7BC, Jupiter and Saturn passed a degree apart within the constellation of Pisces. Jupiter is considered a royal planet and the constellation Pisces is associated with the Jews. Perhaps Saturn was regarded as an evil planet and equated to the Roman Empire.

2. In the month of September, 7BC, Jupiter and Saturn came together again within Pisces.
3. In the month of December, 7BC, Jupiter and Saturn again came together in Pisces.

So, three times (May, September and December) in eight months, the royal planet Jupiter and Saturn met in the constellation associated with the Jews. In the month of February, 6BC, Jupiter, Saturn and now Mars coalesced within the constellation of Pisces. A conjunction of Jupiter, Saturn and Mars is unusual, occurring only once every 805 years.

To the wise men, this could have been of tremendous astrological significance, since Mars, the blood-colored planet, was a sign of conquest. A great world ruler (Jupiter) was soon to arise from among the Jews (Pisces), who would challenge even Rome (Saturn).

Later in the month, February 20, 6BC, the two-day-old moon passed very close to Jupiter, while Saturn and Mars paired together. This all occurred in the constellation of Pisces and could have meant that a ruler (Jupiter) was going to rise (the new moon) from Judea (Pisces) to conquer (Mars) Rome (Saturn).

Because the Jews had lived in Babylon before Cyrus the Great freed them to return to Jerusalem, then perhaps the wise men were from Babylon and had studied the Jewish scriptures:

> I shall see him, but not now: I shall behold him, but not nigh: there shall come a Star out of Jacob, and a Scepter shall rise out of Israel... *Numbers 24:17*

Now that the wise men had this information, they would have naturally been wondering when this event was going to happen as they studied the heavens every night for more evidence.

Then a little over a year later, Chinese astronomers noted that a new bright star appeared between the dates of March 10th and April 7th in 5BC and lasted about seventy days. This "new star," a bright supernova, appeared between the constellations of Capricornus and Aquila. This unexpected stellar event would have been visible from Babylon and could have signaled to the wise men that the king had arrived. From the wise men's perspective, this last heavenly event was a signal to get on their camels and ride, Jerusalem being the logical destination.

Following the Euphrates route, a caravan from Babylon could have traveled the seven hundred miles and reached Jerusalem in forty-seven days, well within the seventy-day visibility of what the Chinese astronomers recorded. The Bible tells us that the wise men came to Jerusalem and met with King Herod, and from Jerusalem then traveled to the City of David (Bethlehem).

One interesting aspect of Mr. Kidger's scenario is that the star (the bright supernova), which at first they saw in the East at dawn, would have risen an hour earlier every two weeks until it was almost exactly due south at dawn. So, when the Magi set out for Bethlehem, traveling south from Jerusalem, they would have once again seen the star (a bright supernova) before them, appearing like it hovered right above Bethlehem from the angle at which they were traveling.

All of this actually happened in 5BC, a year before Herod died. This may be why Herod ordered the killing of all boys under the age of two years old. The wise men would have explained to Herod that the unusual stellar events started about eighteen months ago, and Herod wanting to be thorough, ordered all boys under the age of two to be killed.

These are all factual astronomical events that took place between 7BC and 5BC. And the fact that they all coincide within the time frame that Jesus was born, is indeed miraculous. Therefore, looking for astronomical events in 2BC and 1BC is unproductive. But looking for astronomical events in 7BC to 5BC is an eureka moment. You see, the gospel always ends up fitting together, we just need the big picture.

The great Roman record keeper (Josephus) tells us that Herod died sometime after the eclipse of the moon visible in Palestine on March 13th, 4BC and before the feast of Passover on April 10th, 4 BC. And the Bible also tells us that after King Herod died, Mary, Joseph and Jesus finally return to Nazareth from their hiding place in Egypt.

So this calendar thing, that may have caused some Christians to waiver in their belief in Christ, has now become a positive and presents confirmation that the Bible is true.

Atheists will try to make you doubt the existence and need for a God. Agonistics will continue to use their whole lives attempting to prove a negative, which is an impossible task. Anti-Mormons who claim to be Christians, will spend their entire lives telling Mormons that they are not Christians, instead of spending time with Jews, Muslims and atheists to testify about Christ.

> Note: Of the top twenty largest churches or religions that exist today in the United States of America, the very first one to name their church after the name of Christ was Joseph Smith's in 1830. Wow! That is something! The irony is so thick when someone says that the Latter-day Saints are not Christians, when the fact that Christ's name is on our church, and we were the first of the twenty largest churches to do it.

If someone in my home was Muslim and they pray to Allah, it would not bother me. Bottom line, I am just glad they are praying, because I salute any person who is looking to their Creator for further light and knowledge. This is an admirable attribute. Besides, if I were not to allow people of other faiths to pray in my home, then I would not be a very good Mormon. The LDS Article of Faith #11 states that, "we claim the privilege of worshiping Almighty God according to the dictates of our own conscience, and allow all men the same privilege, let them worship how, where, or what they may."

To be a good Mormon, or Christian, by that matter, we must allow anyone to worship God, however they may wish. If we don't, then we are not what we claim to be.

Everyone, just do it. Read the Book of Mormon, pray about it, follow the teachings of Christ, become a disciple of Jesus with all your soul, acts, deeds and thoughts.

You will find the peace for which you are looking, you will not thirst anymore and you will be able to handle times of distress and strife that this life might throw at you.

In your lifetime, you will see Mormon friends leave the church. You will witness some Protestants, Catholics and Mormons stop believing in God because of science. You will also see people you have known for years, who have not had any religion in their life, accept Christ and be baptized and change their life for themselves and their family to become great Christians.

The question is not whether you are going to have adversity in your life. The question is, when you experience adversity, then how will you handle it? I testify to you that it is much easier to handle adversity when you have Jesus the Christ standing next to you.

As my old missionary companion and I can both testify, after thirty years of many adverse challenges, we still have Jesus Christ in our hearts, and basically that is all we really need.

I testify to you that this is all you really need. So get it. Take the Moroni challenge and let your soul accept the words of Christ. Trust in Christ to help you through all adversity. Adversity will come and if Christ is by your side, you can handle anything.

CHAPTER 9
WHO CREATED SATAN?

How can God claim to be perfect when God Himself creates imperfect creations? How can a perfect God be the creator of Satan? How can a perfect God create flawed humans? If God is perfect, then by definition, why does He not create flawless humans? If God created everything, then where did Satan come from? Why did God create Cain, a murderer who killed his own brother? How can God claim to be perfect if He creates non-perfect things like Satan?

The answers to these questions might be relative to your perspective; meaning there might be multiple correct answers for the same event. Remember the word "relative" and we will come back to it later in this chapter.

All of these questions consolidate down to one thesis statement or question that one must answer. That is, do you actually believe that God is the Father of your spirit? Really? Let me be more specific. I do not mean, is God the creator of your spirit, like a great chef is a creator of a delicious apple pie. I mean, when the Bible says that God is your Father in heaven, the Father of your spirit, do you believe that God is the same species (in spirit) as you are?

> Note: I am using the definition of the word "species" very loosely, but it is the closest word I have to explain this question.

Said another way, do you believe you are made out of the same spiritual material as that which comprises God the Father?

If you said yes, that God is the actual Father of your spirit, then you are going to like this chapter of my book.

If you said no; (i) that God is not the actual Father of your spirit, (ii) that your spirit (I emphasize the word "spirit" here) is not made out of the same stuff as God, (iii) that the Bible is speaking in a metaphorical way, (iv) and that God is only the creator of our spirits (like a chef creates an apple pie) then you would have to conclude that God just views us like a human views an ant hill. Meaning, the ants look nothing like a human, and the ants are just an amusement to a human observer. An ant hill is just something interesting for the human to observe and be entertained. If that is your answer, then this chapter is not going to be your favorite one of my book.

The very definition of the word "perfect" is that if a person is perfect, then everything that person makes or creates would be perfect. Under that definition, where did Satan come from; who created Satan? Because we know Satan is not perfect. Who created him? How can the God that created Satan claim to be perfect?

To understand this, we must first clear up the issue regarding whether or not Jesus and God are the same person. I am using the word "person" with a very liberal definition. Are they the same person or are Jesus and God the Father two entities but both <u>one in purpose</u>? Most Christian faiths believe that God the Father and Jesus Christ are the same person or the same Individual.

Mormons do not believe that the Father and the Son are the same person or Individual. Mormons believe that God and Christ are two separate entities, but both perfect, one in purpose.

To clarify this, I need to start with the writings of the Apostle John. Because St. John is such a great writer, he always clarifies himself as he writes, and clears up ambiguous statements. Here are a few examples:

> After these things came Jesus and his disciples into the land of Judaea; and there he tarried with them, and baptized. *John 3:22*

This scripture says that Jesus baptized. The Bible says that Jesus baptized. But wait, turn the page of the Book of John; "Though Jesus himself baptized not, but his disciples" (John 4:2). What did the Apostle John just do? He clarified himself. He is writing on a parchment with ink and he is not finished writing, but goes back and reads what he just wrote. He realizes that John 3:22 could be misinterpreted. Rather than take some ink and blot out John 3:22, he just writes another verse to clarify the earlier statement, because St. John assumes that the reader will read the whole book and not stop at Chapter 3:22. If the reader stops at that verse, and does not read the whole book, the reader will think that Jesus did baptize many people. From St. John's perspective, why would any normal person not read the entire work? From St. John's perspective, it is unimaginable that the reader would only read one verse to get a conclusion. Let's read another:

> No man hath seen God at any time; *John 1:18*

But then St. John once again clarifies himself a few pages later:

> Not that any man hath seen the Father, save he which is of God, he hath seen the Father. *John 6:46*

Once again, rather than going back and blotting out Chapter 1:18 with ink, the Apostle John just clarifies himself and writes more words in Chapter 6:46, because he assumes the reader will read the whole book. St. John clarifies himself because he wants to make sure the reader understands the whole concept in full, which is why he writes more words and clarifies an earlier statement. This is a rational assumption. This makes perfect sense.

My point is that you must read the entire book in its totality to understand the answer. You have to read all of the scriptures to get the answer. If you only read one verse, you will not understand what St. John is talking about in the Book of John.

My protestant friends tell me that the Bible says that God and Jesus are one.

> I and my Father are one. *John 10:30*

> He that hath seen me hath seen the Father; *John 14:9*

These two verses imply that Jesus and the Father are the exact same person. However, the Apostle John once again clarifies what he said in Chapter 10 and Chapter 14 with what he says in Chapter 17. In Chapter 17, Jesus is praying to the Father for His apostles, as He explains what it means when He said in Chapter 10, "I and my Father are one."

Jesus prays to God the Father and says:

> Neither pray I for these alone, but for them also which shall believe on me through their word; That they all may be one; as thou, Father, art in me, and I in thee, that they also may be one in us: that the world may believe that thou hast sent me. And the glory which thou gavest me I have given them; **that they may be one, even as we are one.** *John 17:20-22*

Here you have two options or lines of logic to understand this scripture:

Option 1: If Jesus and the Father are the exact same person, then that means that Jesus is praying for all of His apostles to somehow all mesh themselves and combine themselves into one person, because Jesus said, "that they may be one, even as we are one." Remember, Jesus is talking to the Father when He prays for this.

Option 2: If Jesus and the Father are two separate entities, two perfect entities, but not the exact same person, but both are perfected, then Jesus is praying to the Father in hope that all of His apostles will become one in purpose (a perfect oneness), just like Jesus and the Father are one in purpose.

When I explain this scripture in John 17: 20-22 to my Protestant friends, they always say, "Yes, but the Book of John Chapter 10 says that Jesus and God are one." And my reply is, Yes, the Book of John does say that, but the Book of John Chapter 3 also says that Jesus baptized! The writer of the Book of John assumed you would read the whole thing, not just one verse. St. John assumed you would give him time to clarify himself.

When John Chapter 10 says that, "I and my Father are One," then just a few more pages over in John Chapter 17, Jesus prays to the Father that all the apostles may be one, just like Jesus and God are one, it all makes sense. Option #2 is the only viable conclusion. This is one reason I had to leave the Protestant faith years ago. My reading of the Bible says that they are **one in purpose**, and the trinity doctrine never really resonated in my soul.

The Apostle John does not stop there; he continues to write and write and write to clarify that Jesus and God are two entities.

> For I came down from heaven, not to do mine own will, but the will of him that sent me. *John 6:38*

> For the Father judgeth no man, but hath committed all judgment unto the Son: *John 5:22*

Now really focus on what St. John says in this next scripture when Jesus says;

> For my Father is greater than I. *John 14:28*

Also, Jesus says to Mary on the morning of the resurrection:

> Go to my brethren, and say unto them, I ascend unto my Father, and your Father; and to my God, and your God. *John 20:17*

As you can see, the Apostle John once again, clarifies himself. Jesus and God are separate entities but one in purpose.

When I was first taught by the Mormon missionaries, they told me that God and Jesus were two separate people. This was something that I already believed, but I was in a church that taught that Jesus and God were the same person. The Mormon doctrine was sweet music to my soul. Back then, my personal question was, why did my Protestant religious leaders continue to teach me about the trinity concept?

Here is one reason; I refer you to a couple of verses in the Book of First John that were added to the Bible in the 3rd and 4th centuries. In the early 1500s after the invention of the printing press, several translators, including William Tyndale, printed some of the first English translations of the Bible and erroneously retained these two verses. The King James Version, in 1611, once again retained these two verses.

> For there are three that bear record in heaven, the Father, the Word, and the Holy Ghost: and these three are one. And there are three that bear witness in earth, the Spirit, and the water, and the blood: and these three agree in one. *1 John 5:7-8*

Those two verses are not in the oldest-known text of St. John's writings. They were added to the Bible three hundred to four hundred years after the birth of Christ. I need to make the point that someone, some religious monk, thought that the Apostle John needed a little help. Someone thought that a man who walked with and was taught by Jesus for about three years needed a bit more clarification on the doctrine of the trinity; a doctrine that was introduced in 325AD by the Nicene Creed. Someone must have thought that they were just helping the Apostle John out. Wow, as if he required help? As we can read from his writings, St. John was a very good writer, and when something was written in an ambiguous way, St. John always clarified himself with multiple examples. So, I am not blaming anyone for believing in the concept of the trinity, because it is inferred in the King James Version of the Bible and other translations. However, the doctrine of separate but one in purpose is very clear and easy to understand if you just;

1. Believe John..... Just read the entire Book of John.

2. Believe Stephen.... The disciple Stephen had a vision that is written in Acts 7:55-56 where it says that Stephen "looked up stedfastly into heaven, and saw the glory of God, and Jesus standing on the right hand of God." So was Jesus actually standing on God's right hand, or was Jesus standing on the right side of God? Either way you read this verse in the Book of Acts, figuratively or literally, there are two beings in the vision, not one. This is an eyewitness account from Stephen.

3. Believe Joseph Smith.... The most compelling case is a more recent eyewitness account. Joseph Smith met God and Jesus Christ when he was fourteen years old and he said that there were two beings, because he said that one turned to the other and said, "This is My Beloved Son, Hear Him."

We have the Apostle John's written account; we have the disciple Stephen's eyewitness account and Joseph Smith's eyewitness account; all testifying that they are two separate beings. Both are perfect and therefore, perfect in purpose.

When my non-Mormon friends tell me that they don't believe the Joseph Smith account, I understand, because they are not Mormon. It makes sense that they would not believe Joseph Smith. But what I don't understand is - why don't they believe the eyewitness account of Stephen, or the Apostle John in the Bible? St. John is so clear on this subject. I continue to ask my Protestant friends why they don't believe the Apostle John. In the end, my friends never have given me a satisfactory answer to this question.

Therefore, Joseph Smith, the disciple Stephen and the Apostle John have established that God and Jesus are two separate individuals. This concept is essential to answering the question, is your spirit the same species as God the Father? Is God the actual Father of your spirit?

Think about this, if He is not, then why is there this verse in St. Matthew which says; "Be ye therefore perfect, even as your Father which is in heaven is perfect" (Matthew 5:48).

Why would Jesus <u>command</u> us to do this, if it was not possible?

If a human is looking down at an ant hill, with millions of ants running around, the human would not say to the ants, "become like me." Why? Because that is not possible, an ant cannot become like a human being. But Jesus tells us, "Be ye therefore perfect, even as your Father which is in heaven is perfect."

If we truly are not the same species, in spirit, then this commandment would not make any sense. In fact, it would be a lie, commanding us to become something that we could never accomplish. However, Jesus is not lying, He is telling us that God is His Father, and God is our Father. Jesus also tells us that we need to become perfect, just like our Father in Heaven is perfect. If God is not truly the Father of my spirit, then I could never hope to become perfect like He is. Just like an ant on an ant hill could never become a human being, because humans are not the fathers of ants. They are a different species.

Why are we commanded to become like God, if we are not His actual spirit children? Matthew 5:48 does not make any sense, unless you believe that God is the Father of Jesus, and God is the Father of your own spirit.

Here are a few more scriptures to help understand this concept:

> Furthermore we have had fathers of our flesh which corrected us, and we gave them reverence: shall we not much rather be in subjection unto the Father of spirits, and live? *Hebrews 12:9*

The Book of Hebrews makes a distinction between the father of our flesh and the Father of our spirits.

> For in him we live, and move, and have our being; as certain also of your own poets have said, For we are also his offspring. Forasmuch then as we are the offspring of God, we ought not to think that the Godhead is like unto gold, or silver, or stone, graven by art and man's device. *Acts 17:28-29*

The writer of the Book of Acts uses the term, "offspring of God." Why would the Book of Acts use the term, "offspring of God?" And why does it also use the term "Godhead?" It is for the same reason that Genesis uses the term "us" and "our."

> And God said, Let us make man in our image, after our likeness: *Genesis 1:26*

The Bible tells us that we are His offspring and heirs to the throne; that is, joint heirs with Jesus Christ.

> The Spirit itself beareth witness with our spirit, that we are the children of God: And if children, then heirs; heirs of God, and joint-heirs with Christ; if so be that we suffer with him, that we may be also glorified together.
> *Romans 8:16-17*

> To him that overcometh will I grant to sit with me in my throne, even as I also overcame, and am set down with my Father in his throne. *Revelation 3:21*

Therefore, Romans Chapter 8, and Revelation Chapter 3 have established that all of us can be joint heirs with Jesus Christ.

Now, here is another important question: how can we be joint heirs with Jesus Christ, if we are not of the same lineage? Listen to the following sequence of events in the Book of John when Jesus says:

> I and my Father are one. Then the Jews took up stones again to stone him. *John 10:30-31*

Then Jesus asks why they are going to stone him?

> Because that thou, being a man, makest thyself God. Jesus answered them, Is it not written in your law, I said, Ye are gods? *John 10:33-34*

Hee, hee, hee! Jesus uses their own logic against them because Jesus is referring to the Book of Psalms which says;

> I have said, Ye are gods; and all of you are children of the most High. *Psalms 82:6*

Bam! Jesus stopped them in their tracks. This scripture makes sense if you believe that you are actually a child of God. But if you don't, then Psalms 82:6 does not make sense to you. Once you grasp this concept, then answering who created Satan is obvious.

The term "most High" is reference to the term "most High God." This term is written all through the scriptures. In Genesis Chapter 14, Melchisedec is a priest to the Most High God, and Abraham was blessed by the Most High God. In Daniel Chapter 3, Shadrach, Meshach and Abednego were all servants of the Most High God. In Acts Chapter 16, the Apostle Paul said the men were servants of the Most High God, and Mark Chapter 5 says a wild man named Legion ran to Jesus and cried with a loud voice, and said, "What have I to do with thee, Jesus, thou Son of the most high God?"

My point is, why did the writers of the Bible require the term "most High God?" Why did the writers of the Bible need to make that distinction? It is because there are scriptures like Revelation 1:6. Listen to this very carefully;

> And hath made us kings and priests unto God and his Father... *Revelation 1:6*

Also in Hebrews 1:8, God the Father actually uses the term "**O God**" to describe Jesus, and in 2 Corinthians 4:4 it says that Satan is "**god of this world**." This is why the Bible needed the term "most High God." Therefore, we have established the following;

1. Jesus Christ is the Son of God
2. We are all spirit children of the Most High God.
3. We are joint heirs, or can be joint heirs with Jesus Christ upon Jesus Christ's throne.
4. Jesus himself and the Book of Psalms say that we are gods and children of the Most High.

Is it not logical to believe that Satan and the fallen angels from heaven are also a creation of God; that they are also His spirit children? This is one reason Mormons refer to Jesus Christ as their older brother. They are doing so because of the biblical-based scriptures that define who the spirit children of God are. From the Mormon perspective, all humans are brothers and sisters with Jesus Christ. Also, all humans are brothers and sisters with Satan, from a certain perspective, in the same context that all humans are brothers and sisters with Adolf Hitler and Mother Teresa.

However, Jesus is very different from all of us. Jesus is the only person to ever live on this earth and never commit a sin in His entire life. Jesus Christ is the perfect one. We are not perfect, but we have been commanded in Matthew 5:48 "Be ye therefore perfect, even as your Father which is in heaven is perfect."

So, how does God claim to be perfect when God is the one who created Satan? This is a very deep question, but somewhat of a simple answer. God creates and is the Father of perfect <u>spirit</u> children who have the potential to become like their Father. They do not have the right to become like their Father or their brother Jesus Christ. They are not entitled to become like Him. They just have the perfect ability to become like Him. God never caused Satan to rebel against Him. Satan chose that, upon himself, all by himself.

If you do not accept the theory that you are the same species as God, then you must accept the only logical alternative; that sometime way, way back in the past, before the earth was created, before God separated the light from the darkness, before God created the heavens and the earth; back when there was nothing, God was sitting around as an Omnipotent Being, and He must have been bored out of His heavenly mind. Because He created us, and if we are not His children in spirit, then He just decided to create an earth and put human beings on that earth who are nothing like Himself. Because, I guess, He wanted to have an earth where people like us can walk around, and function like an ant hill and worship Him.

You'd have to accept that an Omnipotent Being is creating worlds of humans that can never be like Himself. And you'd have to accept that a perfect being is commanding those humans to become perfect like Himself, fully-knowing that they can never achieve this command. You would have to accept that God was just lonely and needed something or someone to worship Him. You would have to accept that instead of God deciding to create someone like Himself, He decided not to create beings that had the potential to become like Him. No, He decided to create an ant hill called Earth and command the humans to become something that He knows they can never achieve. You would have to accept that the Bible, when it says that we are the offspring of God, (i) is just talking in a metaphoric way, (ii) that the Bible just uses words like "offspring," incorrectly, (iii) just wants to lead us to believe we can become like God, (iv) is a lie, if you don't believe we are His spirit children.

Adam's physical body vs. Adam's spiritual body

The physical body that was created for Adam came from the dust of the ground of this earth. In the Book of Genesis, Adam's body came from the dust of the ground. God created the earth, and once the earth was created, God used **pre-made** materials, listed in the Book of Genesis, to make a body for Adam's spirit to dwell in. The materials listed in Genesis are the ground, the dust of the ground and a mist over the ground, H_2O (water).

Adam's spirit was not created inside of the Garden of Eden. Adam's spirit existed long before the Garden of Eden. Adam's spirit existed long before Adam's body was created.

Therefore, humans are made up of two things: a body and a spirit; the spirit part being the offspring of God, and the body part being a creation of God.

Genesis says the plants came from the ground; the beasts came from the ground; the fowl came from the ground and the man—or more precisely—the body of the man, came from the dust of the ground.

> But there went up a mist from the earth, and watered the whole face of the ground. And the Lord God formed man of the dust of the ground, and breathed into his nostrils the breath of life; and man became a living soul.
>
> *Genesis 2:6-7*

Once God put a mist over that ground, meaning water or H_2O, He then mixed those materials together to make Adam's body. That's a creation!

Here is a scriptural issue that I have. I am <u>unable</u> to find a scripture that says that God is the Father of Adam's body. I can't find it. Though, I can find multiple scriptures that say that my spirit is the offspring of God, God is the Father of my spirit, we are all gods, we are children of the Most High and that we are joint heirs with Jesus. God is the creator of Adam's body with mist, water and dust of the ground. In contrast, God is the Father of Adam's spirit. There is a huge difference. It appears that the Bible does make this distinction. In this context, I am not using the words "creator" and "father" as synonyms. I am making a distinction between the two words, just as the Bible has instructed me, because, the creation of a physical body and the fathering of a spirit are two very different things.

God is the Father of Jesus.

Jesus and God the Father are two separate entities and Mormons know this, because Mormons only pray to the Being that Jesus Christ prayed to while He was in the Garden of Gethsemane. When Jesus Christ was in the Garden of Gethsemane (Matthew 26:39-44), Jesus asked the Father three separate times for the task to pass from Him, and three separate times Jesus was denied His request. The divine Being to whom Jesus was praying basically said no to Jesus three separate times. Whoever that Being was, whatever you want to call Him, whatever name that He might go by from your perspective; whoever was listening to Jesus's prayer that night, that is to whom Mormons pray. Jesus taught us to pray to God.

No place in the Bible does Jesus teach us to pray to Jesus. That is why we do not pray to Jesus.

Even though Jesus was denied three times, He still agreed to do the will of God the Father, because Jesus and God are one in purpose, not one person.

Lucifer chose to be a satan.

Lucifer chose not to do the will of the Father. Becoming a satan was not an assignment, or a calling.

> Note: This concept is discussed in greater depth in Chapter 12: Was Adam Set Up To Fail?

Lucifer was just one of God's angels who thought he could be equal to God. Now, get this; Lucifer thought he had a better plan than God had. I have to give some credit to Lucifer, as he was able to convince a third part of heaven to follow him. Think about this; God, being perfect, had a third part of heaven fall from Him because of Lucifer. This is a very perplexing part of the story; how did a perfect Being lack the ability to convince so many that Lucifer was a liar, short-sighted and ill-versed on what it takes to become perfect? This begs the question; how does a perfect Being, create imperfect things?

Here is some additional information that will help with this question. The word "perfect" in the Book of Matthew is translated more precisely to be the word "complete." Therefore, the translation could be, "Be ye therefore complete, even as your Father in heaven is complete." If you are truly complete, then you are truly perfect, because you have nothing that is missing. If you have nothing that is missing, then you are by definition, perfect, or fulfilling your full potential. Perfect in this context does not mean you can do anything. It just means that you have fully-completed or fulfilled your full potential; that you are complete and have nothing that is missing.

Our Father in heaven has provided an opportunity for each one of us to become complete, as He is complete.

Lucifer thought that he had a shortcut to becoming complete. Lucifer thought he had a substitute for actual experience.

What I want to say to Lucifer is this; "The reason that you keep going in circles, is probably because you are cutting corners. There is no short cut. There is no substitute for experience."

Some children plant wheat in the spring and expect orange trees to grow in the fall—even though their parents tell them that this course of action will not produce orange trees. Yet, some children must experience things for themselves before knowledge will penetrate their sculls. Conversely, sometimes our Father in heaven has to sit back and painfully watch His children fail, so that they can learn. Some children cannot learn any other way; experience has no substitute.

My Protestant friends tell me that if I claim to be the same "species" in the spirit as God, then I am committing blasphemy. I have two answers to that accusation.

1. Jesus said, in John Chapter 10, that the scriptures say that we are gods, and Psalms 82 confirms that we are gods and children of the Most High.

2. I remind them of the theory of relativity taught by Joseph Smith in 1843 (Doctrine and Covenants 130:4) which says, that time is relative to the planet where you reside. Joseph Smith taught this concept about three quarters of a century before Albert Einstein figured out the mathematical equation and became a Nobel Prize winner.

Joseph Smith taught in the Doctrine and Covenants 130:4 that the "reckoning of God's time, angels' time, prophet's time and man's time, [is] according to the planet on which they reside." Joseph Smith taught the theory of relativity long before Albert

Einstein was even born.

Here is an example or metaphor of the theory of relativity:

You are standing on the side of the train track and there is a flatbed train car coming down the train track traveling at a speed of thirty miles per hour. I am standing on the flatbed of the train car, holding a golf ball about the height of my nose. As the train car comes close to where you are standing I drop the golf ball so that it bounces at my feet. Then the golf ball bounces up, I don't catch it, I allow the golf ball to bounce again and then I catch it. From my perspective the golf ball bounced straight up and straight down, but from your perspective the golf ball bounced approximately thirty feet down the direction that the train was moving down the track.

Now, here comes the confusion. You and I are standing in front of a judge in a court of law and you testify that the ball bounced thirty feet and I testify that the ball only bounced straight up and straight down. Who is the judge supposed to believe? Did the ball bounce thirty feet, or did it bounce straight up and straight down? Who is telling the truth? The answer is that two people can see the exact same event and have two totally different conclusions, and both conclusions can be correct. That is the theory of relativity, taught in a metaphor.

Albert Einstein taught us that time is the same way. Two people traveling at two different speeds can view the same event and one person traveling at the speed of light would age two years, while the person not traveling at the speed of light would age thirty years. The person on the earth watching the person traveling at the speed of light would appear to be moving very slowly. That is relativity.

So my answer to the blasphemy question is that, Joseph Smith taught—and Albert Einstein discovered the mathematical equation—that two people can witness the exact same event, have two totally different conclusions and both can be correct.

I read the scriptures and they tell me I am a child of God. My Protestant friends read the scriptures and it tells them that they can never comply with Jesus commandment to be perfect even as your Father in heaven is perfect. My friends have a commandment in the Bible with which they cannot comply, because they do not believe that God is actually their Father.

It is an interesting note that in the New Testament, before Jesus is resurrected, He commands us to be perfect like the Father. But after He is resurrected He says; "I would that ye should be perfect even as I, or your Father who is in heaven is perfect" (3 Nephi 12:48). After He is resurrected, He includes Himself, along with the Father, as being perfect. A very interesting change in contrast to Matthew 5:48.

So, who created Satan? From a certain perspective, Satan created himself. Lucifer made himself into "a satan." Also, from a certain perspective, you have created yourself. Satan chose to be bad and therefore created an evil self. In contrast, you have chosen to follow Christ. If you continue to follow Christ and never quit, even when you make a mistake, you will one day become complete. Never quitting is the faith in Jesus that saves you so that you can go to heaven. You only need to believe that you will never give up on trying to follow Christ. And from that perspective, you have created yourself and can create a perfect, complete self, with the help of Jesus Christ.

CHAPTER 10
GOD'S MULTIPLE METHODS OF COMMUNICATION

Over many years of teaching Sunday school and priesthood classes, one question that continues to come up as a very common concern among all types of religious people is, how do I get answers to my prayers? Or, why can't I get answers to my prayers? I guess the real question is, how do I know when God is talking to me?

First of all, I believe that there is no wrong way to pray to your Heavenly Father. However, I do believe that the way you pray can affect the way God can answer those prayers. There are seven billion people on the planet and therefore, there are seven billion different ways to pray to God; some of which are better than others, but if a person is truly opening his or her heart to their creator, in humble communication, then I believe each person can and will be answered. However, the answer might not always be what you expect. God answers all prayers, but sometimes the answer is, NO! If you can't deal with that concept, you're going to become very frustrated.

Even Jesus Christ, while He was praying in the Garden of Gethsemane, was told "no" from God three times; (i) let this cup pass from me, (ii) is there another way and (iii) that the hour might pass from Him. God basically said no to all three requests. This is the Savior of the world asking God for the desires of His heart, and Jesus is basically told no three times. If Jesus can be told no, then who are we to think that we are more deserving?

Even with many years of studying about Jesus Christ, I still have a mountain of learning ahead of me when it comes to understanding answers to prayers. Over the years, I have prayed while driving in my car, walking down the street, or kneeling at my bedside. All of these prayers are to my Father in heaven. Each time I pray, it seems that the answers come to me in a multitude of different ways. These personal experiences are not easy to articulate and thus difficult to share in a book like this, which could be God's objective. Knowing who God is through prayer becomes a process where you come to know yourself. Maybe that is the way God wants it.

The first thing I would recommend to a person who wants to receive and understand answers to their prayers is, stop asking God ridiculous questions. What do I mean by ridiculous questions? I mean, that in many instances, we ask God questions and then we can't do anything with the answers. If, for example, we ask Him questions that are negatively-phrased, then He is bound to give us truthful answers that will never give an actual solution to the person asking the question. In a negatively-phrased question, God does give us what we asked for; however, the answer can do us no good and is worthless to the person who prayed for it.

An example would be something like this; "Heavenly Father, why am I so stupid?" Has anyone ever asked this question? I HAVE! Has anyone ever been walking down the street and asked; "Father in heaven, why am I such an idiot?"

Come on be honest, I've done it myself many times, I've asked God, "Why am I so stupid?" Now, why would anyone ask this question? Better yet, why would I ask this question over and over again in my life? It sounds funny, but I keep asking the same question.

The definition of insanity is doing the same exact thing over and over again, but expecting a different result.

Here is another question that I've asked many times; "Why can't I learn a new computer program at my work?" Has anyone ever asked that question to God? How about, "Why can't I live the law of tithing?" Has anyone asked this question?

There is a true fact that everyone needs to realize; universal to every person living on this earth. The fact is, the Light of Christ is within each person. The Light of Christ is extremely powerful and a personal answering device. This Light of Christ has the ability to teach us right and wrong relative to almost any circumstance. It was given to us the day we were born and is with us, if we allow it to be, for the remainder of our lives. The Light of Christ is inherently within every single human being on the planet, and will eventually answer almost any question that you ask it. It is always on and always running for us to appeal to when we need it. Therefore, the fact is, if you ask it negative questions it will give you negative answers; you will receive answers that will do you no good whatsoever. And the only reason the answers will not benefit you, is, because of the way you originally phrased the question. When I ask Heavenly Father, "Why am I so stupid?", I am going to get an answer and when I receive the answer to that question, I will not be able to use the answer to help myself. The reason is, because it is a negatively-phrased question.

Here's another example: "Why can't I learn the new computer program at work?" Let's think about all the answers that could come from that question. Each and every answer would be negative and would reinforce all of the reasons why I can't learn that program. It would also solidify in my mind that I am not able to learn it. Nevertheless, the Light of Christ will answer the question I ask it.

Each of us needs to learn to phrase our questions positively, so that when the Light of Christ answers the question, it enables us to use the answer to our benefit. Instead of asking why we can't learn the computer program, we should ask the question, "How _can_ I learn the new computer program at work?" At some point, when the Light of Christ answers this question, you will have an action list on how you can conquer this problem.

The answer might be;

- You _can_ learn the new program by asking one of your co-workers to help you.
- Or you _can_ learn the new program by purchasing a CD-ROM tutorial.
- Or you _can_ learn the new program by taking a computer class at the college.
- Or you _can_ learn the new program by studying a certain book.

All of these answers allow you to overcome your problem and they also reinforce the notion that you _can_ learn the new computer program. If you continually ask negative questions, then the Light of Christ will give you an answer that disables the positive and reinforces the negative. On the other hand, the positive questions of how someone can overcome their obstacle will enable that person with a to-do list.

A to-do list is an empowering action list, and therefore, accelerates your progress in becoming something that you are not. Thus, the miracle of Jesus Christ is not in helping humans to see themselves as they are, but rather to help them envision themselves as what they can become.

I already know what I am. I already know that I am an idiot: you don't have to tell me that, I already know it. But what I really want to know is, how can I become smart? Wasn't that the true core message of Jesus? He wanted to teach us what we could become, not what we currently are.

Most humans are selfish and they know it. Jesus Christ says that you don't have to remain where you are, because if you come unto Christ, you eventually become charitable. The big difference from being like an animal, or to only care about eating, sleeping and drinking, is to become a being that cares for and loves his fellow men with the pure love of Christ. How can you do this? It might all come down to how you phrase your questions and what you do with the answers. You must ask how you can become charitable.

Take, for example, the question that troubles some people; that is, why can't I live the law of tithing? This is a negative question that will result in negative thoughts and answers. The person who asks God this question will receive a truthful answer. Doesn't everyone expect a truthful answer when they're talking to God? But think about it, do you really want God to tell you the truth to everything you ask Him? That's a dangerous game, because He just might tell you the truth. What a concept! The truth sometimes cuts right to the core and we usually do not like answers that are so completely honest.

When I asked this question many years ago as to why I could not live the law of tithing, this is the answer I got back: "The reason you cannot live the law of tithing is because you are greedy, self-centered, and lack charity." Wow; that kind of hurt a little. Once I got this answer I repeated it in my mind many times over. I am greedy, I am self-centered and I lack charity. I walked around repeating this to myself over and over again. I am greedy, I am self-centered, and I lack charity. Let me ask you, what good does it do to remind myself over and over that I am greedy, self-centered, and lack charity?

The answer is, it does me no good at all! I get no benefit from a completely truthful answer that God gave me because of the way I phrased the question. God did tell me the truth and I finally accepted it. Then I realized, I already knew that. He wasn't telling me anything I didn't already know about myself. This was a great <u>turning point</u> in my life. At this moment <u>I stopped asking God what I was and I started asking Him about what I could become.</u>

What I should have been asking is, "How can I learn to live the law of tithing?" Or, "How can I get the spirit of tithing?" When I received an answer to those two questions, I was on my way to living one of God's laws and improving my charitable qualities. Because I received an answer to a positively-phrased question, it allowed me to do something with those answers and I could make a to-do-list; an empowering list that helped me to become something that I currently am not.

In the Book of 1 Corinthians 13:13, it says that the greatest of all the gifts is charity (which I believe is the true love of Jesus Christ). Many men seek for the gift of charity, but few ever really obtain it.

Basically, just be aware of what you are praying for and how powerful the Light of Christ is. Are you praying to receive a direction and a way to overcome the obstacle in front of you? Or, are you praying for the obstacle or challenge to be removed?

If you continue to pray for all of your obstacles to be removed, then you really do not understand why you are here on earth.

Let's move on and talk about the Holy Spirit or Holy Ghost. There are many scriptures that refer to the Father and the Son. But the subject of the Holy Ghost is somewhat lacking in scriptural volume and the Holy Ghost is the most elusive member of the Godhead.

To learn about the Holy Ghost, or the Holy Spirit, we have to piece together and coalesce scriptures to obtain a good understanding of the importance of this heavenly Being, who is a member of the Godhead. We know for certain that He is very important because He is mentioned in the baptismal prayer. When we are baptized, we are baptized in the name of the Father, the Son and the Holy Ghost. He is referred to as a spirit or a ghost, because He has not received a body in the flesh. However, He is made up of matter.

> There is no such thing as immaterial matter. All spirit is matter, but it is more fine or pure, and can only be discerned by purer eyes; We cannot see it; but when our bodies are purified we shall see that it is all matter.
> *Doctrine and Covenants 131:7-8*

The definition of matter is that it fills up space. Something can be very small or insignificant, but if it fills up space, in this context, it is defined as a matter. One of those real creations is the Holy Ghost, the Holy Spirit, or also known as the Comforter. We are told that the Holy Ghost is able to give us promptings and suggestions which are predicated on our worthiness and our inward true love of Christ. These types of answers are much more enhancing than the Light of Christ answers. These answers, promptings and suggestions are profound.

The main question you need to ask yourself is whether or not you want to live your life pure enough to be a conduit to receive the promptings of the Holy Ghost.

If that is the case, then you can and will receive revelation for your personal life, for your family and for those people with whom you come in contact; all with charity being your standard, the underlying theme.

In my first year of college I was filled with the desire to serve God and was asked by the bishop of the LDS student ward to become a "home teacher."

In the Mormon Church, home teachers visit other members of their ward once a month to share a spiritual message and check-in on how those members are getting along in their temporal and spiritual needs. In September, the first month of school, my home teaching companion and I were assigned to check-in on a girl named Cindy. Her name had popped up on the bishop's ward list, but he had never seen her in church. We went to her apartment, knocked on the door, told her who we were and she invited us in. There in the room with Cindy was her cousin who was visiting from across town. Both of them were about nineteen years of age.

We were basically there just to introduce ourselves and had a few minutes to say hello. Cindy stated that she had not been to church since she was about eleven years old. Something had happened back then and her family just stopped going to church. Then out of the blue, her cousin started to explain to us why he did not go to church. He told us that he did not go to church because in his ward there were no young people his age. Then he clarified that statement by saying that there were some young people, but he did not get along with any of them, so he stopped going to church. And at this moment I had a prompting.

I don't know exactly why, but I said to him, "That is a pretty bold statement." The cousin looked at me quite strangely and said, "What do you mean a bold statement?" My answer was, "Do you realize what you are saying to God? You are saying, 'God, when You get some young people, that I like, going to church, that is when I will show up. But until then, You won't see me at church. So God, when You make it enjoyable for me, then I will come to church.' That's what you're saying to God and that seems to be a pretty bold statement."

Right after that, we left the apartment and went on to our next home teaching appointment. We were really only at Cindy's apartment seven to eight minutes, total. This was literally eight minutes of my life doing something for the bishop of our ward. This visit seemed like nothing to me, except for the fact I didn't really know why I had said that to Cindy's cousin and put it so bluntly. I wasn't being rude; I just thought I was telling the truth.

In the Mormon Church you're supposed to do your home teaching at least once a month. Well, two more months went by and I had not completed any more home teaching visits. Then, I got a call from the bishop's secretary asking me to come see the bishop at his office. I didn't know what he wanted to talk about. As I started to sit down in his office he started talking about home teaching and how important it was in the lives of all Latter-day Saints. As the words "home teaching" came out of his mouth, I can tell you my gut started to cringe, because I had missed home teaching the last two months. So I sat there waiting patiently for a reprimand but I could not believe my ears. He started praising my valiant efforts as a home teacher. I thought that he must be confusing me with some other home teacher. I sat there and listened as he talked about Cindy. He said that Cindy came to see him with tears in her eyes. She told him about her years of inactivity from the gospel of Jesus Christ and that she had become activated because of my home teaching visit. What the bishop did not know was that it had been my ONE and only visit. Cindy said that the words and message that we shared with her had brought her to a point in her life that she had to allow Jesus Christ to take over.

She basically said that since my home teaching visit, she had accepted Christ and will never leave Him again. The bishop stated it had been eight weeks and Cindy had not missed a single Sunday of church. The bishop had brought me to his office because he wanted to thank me for being such a great home teacher and praised me. He said it was a miracle. A miracle?! A miracle? I thought to myself, did he just use the word miracle? During the whole meeting, I said maybe two words. I was dumbfounded. As I walked back to my dorm room, I reviewed in my mind the whole eight-minute visit, over and over trying to find what the bishop called "a miracle." As I laid in my bed that night, looking up at the ceiling, the thought that I continually had was, is the gospel of Jesus Christ that simple? I mean, is that all you have to do; just ask someone to come to Christ and they'll do it? There is no huge feat of strength I must do, or climb some huge mountain and pray by a burning bush? Because, if there is a huge mountain or some feat of strength, I would surely do it for Jesus Christ! But just knock on a door once a month and ask people to come to church, I'm not sure I'm up to that level of commitment. It's too simple, it will never work. God must be much more complex than that. Just knock on the door and ask people to come to church. I don't know, it sounds too complicated! Ha Ha.

If the story had ended there, I think I would've been just fine with it. To my surprise, that next Sunday, Cindy got up in front of the congregation and told the story of how she had been activated by her home teacher. To exponentially make it even more difficult for me, the next Sunday the bishop came in the elder's quorum and recounted the story about me being a wonderful home teacher. I sat there and let it go on and on and on. Then, for the next three to four months, any time that the subject of home teaching came up, my name was mentioned as an example to all the others in the student ward. Oh my heavens, since that day in college, I had to make sure to do my home teaching each and every month.

The guilt was killing me. Basically, I was guilt-ed into becoming a consistent home teacher. God works in mysterious ways! Guilt, not being that mysterious!

The point of this whole story is that the promptings of the Holy Spirit are very powerful and can have lasting meaning in someone's life. It doesn't take a profound action or statement to do so. Seriously, can eight minutes change someone's life? Apparently yes, anything is possible when the person is ready to receive the Holy Spirit. Cindy became a stalwart Christian and I became a consistent home teacher. Maybe that was God's plan all along. He did this so I would never forget that when the bishop asks you to do something and you don't do it, then the exquisite punishment might just be overwhelming unjustified praise. Ha!

In some cases, as this next example will illustrate, the Holy Spirit sometimes will teach you a truth and you will not accept it, even though it is true. I will first give you an example of this so as to build up the subject before I give you one of my life's experiences to make the point.

Here is the example. When you look at a map of the entire world, you see it as a flat accurate representation of a spherical object. The earth is a sphere and a map is a flat plane (a flat map) hanging on the wall. On the flat map of the world, move your eyes down to the equator and imagine yourself flying in a jet with a trajectory of due east.

If you were flying due east on the equator you would fly along the equator in a straight line, and continue until you arrive at your starting point. You would stay on the equator line during the whole flight of the jet.

Now we know that this is not a straight line, but it is a circle around the earth. But when you look on a flat map, the equator appears to be a straight line going directly east and west.

Therefore, in this example, if you were in the country of Ecuador, which is on the equator, and you flew due east and stayed on that same trajectory, you would eventually end right back up in Ecuador, on the equator.

Now, take that same scenario in your mind and fly in a straight line around the earth starting in NASA, Florida, headed to a place 42 miles south of San Francisco. If you continued on this same trajectory around the world, what do you think the next major land mass would be that you would fly over? That is to say, except for a few islands in the ocean, if you fly from NASA, Florida, in a straight line to a point just south of San Francisco and maintain that course, where do you end up? The answer is, the next major land mass that you fly over is Florida. Let me draw this line up on the world map. This straight line would go up over the North Pacific, then curve down through the islands between Asia and Australia continuing south into the Indian Ocean, then curve around South Africa, and go north across the Atlantic straight back to NASA Florida. Basically, you would be over the ocean the whole time. That is a straight line around the earth in the same context that the equator is a straight line around the earth. However on a flat map, the line appears to be two huge waves of an up and down motion. The line looks like a big curve up and down, but when I tell you that this is a straight line, you don't believe me. I am telling you the truth that this wavy line on a flat map is a representation of a perfectly straight line, or as straight as the equator is a straight line around the earth; both of which are actually circular lines that encompass the earth.

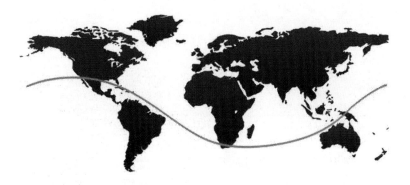

Now, what I have just taught you is true, but your mind does not want to believe it, because you have been taught your whole life that this flat map of the world is accurate. I am teaching the truth, but you are not accepting it. In the same way, the Holy Ghost will tell you truth, but you will not accept it, because of pre-conditioning. This is a simple concept, but you won't let it in because you are confused. Hold this thought and we will come back to it shortly.

Below is a picture of five sides of a globe which will illustrate how this straight trajectory will end up back in Florida.

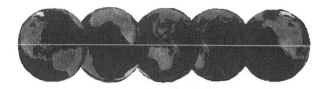

A second example, on a "flat" map, is that the country of Greenland looks extremely large. It is huge, but Greenland is really about the size of the country of Mexico. It is a similar optical challenge just like the straight line theorem from Florida, to San Francisco, and around the world back to Florida.

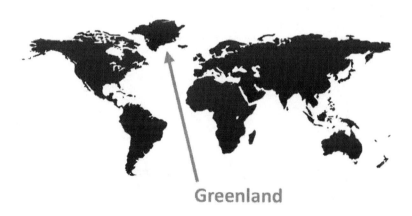

You might need to find a globe and look at it for yourself before you will believe the truth I just taught you. The question is, why do you need proof? Why can't you just believe me? Why can't you just feel in your heart that I have told you the truth?

In a similar way, the Holy Ghost tells us truth, but we do not accept it, because of our complicated, preconditioned minds.

Our complex brains believe that anything from God cannot be simple, it must be deeper. Simple answers cannot be the way of the Creator of the universe. The universe is complex and He must be complex also. However, in these two examples, the most simplistic answer appears to be complex or erroneous.

It is so simple and academic that your brain can't believe it. In this same manner I have had answers to my prayers, but I did not want to accept the answer, because the answer was too simple. So, I have contended with my Father in heaven to correct the answer. In my contention—now get this—I basically told the Creator of the universe that He was wrong.

Here is the story:

A few years ago I was at work and the subject of the Sabbath day came up in conversation. I told the group that I thought the best place for me and my family on Sunday was to be at church. I stated that I learn a lot from going to church and it benefits me and my family. One gentleman, who I did not know very well, spoke up and said, "Church is a waste of time." As we conversed back-and-forth, I came to realize that this man has had this discussion many times before with other church-going people. His statements and questions were very calculated. It was as if he were playing a game of chess, in which he was purposefully trying to corner me. He was not a novice, and this became apparent when he asked, "If you learn so much at church and you don't think it's a waste of time, then what was the subject of your Sunday school lesson three weeks ago?"

At that moment my mind was blank. I could not think of what the subject was in my Sunday school class three weeks ago. But I can tell you, I offered a quick prayer to God and asked Him to help me remember so that I could show this guy up. I wanted to prove to him that church was the right place to be on Sunday. This was my big chance to prove him wrong, and the answer was not that difficult. I figured this was going to be a very satisfactory conversation from my side and not so gratifying from his side. So, I said a quick prayer to God to help me, and you know what happened? I got an answer from God. The answer said, "It does not matter." My reply to God was, "Wait a minute, God, You have told me through Your scriptures that a righteous prayer will be answered. So, I ask You again to help me in answering what was the subject of my Sunday school class three weeks ago?" And the answer came once again, "It does not matter." I said to God, "May I remind You that in Your Holy Book, You promised that for those who knock You would open the door, to them that seeketh, they shall find, and to him that ask they shall receive." And once again I was obliterated with the answer, "It does not matter." I said to God, "What about that scripture saying, 'If any of you lack wisdom, let him ask of God, that giveth to all men liberally, and upbraideth not; and it shall be given him.' (James 1:5)?"

Then, after I proved to God that I knew the scriptures, what do you think happened? You got it, the answer came back, "Tell him it does not matter."

This conversation between me and God happened inside a whole of about five seconds. That is, me asking Him and His answering, me asking Him again, His answering me again, me quoting a scripture and His final answer. All I really know is that it was so fast, but so simple. I knew it was God talking directly to my spirit.

Well, what can I do? What would you do? Stand there and make up an answer and see if the Holy Spirit would bear witness to the man's soul that this made-up answer was true? That would never work, because it would be a lie. I realized that any type of lie would not allow the man to feel the power of the Holy Ghost. Finally I gave into what I thought would be a disastrous answer.

I said to the gentlemen, "You know, it really doesn't matter if I can't remember what the subject was of my Sunday school class three weeks ago."

The moment I said those words, I remembered my previous next-door neighbor Dan, and about a similar encounter he had years ago. I remembered how he answered this question, and it all came to my mind within a split-second.

So I said, "Just like I can't remember what I had for breakfast three Sundays ago, but I do know that whatever I did have for breakfast three Sundays ago, it filled me that morning and gave me substance which sustained my body throughout that whole day. I testify to you, that whatever I was taught in Sunday school three weeks ago, even though I can't remember it, I do know that it gave me substance, filled me spiritually throughout that next week, and helped me to be more charitable to my fellow man. Therefore, it doesn't matter if I remember what I ate for breakfast or what was taught to me in Sunday school. What does matter is that it sustained me and made a difference in my physical and spiritual well-being."

The man had no reply to this answer as he sat there and was dumbfounded. God knew exactly what He was doing all along. God was just trying to allow me the opportunity to trust Him and His simplistic truthful communication methods. God gave me a simple answer and then prompted a very old memory. This was not the answer that I had prayed for, but it was the exact answer that the gentlemen needed to hear. Sometimes you just have to have faith, and you've got to go with "it."

Whatever "it" is, you need to go with it and stop fighting it. You need to allow God's simple gospel to be taught.

Learn to recognize when truth is being taught and no matter how confusing or complex it seems, the key is to know what truth feels like. With the Holy Ghost, you do not need to know the whole equation, you just need to know the answer and then believe and go with that answer.

Sometimes in my life, God is trying to give me an answer and I will not accept it; (i) because it is too simple, (ii) because I want to complicate it, (iii) because I think I'm so smart. In this example I wanted to show that gentleman I had a good memory and that church did make a lasting impact on me and my family. However, God needed to show me that it wasn't about me. Therefore, when I take myself out of the equation and only think about others, then and only then do I seem to get fast, simple, and accurate answers to my prayers.

For all of those questioning people who are seeking answers to their prayers, let me summarize how it works for me. It might not work the same for you, but maybe you can glean something from my experiences. Summary;

1. Phrase your questions to receive positive answers.

2. Rely upon the Light of Christ; it is powerful.

3. Promptings come to those who are seeking to keep the commandments.

4. When truth is presented, just accept it, it is usually very simple. Don't try to over think it.

5. Arguing with God about the answer is a waste of time.

6. Always remember that even Jesus the Christ was denied His prayer three separate and distinct times in the Garden of Gethsemane.

Follow the Light of Christ and continually ask questions, then live righteously to become a tool in God's hand. He will use you for His purposes, and those experiences will help you to know what the Holy Ghost feels like. You will actually be able to recognize promptings and speak with the power of the Holy Ghost. This is when you grow and become familiar with how the Holy Ghost works His plans. And most of the experiences, after you look back on them, when they are all finished, will allow you to know yourself.

When Abraham was asked to sacrifice his son Isaac, it was not so God could know a little more about Abraham, it was so that Abraham could know a little more about Abraham.

Prayer can do that for you. As you discover more about God you eventually ascertain more about yourself. Prayer allows you to find out what you can become and that is the real answer that God wants to give you. Forget about what you are and find out what you can become. That is an answer that will empower you and fill the void in your soul.

CHAPTER 11
DO YOU REALLY WANT THE TRUTH?

Most people want to know the truth only if it will bring peace and calmness into their lives. But, as we read the scriptures, once some people find the truth, their lives are turned upside down. Take for instance the Apostle Paul. Before he was an apostle his name was Saul and he was hunting down the original apostles to kill them. But once Saul found the truth, he became an apostle and was eventually killed for his belief in Jesus Christ. Have you ever heard the saying, "Be mindful of what you pray to God for, because He just might LET YOU HAVE IT!"

A good number of people are not like St. Paul. Once they find the truth, they will do nothing with it. They will not change their lives. They will set the truth up on a shelf like an old dusty trophy. The reason is usually because the new-found truth does not fit into what their preconceived notion had been. The new information is so far out of the realm of previous rationale that it is difficult for the recipient of such information to digest and use it. There are a number of reasons for this. One might be the rejection of long-time friends and family who do not share the same information or belief. Another might be the daily mental challenge of knowing how to solve a problem, because you know the truth, but the people around you do not see it.

You have to painstakingly sit and watch for years and years the people you are trying to help, fail and fail again because they refuse to take counsel from anyone other than themselves. Sometimes knowing the truth is a very lonely place to be.

In the 3rd century before Christ, there was a man who was a seeker of truth. His name was Eratosthenes. He was not just a seeker of truth, but he was a truth-finder. It is one thing to be a seeker and it is a whole other thing to be a finder. He was a brilliant man and the curator of the library of Alexandra in northern Egypt.

Also in Egypt, in the Egyptian language, there was a city known as Swenet. It was also known as Syene in the Greek language. Today, it is known as the city of Aswan, which is located near the Tropic of Cancer in Africa.

One day, Eratosthenes read on a papyrus that in Swenet, a city far to the south, on June 21 (summer solstice) as it came to noontime, the sun would rise to the zenith directly overhead. The light from the sun would then shine directly down into deep water wells and at the same time a straight up and down column would not cast a shadow. This "zenith" sun light only happened on one day of the year at noontime.

Eratosthenes did not understand how this light beam from the sun could shine directly down into deep water wells on one day of the year in Swenet and on this same day of the year, in the city of Alexandra at noontime, the light beam from the sun did not shine directly down into deep water wells, and a straight up and down column did cast a shadow. However, at the same exact time, in the city of Swenet, the straight up and down columns simply did not cast shadows.

Hmmm, this was an observation that did not make sense. Eratosthenes theorized that the sun was very far away, and if the earth was flat, then how could one perpendicular column cast a shadow and the other perpendicular column in another city not cast a shadow at noon on the same day?

This was a good question but it just did not make sense, seeing that the world was flat. This anomaly worked on his mind until he narrowed the possibilities and recognized some other possible answers. (Remember, Eratosthenes was not only a seeker of truth but also a finder of truth.) He would observe that in the night sky the moon was round in shape and he could also see that the sun was round in shape. So, he dared to think that maybe the earth was also round, or a sphere-like shape. If that was true, then it would make perfect sense as to why one column could cast a shadow in the city of Alexandra when the same column in the city of Swenet did not.

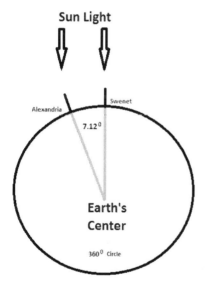

He conducted an experiment. At noontime, on the summer solstice day of the year, Eratosthenes measured the angle of the shadow that a column cast in the city of Alexandra and discovered that the angle of the shadow was about 7.12 degrees apart. That is, if the earth is a circle, and both perpendicular columns—one in Alexandra and the other in Swenet—kept going down into the earth, they would meet in the center at the earth's core. Then, that would equate to these two diverging columns having a mathematical angle. Thus, if you draw a circle on a piece of paper and divide that circle into 360 equal slices (a 360 degree circle) and draw a line from the center of the circle straight up so that it is pointing directly at the sun, that line or column would not cast a shadow. Then you draw a second line from the center of the circle with enough angle to cast a shadow on the edge of the circle that matched the angle of the shadow that Eratosthenes measured in Alexandra. Therefore, that column or line from the center would be approximately 7.12 degrees of a 360 degree circle or 7.12 degrees apart from the line that is perpendicular to the sun's light. 7.12 degrees is about 1/50th of a full 360 degree circle.

Once Eratosthenes found the angle, he then hired some men to measure the distance between Alexandra and Swenet; he also used well-documented Egyptian records, which dated back thousands of years, to determine the distance. Once he had the measurement of the distance between the two cities, he then multiplied that distance by 50 (7.12 degrees is about 1/50th of a 360 degree circle) and came up with a number of 39,690 kilometers for the circumference of the earth.

WOW... No... Double WOW! This is all taking place in the 3rd century BC! Eratosthenes not only proves the earth is round, (as if that was not good enough) but he goes on to measure the earth's circumference with an error of less than two percent, without ever leaving the city of Alexandra. WOW! Does anyone else think this story is absolutely amazing? This was definitely a man who wanted to know the truth.

Now, let me ask you a question. Was this a good day or a bad day for Eratosthenes? The day he figured it all out, knowing "the truth," was it a good day? Or was it a bad day? He found out the truth and got what he wanted.

Hypothetically, Eratosthenes walks down the street and talks to his friend who has been a goat herder all of his life. He explains that he now knows the earth is round and tries to explain how he came up with his measurement of the circumference of the earth. The goat herder says to Eratosthenes, "I love you like a brother, but that simply cannot be true, because wouldn't the people on the bottom of the earth just fall off?"

Eratosthenes then goes to his friend who is a farmer and tells him the great news. The farmer says to Eratosthenes, "I believe you, I have never taken one math or science class in my entire life, but I just know you and you would not come to me unless you knew you were right. Hence, I am just going to believe you."

Eratosthenes probably had these same types of conversations with his aunt, cousins, priests, contemporary scientists, etc. He probably received different reactions from many different points of view.

One of these might have said, "Eratosthenes, I will not believe this until you prove it to me. Until someone goes in a ship and sails all the way around the earth and proves your theory true, then and only then will I believe you. But until you prove it to me, I will not believe."

Do you think this conversation ever happened? Sure it did. Eratosthenes has the truth and he is sharing it, but some people will not accept it, because it is outside of their realm of thinking or rationale. It is outside of the fundamentals of what they have been taught their whole lives.

So is it a good day or a bad day when you know the truth?

A young teenage boy wanted to know the truth, so he went into a forest to pray. This boy, whose name is Joseph Smith, walks out of a grove of trees and knows the truth. He tells his friends the farmer, the herder, the priest and many others about what he now knows to be true. This boy Joseph spends almost the next two and a half decades of his life telling about his experience and this truth, and is eventually murdered for teaching the truth. Was it a good day or a bad day when Joseph Smith found the truth?

The Apostle Paul also found the truth and had to change his profession from being a hunter of the apostles to actually becoming an apostle, and was eventually killed for telling the truth. So, is it a good day or a bad day when you find out the truth? Deep question!

Do you really want to know? Because the answer might cause you to have a great test or struggle in your life. Finding the truth, is it a good day or a bad day? Truth may require change and sometimes people do not want to change. Change is difficult and improvement takes effort. Effort requires determination. Determination can bring order to your life. The problem is that "order" is constantly in conflict with "chaos," and finding "order" in essence is the expedition of truth.

Here is a truth that many people have a difficult time accepting; God does not care what you are. Many people reading this will be unable to accept that statement, but it is true. Right this instant, God does not care what you are in this one moment, but He does care about what you can become. Just keep reading and let me explain.

We humans like to tell God what we are, as if God does not already know this. God, I am not a good person, God's answer, I know. God, I am an adulterer, God's answer, I know. God, I am addicted to pornography, answer, I know. God, I am a mean and uncaring husband to my wife, answer, I know. God I am an alcoholic, answer, I know. We tell God what we are as if He did not know it already.

God probably says back to us in a patient voice, "I don't think you remember this part of the Bible, but I have left all of the judging to My Son. I am not your judge because that task is left to Jesus Christ, My Son."

> For the Father judgeth no man, but hath committed all judgment unto the Son: *John 5:22*

I am your Father in heaven and I am not here to judge you, but I am the provider of programs that can help you. I don't care what you are right now, but what I do care about is what you can become tomorrow. I care about what you are capable of becoming. Your current state of affairs is gruesome, chaotic and lacks order. But you are worthy of a chance to become the best **you** that you can be. I will let My Son judge your actions, but what are you going to do right in this moment of time to improve yourself or your situation?

This is what God cares about: not what you are, but what you can become. Is this a good day or bad day, for you?

In the story of the talents in the Book of St. Matthew, the Lord gives one man five talents and he turns it into ten talents, and the Lord is pleased. Then the second man is given two talents and he turns it into four talents, and the Lord is pleased. Then the third man is given one talent and hides the talent and when the Lord returns, the third man gives the one talent back to the Lord, and the Lord is angry and refers to third man as "slothful."

From God's perspective, it does not matter to Him if you are currently an alcoholic or an adulterer; likewise, God does not care if you are a bishop or a leader in your community. He just wants to know, what you are going to do now.

For instance, let us say that the first man in the parable of the talents had been born into a wealthy family, educated at the best schools and was very tall, handsome, robust and a picture of good health. God is basically saying to this man, "I gave you five whole talents; now let us see what you can do with them. Therefore, I do not care what you are; what I care about is what you can become. Can you take whatever you currently have and double those talents?"

People reading this book right now probably have more talents given to them by God than most people on earth. Compare your life to the boy who is born in Mongolia in a grass hut or "yurt." Compare the educational opportunities that you have received in your life to his. How about comparing yourself to the boy in Mongolia with your knowledge of Jesus Christ and the availability of scriptural truth? You might make the analogy that you are the one with five talents and he is the one with two talents. God does not care if you have five or two; what He cares about is what you are going to do with them.

This is why Mormons believe that you must be "born again" in this life to really understand what God wants you to do in this life. In the Book of Mormon it calls people to be born again.

> And the Lord said unto me: Marvel not that all mankind, yea, men and women, all nations, kindreds, tongues and people, must be **born again**; yea, born of God, changed from their carnal and fallen state, to a state of righteousness, being redeemed of God, becoming his sons and daughters; *Mosiah 27:25*

Then, in the Book of Alma, as Alma is speaking to the old, middle-aged and rising generations, he says;

> Unto them that they must repent and be **born again**.
> *Alma 5:49*

What I have explained in the above paragraphs is true. There is substantial evidence, but many will not believe. Some people on this planet have decided that even with fantastic evidence they will not believe until there is conclusive proof first. Just like some people did not believe Eratosthenes for 1,800 years, that is, until Magellan circumnavigated the globe in 1522AD. Imagine how much more fulfilling their lives would have been in the 3rd century BC, if they would have believed.

Are you going to wait 1,800 years before you will believe? If I tell you that if you read five minutes a day in the scriptures and pray to your Father in heaven every day that you will be able to overcome all obstacles that this life can throw at you, will you believe me? That is a true statement, but some people will not believe this until some big university does a huge study, spending thousands of dollars to prove that people of all faiths, who study the scriptures on a daily basis, and pray regularly, cope better with the challenges of life than people who do not. Do you really need a university study to prove to you that studying and digging into the scriptures can help you find truth?

If Eratosthenes can figure out the circumference of the earth within two percentage points without even leaving his home town of Alexandra, then I believe you have the ability to understand that reading scriptures can help you overcome life's obstacles. You do not need to wait 1,800 years for someone to actually prove it for you.

Another way to become not only a seeker of truth but a finder of truth is to learn to clarify what you are trying to say. You must learn to discuss issues until you understand the true root of the problem. Actually finding the precise problem or issue in a dispute is an attribute of someone who is a finder of truth. This simple function will attract truth from those that are around you. If you can learn to do this, you will be able to learn more about life than you ever thought possible and the design in which God deals with His children. I realize that this statement may not make sense to those who are reading this, but it is true. Let me give you a few examples.

A few years ago, I was riding in my friend's big truck and he needed to fill up on gasoline. He proceeded to drive 2.5 miles past three other gas stations to go to his favorite gas station. He said that this gas station always had their gas ten cents cheaper per gallon compared to the other stations.

As he was driving, I said to him that I thought it was stupid to drive five miles round trip, out of your way, to save a dime per gallon. My friend then lit into me about the value of saving money and that in his family it was a valuable trait to be a saver and not such a high-spender. He said that he had been doing this for years and the savings had really added up.

I then replied; "Let me clarify myself. What I meant to say was that your truck gets twenty miles to a gallon and gas is $4.00 per gallon, and you are driving 2.5 miles to the gas station and 2.5 miles back from this gas station. When you fill up your tank at an average of twenty gallons you save ten cents per gallon, times twenty gallons is a $2.00 savings. But since your truck gets twenty miles to the gallon, it therefore costs you a quarter of a gallon for the round trip to and from the gas station. Thus, a quarter of a gallon costs $1.00 of gas and therefore, you are saving $1.00 every time you drive by the gas station that is one block from your house to this cheaper gas stations that is 2.5 miles away. Therefore, if you fill up twice a month you are saving approximately $24.00 per year. That is all I was trying to say. I am sorry I said what I said, and the way I said it. Using the word 'stupid' and my tone were wrong, but I am now glad you allowed me to clarify myself, and what I really meant to say."

If you can develop this skill of talking through issues, instead of arguing and letting emotions get in the way and not offend people when asking questions; if you can learn this skill, then you are on your way to becoming a finder—not just a seeker—of truth.

In the above example, developing this type of communication expertise becomes a magnet for truth. The discovery and development of this type of skill set elevates your probability of success in finding the truth. Its natural gravitation will develop into an unstoppable chain reaction once you embrace this form of explorative conversation with the people whom you come in contact with. Not being afraid of conversations that clarify difficult issues is a key theme for finding truth.

Another example of becoming a finder and not just a seeker of truth is when Mormons and Protestants or Mormons and Catholics both pull out their scriptures and begin talking about salvation. It is very frustrating to watch, because Protestants and Catholics are quoting scriptures that are the requirements of getting into heaven, and Mormons are usually quoting scriptures that are the requirements to receiving huge responsibilities once you are in heaven, referred to as becoming "exalted." The scriptures for getting into heaven are all about faith in Jesus and grace from God. And the scriptures for getting into the exalted part of the celestial kingdom are mostly about being judged for your good works. It is very frustrating to watch, as these two groups believe they are talking about the same event, and therefore the disagreement.

Getting into heaven just takes the grace of God and faith in Jesus, along with an attitude that you will never give up on trying to follow Jesus. Even when you realize you have committed a sin, the very next moment you are still committed to trying to follow Jesus. This is the faith in Jesus that saves you. There are not any good works that you can complete on earth that guarantee your entry into heaven. Baptism is the lone exception, but even if you are baptized you still need faith in Christ to get into heaven. Baptism without faith in Jesus will not get you into heaven. No good works get you into heaven. However, once you do get into heaven, then your good works will count as you might be able to have a different mansion, or different responsibilities.

The movement from the bottom one-third of heaven to the middle one-third part of heaven requires good works, and moving from the middle part of heaven to the exalted part of heaven requires even additional completed works. Everyone who is in heaven has access to, and is living with, God the Father; but there are some who will have increased responsibilities in heaven based on the good works they have completed. Most of those good works are directly related to whether or not the person (the individual) really, truly understands the word "charity."

Accordingly, when Protestants and Catholics are reading their scriptures to describe how someone gets into heaven, Mormons should not make the mistake of then reading scriptures about what it takes to become exalted. Please make sure you clarify yourself before you get into an argument about faith vs. works. There is no faith vs. works. Faith and works are just two separate rungs on a ladder as you make your way to exaltation.

I have witnessed Mormons make this scriptural mistake, over and over again. It is very frustrating to observe, because they believe they are talking about the same event. These are two separate and distinct events requiring different and distinct attributes. Protestants are exactly correct on the requirements of getting into heaven through baptism and then faith in Jesus Christ. All it takes is to recognize that you both are talking about two different subjects.

The skill of clarification is a magnet for discovering truth. Learn how to clarify what you are saying, without offending others and witness truth flow toward you faster and more clearly than you ever thought possible.

If you really want to know the truth, then I am going to tell you. Here it is; the best life that we can achieve here on earth comes from keeping the commandments. Even an atheist will have a better life by keeping the commandments, than if he or she did not keep the commandments, and that is the truth! Keeping the commandments will not make your problems or challenges go away. All that it will do is help you cope with and overcome your problems and challenges with an ease and peace that you did not have before. This is truth that I am speaking.

Some people waited 1,800 years from the time of Eratosthenes until Magellan circumnavigated the earth in the year 1522 before they would believe the earth was round. Are you going to wait 1,800 years before you will believe that daily prayer, daily scripture study and continual discussions with your spouse, children and friends will bring growth and happiness to you? Are you not going to move, or enact change, or become pliable until someone gives you proof that Jesus is the Christ? Really?

Are you going to wait 1,800 years before someone proves that the gospel works? Or, can you deduct from simple observations that this is true?

This starts with accepting Jesus Christ as your personal Savior, asking Him to come in and take over, taking on His mantle, becoming His disciple and pupil. Once you do this, you are on the path to eventually overcoming all things that this life will throw at you. Here is the truth and this is the way to find your true self; not just your true self, but your true BEST self.

Christ does not just show you who you are, He already knows who you are, He shows you who you can become. That is the core of His messages. That is, we all know what we are, but what we can become is magnificent.

This is how we find truth. We find the truth in ourselves with the assistance of Christ and the outcome is a fountain of truth that flows to us every day. It grows and multiplies.

Another way to find truth is to understand the big picture. Here is an example. In the Book of Matthew Chapter 22, there is a scenario in which a question is asked of Jesus about marriage in the resurrection and it goes like this: There were seven brothers and the first brother marries a woman, has no children and he dies. Then the second brother marries the woman and has no children and he dies. This continues for all seven brothers. Then lastly the woman dies. The question is asked to Jesus;

> In the resurrection whose wife shall she be of the seven? *Matthew 22:28*

And then Jesus answered and said unto them;

> Ye do err, not knowing the scriptures, nor the power of God. For in the resurrection they neither marry, nor are given in marriage, but are as the angels of God in heaven.   *Matthew 22:29-30*

People who are not Mormon continually misinterpret this scripture to mean that there are no marriages in the afterlife. They misinterpret it because they do not have the overall understanding of the truth. Only from a Mormon perspective can you receive the meaning of what is being said here. Non-Mormons use this scripture to conclude that there is no marriage after death. But to a Mormon, this scripture makes perfect sense, because a Mormon understands the context in which the question was asked. The context is eternal marriage, because the question itself assumes, as common knowledge, that marriage does exist in the afterlife. That assumption is obvious, just based upon how the question was posed to Jesus.

So, in that context, if you ask any Mormon who understands temple marriage and you say to him; "There was a man, who married a woman in the temple for time and all eternity, and he died and then his brother married the women and he died and all seven brothers married her and died each one of them, and then she eventually also died. The question is, who will she be married to in the resurrection?"

Any Mormon would answer the same way Jesus answered the question by saying, "You do not know your scriptures very well, because there are no marriages taking place at the time of the resurrection. Eternal marriages are performed on earth, long before the resurrection. And if you knew your scriptures you also would know that she will be married to the first husband, because they were married in the temple for time and all eternity, and all others who are not married for time and for all eternity, become angels in heaven."

In the Book of Matthew, Jesus is not saying that there are no marriages in the afterlife. Rather, He is saying there is no giving or taking of spouses at the time of the resurrection. All marriages are decided way before the resurrection, and if you do not understand this, then you do not understand either the temple or the scriptures.

My point here is, when you understand the overall big picture of truth, as Mormons do, then Bible stories like this make perfect sense, and truth is easier to obtain and understand. People who have not received the fullness of the gospel have a difficult time understanding stories like this, resulting in the misinterpretation of what question Jesus was actually answering. Therefore, from those misinterpretations of what is actually being discussed, faulty assumptions lead people to erroneous conclusions. You see, the truth is much simpler to acquire once you accept the fullness of the gospel. Mormonism allows for all the scriptures to fit together.

Here is another scripture that would only make sense to a Mormon. It is St. Peter speaking about a "figure."

> The like figure whereunto even baptism doth also now save us... *1 Peter 3:21*

Ok, what <u>figure</u> is St. Peter talking about? In the verse preceding this scripture, St. Peter says that **eight** souls were saved at the time of Noah. This is the only number or figure that is used in any of the previous verses. Therefore, when Peter says, the like figure (which is the number eight) whereunto baptism doth also now save us, we must conclude that the figure eight, or number eight has the power of baptism to save us.

Mormons baptize their children at the age of eight years old. And this scripture in First Peter says that eight is the figure that baptism does now save us. I realize this is an obscure scripture and you will need to look it up yourself and study it. But my point is, if you know and understand Mormonism, scriptures like this are understandable. Mormon doctrine gives the core basis to actually obtaining a complete understanding of the Bible within the Joseph Smith perspective of the scriptures.

Here are a few more examples. 2 Corinthians 12:2 talks about a third heaven. Only Mormons know how to explain what is meant by the third heaven comment in 2 Corinthians 12:2.

Here is another; 1 Corinthians 15:29 talks about baptism for the dead. Mormons have a complete answer for this scripture and the explanations offered by other faiths are weak on this subject.

Another one is in Psalms, which says; "Ye are gods; and all of you are children of the most High" (Psalms 82:6). If you are not a Mormon then this scripture is confusing.

Another is Hebrews 7:12, as it talks about the Melchizedek and Levitical priesthoods. Verse 12 says that the priesthood was changed. Only under Mormonism can anyone understand the difference between those two priesthoods. No other Christian faith has a complete answer to this.

Then there is Exodus 28:42 where it says that the only people who are allowed to go into the tabernacle must wear linen breeches that reach down to their thigh. Exodus 28:42 is confusing to non-Mormons, and they are handicapped when trying to completely understand this scripture.

I am so glad my Mormon friends sent the missionaries to teach me the restored gospel. If they hadn't, I would have spent the last thirty years being scripturally frustrated. But, because of Joseph Smith and the Mormon overall general understanding of God's plan, the scriptures make much more sense and fit together as they help me understand truth. Once you have the overall big picture, then understanding doctrine is much easier.

It is easy for someone in the 21st century to understand Eratosthenes' calculation, because we already know the story of the solar system and therefore it is easier for us to accept that type of truth. This is in contrast to the many people living in the 3rd century BC who did not have a basic understanding of the cosmos and the solar system. The truth that the earth is a sphere would be difficult for them to accept.

Plants created before the sun and moon

The following is an example of unlocking the mysteries of heaven. The Book of Moses and the Book of Genesis both state that the plants were created on the third day and the moon and sun were created on the fourth day. It seems odd that plant life is created before the sun is created. Also, we now know that the moon was created by a very large object crashing into the earth and turning everything into molten rock resulting in a piece of the earth separating and forming the moon. Therefore, the assumption that plants could not have existed before the moon was created, is understandable.

However, there is a controversy in science on how life began here on earth. One group of scientists claims that microbial life came here attached to the side of an asteroid. Another group says that life began here on earth with a mixture of elements and some burst of energy.

However, all scientists agree that all life on earth can trace its existence back to one single "genesis" of life moment or event. Everything alive can trace its roots back to one single event, a "genesis." This is a common agreement from all schools of science and that as soon as life could start on planet earth, it did start.

Life on earth started almost as soon as it was possible. And if life did start as soon as it was actually possible for any life to begin on earth, then how come it didn't start again on a different part of the world? And how come we don't see life springing forth from elements today? Why was there only one single burst of life over a 4.65 billion-year time period? Why aren't there multiple bursts of life on earth?

It does not seem logical that if life can begin on earth over four billion years ago; then why didn't a new different strain begin three billion years ago, and another strain begin two billion years ago and at many other times or places on earth? Why does every living thing that lives today trace its existence back to one single "genesis" event? Why does all life on earth go back to a single point?

Using this type of deduction, one group of scientists now believes that life should have started multiple times on earth; and since it did not start multiple times, but only started one time, and because we have no evidence of any other "genesis" of life on earth, then they conclude that life came here on an asteroid from another planet.

If this is true, then Joseph Smith writing in the Book of Moses, and Moses writing in the Book of Genesis states that plants were created on the third day, before the sun and the moon were created on the fourth day, would be proof that God talked to Moses and Joseph Smith.

If science ever does prove that asteroids brought life to the earth, then they will be proving the Genesis timeline; that plants were created before our moon was created. Our moon was created about 4.65 billion years ago when a large object crashed into the earth and turned the earth to molten rock. Then, after the moon was formed and the earth cooled down, an asteroid delivered microbial life to the earth. That microbial life must have existed long before the moon had been created.

The life may have come from Mars or maybe the previous earth. If microbial life came from a previous earth, then the statement for Adam to <u>replenish</u> the earth, as stated in the Book of Genesis, would finally make sense. (I have always wondered about the word "replenish" in the Book of Genesis, as if to re-fill or re-establish. This word seems out of place in the story.)

If the microbial life came from a previous earth, Mars or somewhere else, attached to an asteroid, all of these scenarios would mean that plants existed before our moon was created. And if science ever proves that, then they would prove that Moses and Joseph Smith must have talked to God and were not just writing fiction.

Remember that Genesis and the Book of Moses are describing the beginning and creation of the universe all the way up to creating Eve. And in that context, having plants being created on the third day and the moon created on the fourth day is a correct time line, if science proves that an asteroid brought microbial life to the earth.

However, if someone was only trying to describe the history of the earth, they would have a time line that the earth was created first, then the moon was created, then plants came into existence.

Therefore, when you describe just Earth's history, plants are definitely created after the creation of the moon. But, when you describe the universe, plants definitely existed before our moon existed.

Remembering these two stories, of the universe and of the earth, both stories might have the existence of plants in a different order, or sequence of events, as compared to the time or creation of the moon. BOTH STORIES AND BOTH TIME LINES WOULD BE CORRECT!

In the universe's time line, plants existed before our moon existed. However, on the earth's timeline, plants existed after the moon was formed. Both order of timelines are correct depending on which story you are trying to explain.

Once again, if you can accept the overall fullness of the gospel, then truth is easier to acquire.

Here is another truth that the Apostle Paul teaches us. In the Book of Galatians, Chapter 5:19-22, the Apostle Paul tells us that people who are adulterers, fornicators, who live lasciviousness lives, who are haters, who are always envying others, who are murderers and who continue in drunkenness will NOT inherit the kingdom of God. By contrast, if you keep the commandments you will have the spirit of love, joy, peace, goodness and faith. Doesn't that sound like a great life?

The Apostle Paul has just told us that the truth can make our lives better, happier and more at peace. Maybe when you asked God to tell you the truth, He led you to this chapter of *Mr. Mormon*. This chapter is a formula for developing a fountain and flow of knowledge and truth. Ninety-five percent of all people who read this chapter will not believe it, or will not use it in their lives. They will say, yes, that works for other people, but not for me; or they will say that they have a special circumstance. Or, they need to get their friend's opinion to see if they think these things are truth. Well, you just need to be among the five percent that does use it in life and not the ninety-five percent that doesn't.

When the Apostle Paul found out the truth; when Eratosthenes found out the truth; when Joseph Smith found the truth; was it a good day or bad day for them?

Do you have the fortitude to act on the truth? If not, then don't ask God to give you the truth. If you are not going to dedicate your life to Christ, then don't ask God to send light and enlightenment into your life. If you are not going to do anything with it, (i) if you're not going to get baptized, (ii) if you're not going to pray, (iii) if you're not going to come to church, (iv) if you're not going to fast, (v) if you're not going to pay tithing, (vi) if you are not going to truly look after all of God's creations; then don't ask God to give you the truth.

The Apostle Paul's and Joseph Smith's lives were much more **rewarding** and also much more **difficult** after God told them the truth.

Here is a review of the truth for happiness in your life:

1. God only cares about what you can become, not what you currently are.

2. You must be born again in order to understand what this life is about.

3. You must continually clarify yourself. Learning the skills of clarification is like having a magnet for truth.

4. Keeping the commandments is the shortest way to happiness, even if you are an atheist.

5. No matter what religion you are in, daily scripture study and daily prayer is like a daily multivitamin.

6. Accepting the overall Mormon doctrine will make your understanding of the scriptures much easier.

7. Ninety-five percent of all people who read this chapter will never think about it again. You just need to be among the five percent who uses it.

8. Once you find the truth, life is usually much more challenging. (But would you want life any other way?)

9. Be mindful of what you ask God for, because He just might "LET YOU HAVE IT!"

Ok, so if a man in the 3rd century BC can accurately measure the circumference of the earth with just a few observations, then we should be able to figure out how to manipulate our own lives to find truth and happiness along with it.

Here is the question I want you to answer: Is today a good day for you, or a bad day for you?

That answer all depends on what you do with the information. Accept Jesus Christ; accept the words of the prophets/apostles, and act upon them. Don't sit on the sidelines. Start today.

CHAPTER 12
WAS ADAM SET UP TO FAIL?

One of the first questions in the universe that we must try to answer is; why are the numbers "one" and "two" spelled like they are? When you are a little child trying to learn how to spell in the English language, you learn what the properties and sounds of individual letters are in the alphabet. Then, after you think you have it down perfectly, some grown person tries to teach you how to sound out and spell the numbers "one" and "two." They utterly confuse you right from the start of your life. There is no "W" in the number "one" but for some reason the number one has a "W" sound in it. However, the next digit, the number "two", has the letter "W" but doesn't use any of it. So right off the start, when you are a child trying to learn how to spell, you are completely confused by "one" and "two." The pronunciation is illogical. It does not make sense and needs complex explaining. As you can see, this is probably the number one (and number two, Ha!) question in the entire universe.

Right behind that question is the Adam and Eve paradox. It is somewhat as confusing as the number one and number two examples. Similarly, Adam and Eve's paradox begins in the very first chapters of the entire Bible. The question is, did Adam have to break one of God's commandments in order to keep another one of God's commandments? It is a dilemma.

I have always been perplexed by this paradox in that Adam was commanded not to eat of the Tree of Knowledge of Good and Evil. However, at the same time he was also commanded to multiply and replenish the earth. Also, it clearly states in the Bible, that before he ate of the forbidden fruit he did not know he was naked and was innocent like a child. Therefore he could not, at that point, multiply and replenish the earth with Eve. The question that begs the mind of the reader, who is trying to contemplate the very first chapters of the Bible, is the fact that Adam seems to have to make a choice between two opposing commandments from God.

This seems to be a dilemma and if that is true, then God set up Adam in a paradox in which he would eventually have to break a commandment in order to correctly adhere to another commandment. This has always troubled my mind and it never made any sense. However, I do not believe we have the full story, so I cannot accept the traditional answers to this question. It is a paradox that has continued to perplex my soul.

I have three consecutive theories about the story of the Garden of Eden. Theory A, Theory B and Theory C are all designed to make sense of the Garden of Eden story. The three theories are not competing, but complimentary theories. Even if all three of my theories are wrong, it does not matter, because these issues that I am going to talk about really do nothing for anyone's salvation. It is just fun to talk about and may expand our understanding of who God is and how vast His plan is.

When Lucifer was in the Garden of Eden, he was trying to give the fruit of the Tree of Knowledge of Good and Evil to Adam and Eve, because there have been many Adam(s) and Eve(s) on many previous worlds.

> And worlds without number have I created; and I also created them for mine own purpose; and by the Son I created them, which is mine Only Begotten. And the first man of all men have I called Adam, which is many. But only an account of this earth, and the inhabitants thereof, give I unto you. For behold, there are many worlds that have passed away by the word of my power...
> *Moses 1:33-35*

> And Adam called his wife's name Eve, because she was the mother of all living; for thus have I, the Lord God, called the first of all women, which are many.
> *Moses 4:26*

Both scriptures say that there have been many Adams and many Eves and many worlds.

However, once the fallen angel Lucifer successfully gives the fruit to Eve on this world and then Eve gives the fruit to Adam, Lucifer is surprised to find out that he is going to be punished for his actions. Why would Lucifer not have seen this punishment coming? Why had Lucifer not remembered the stories of the previous worlds, that the person who gives the fruit to Adam and Eve is cursed or punished? Satan evidently believes that giving the fruit to Adam and Eve is not an event that would cause himself to be punished by God. Why is that?

Let us back up for a minute. The initial dilemma is that God had given Adam a commandment to multiply and replenish the earth, but He also gives Adam a contradicting commandment not to eat of the fruit. The prophet Nephi, in the Book of Mormon, tells us that if Adam had not fallen he would have had no children:

> If Adam had not transgressed he would not have fallen, but he would have remained in the garden of Eden. And all things which were created must have remained in the same state in which they were after they were

created; and they must have remained forever, and had no end. And they would have had no children...
2 Nephi 2:22-23

The Book of Mormon clearly states that Adam would have had no children if he hadn't transgressed in the Garden of Eden. Other faiths do not believe this and they have multiple explanations for this dilemma which have never been quite satisfactory to me, even before I was a Latter-day Saint.

In the Book of Moses, Eve says that they could not have had children unless they had transgressed.

And Eve, his wife, heard all these things and was glad, saying: Were it not for our transgression we never should have had seed... *Moses 5:11*

> Note: Please remember the term "seed" or the phrase, "we never should have had seed." The word "seed" will be important later on in this chapter.

Both scriptures in the Book of Nephi and the Book of Moses confirm that Adam and Eve could not have had children before they ate of the fruit.

Unique to Mormon doctrine is that this is not the first world that God has populated with an Adam and an Eve. In fact, Mormons believe that God has populated a multitude of worlds and earths with a multitude of Adams and a multitude of Eves. The Book of Moses uses the term "which is many" and "which are many" to describe multiple Adams and multiple Eves on multiple worlds.

Theory A

Here goes Theory A. To accept Theory A, you need to allow for long passages of time in the Garden of Eden. When most people read the Book of Genesis, they do not put in the element of time. But, as I have come to believe, if you place long passages of time into the story, it starts to make sense.

Adam was in the Garden, just walking around and looking around, naming animals and creatures just like Genesis says he was doing. This went on for quite some time. Adam was going to walk around the Garden for a few years, or a few hundred years, or a few million years, until he was bored out of his Eden mind. Then, finally he was going to realize that God had given him a paradox.

Adam would eventually ask, "Is this all there is? Walking around, looking around? There is no challenge here; therefore there is no growth in this beautiful garden. It is just a really, really nice cage, correct? So, how can I (Adam) multiply and replenish the earth without eating of the fruit?"

The answer is, you can't replenish the earth until you eat of the fruit; therefore, the paradox and Adam's dilemma. Eating of the fruit violates God's will, but not multiplying and replenishing the earth is also against what God told Adam to accomplish.

Adam would say, "Heavenly Father, You commanded me to have children, but it appears that I cannot have children until I eat of the fruit. So, Father, how can I have children without breaking one of your commandments? How can I keep both of your commandments?"

When Adam was mature enough to ask these types of questions, then God knew he was ready to understand the consequences, because maturity requires the passage of long periods of time. The answer to this dilemma is that most people do not consider the time factor in the story of Genesis and the Garden of Eden.

The story in the Book of Genesis, about the Garden of Eden, as was told to me for many years, did not make sense, until I applied the following metaphor.

The father of a small child lives in a house on a busy street with many cars and trucks zooming by all day. The father tells his son that he is not allowed to cross the street, play in the street, or even set foot in the street. Also, the father tells his son that he can be anything that he wants in life. He could explore the world, become an important business man, run large governments; he could travel to the South Pole and see penguins, etc. From the little boy's perspective this is a dilemma.

"Hmm... I am told to discover and explore the world, but I can't cross the street?"

Ok, this sounds like a dilemma unless we put the element of time into the story. Allowing time to pass, and the little boy's maturity and understanding to magnify, then the story makes sense as he becomes mature enough to understand the risks of the busy street.

So, fast-forward in time, five, ten, or fifteen years. At some point in the future, the boy is going to say to the father, "Dad, I understand the dangers and risks of the street; I understand how to negotiate the crossing of the street in a safe way; I understand that there are risks involved. I can calculate the speed of cars and trucks and I know when I can cross and not cross the street." At that moment the father realizes that his son has a universal understanding of the risks associated and enough time has passed to allow for real contemplation and understanding of the risks and rewards. Then, and only then, would a good father give his son permission to cross the street.

The child at this point becomes responsible for his own actions and is able to take educated risks. Therefore, if something does not go as planned, then the child will not blame the father, but will take responsibility for everything. He will remember he made an educated choice to take risk. If something goes wrong, then it is not the father's fault, because the father only allowed the crossing of the street when the son was well-equipped to make the choices and decisions. The son might be mature enough at ten years old. However, some sons might not be mature enough until they are fifteen. The point is, an attentive father will know when his son is ready by the questions that he asks. The street is dangerous, but the danger can be mitigated; and once contained, then there are great rewards of personal growth awaiting him. You see, a righteous father will know exactly when to allow his son to cross the street by himself.

This is Theory A, taught through a metaphor. The story just needs the element of time to start to make sense. If they were given enough time to understand the risks and make a knowledgeable decision, then that would have been how the story was supposed to go.

A person really cannot freely choose until the consequence and risk of each choice are fully-understood and comprehended. If he understands completely the pros and cons of the risks and rewards, then he would have no basis to blame God for his problems if something goes wrong. That is why Adam, or his descendants, cannot blame God for anything. We chose to come here; we chose to follow Christ to this earth. Adam, in a true informed choice, would therefore have acquired skills and knowledge of how problems are solved, and thus, becoming more intelligent each and every time he conquered an obstacle. He also would have realized that there is no other way to obtain knowledge and wisdom, except to experience it. This is the only way, but it is first and foremost Adam's choice. He cannot, or should not, be rushed; the father must be patient and allow his child to progress at his own speed.

Theory A uses the assumption that:

1. Adam and Eve could have no children until they ate the fruit.
2. There were many previous Adams and Eves on many

previous worlds.
3. Long periods of time are needed to understand the story completely.
4. The metaphor of the busy street and the little boy helps us understand the two seemingly contradictory instructions from the father.

That is Theory A. OK... buckle your seat belts, because here comes Theory B.

Theory B

Theory B says that God the Father was supposed to give the fruit of the Tree of Knowledge of Good and Evil to Adam and Eve when it was the right time. God was going to give the fruit to Adam and Eve when they were ready.

Let us go back to the metaphor of the boy and the busy street.

The father has to go on a business trip and has an uncle come to the home and babysit the young boy. The uncle is asked to supervise the boy for a few days. While the uncle is babysitting, the uncle decides that the little boy is old enough to cross the street and play in the street and teaches him how to cross the street by himself. And, he tells the little boy that crossing the street and playing in the street is a function of growing up and becoming a successful business man like his father. To become like the father, you must cross the street.

When the father returns from the business trip, he punishes the uncle for allowing his son to play in the street. The uncle's defense is that he says that the boy was going to learn about the street one day anyway. So what is the big deal? And the uncle can't believe that he is being punished for something that the father was going to do anyway.

"That is totally unfair!" says the uncle. "Yes," the father says. "I am going to punish you, because the boy is not old enough to understand all the dangers. You rushed him into it."

The father banishes the uncle, and the uncle feels that he is being treated unfairly. The father didn't punish the uncle for the single act of the boy playing in the street. The Father punished the uncle because it is not the uncle's place to determine when the boy can play in the street. The uncle was trying to be the father; he was trying to walk and talk and act like the father. He is not the father; therefore, he does not decide when it is the correct time to allow the boy to cross the street.

Ok, take that metaphoric story and compare it to the story in Genesis. My Theory B is that in the Garden of Eden, God is not punishing Lucifer for the act of giving the fruit to Adam. God is saying, "I am punishing **YOU**, because **YOU** gave it to him." Not because Adam received the fruit; Adam was eventually going to get the fruit anyway. It's not the act of giving the fruit that is punishable. The act of giving the fruit to Adam(s) and Eve(s) in all the previous worlds was never punishable because God was always the one who gave the fruit to those Adam(s) and Eve(s). He is punishing Lucifer because the act of giving the fruit was not Lucifer's responsibility. It was not his place. That is why Satan was punished. It was not Lucifer's responsibility—not his job or duty.

Lucifer is not God, but he is always trying to be God.

To better understand this Theory B, take this story in context and in a logical sequence of events. Try to remember the situation that Lucifer is in at the time. From Lucifer's perspective, he has just been kicked out of heaven because he had put up a competing plan to God's plan of salvation. Lucifer did not put up a plan to compete with a Jesus' plan. There was no plan from Jesus, it was God the Father's plan and Jesus said he would go and do it. Lucifer thought that he had a better plan than God's plan and he convinced a third part of heaven to follow him. Wow, he must have been quite a convincing public speaker to persuade that many to follow him. Lucifer is trying to be God in the pre-mortal existence. That is why the mighty archangel Michael kicks Lucifer and his angels out of heaven and puts them on the earth.

Think about this, right after the war in heaven, all of Lucifer's followers now have forfeited getting a body. In contrast, all the followers of Christ are going to get physical bodies. The followers of Satan are probably complaining to Lucifer that they lost the war in heaven and are not going to get physical bodies. In an attempt to re-establish himself and regain their confidence, proving that he is just as powerful as God the Father, Lucifer once again tries to play the role of God.

Lucifer says, "I am still going to get everyone of you a body, just calm down. It's just going to take a little bit longer. You fools, don't you see, once Adam and Eve are able to start having children (or more precisely, when Eve is able to start having children) then I have a plan to get everyone who followed me a body. This is just a bump in the road. Just cool your jets and watch me in action. God the Father is not the only one who can get you a body." So, to show off to his followers and keep them in rank and file, Satan once again tries to walk and talk and act like God. And to prove it, he reminds his followers about the stories of the previous worlds and all the previous Adams and Eves receiving the fruit from God the Father. "And remember," he tells all of them, "once God gives them the fruit, then they will be able to have children. Well, watch me in action; I can do everything God can do and I will prove it by giving the fruit to Adam and Eve just as God has done on all the previous worlds before this one."

To show off and regain the confidence of his followers, Lucifer gives the fruit to Eve and simulates what God was supposed to do. Satan is being pressured by his followers, and Satan himself is growing impatient for Adam and Eve to eat of the fruit. It's taking too much time. It is taking too long! When are they going to eat the fruit; when is God going to give them the fruit? Satan grows more and more impatient as he receives pressure from the fallen third part of heaven. Therefore, Lucifer needs Eve to eat it soon, so she can start producing children. So, he compresses the time line by giving the fruit to Eve—just like the uncle did to the little boy on the busy street. What does Lucifer tell Eve?

> For God doth know that in the day ye eat thereof, then your eyes shall be opened, and ye shall be as gods, knowing good and evil.   *Genesis 3:5*

Here, Lucifer was actually telling her the truth, because when we read further it says that after Adam and Eve ate the fruit, this is what the Lord God says;

> And the Lord God said, Behold, the man is become as one of us, to know good and evil: *Genesis 3:22*

The Lord God confirms what Lucifer told Eve. Here is an interesting question; how did Lucifer know that? How did he know Eve would become like God, knowing good and evil? Hmmm... Answer; Lucifer knew this because he knew about all the previous earths, all the previous Adams and all the previous Eves. He knew the story so well that even the Lord God in Genesis 3.22 confirmed Satan's earlier prediction to Eve.

This is a huge clue to understanding what really happened in the Garden of Eden. What do the clues tell me? They tell me that Lucifer knew this story backwards and forwards. He had heard it a thousand times; that Adam(s) and Eve(s) in previous garden(s) on previous world(s) are given the fruit. He knew they would become as gods, knowing good and evil once they ate the fruit. So, if he knew the story backwards and forwards, then the bigger question is, why did he not know that the person who gives the fruit to Adam and Eve is punished? How come he didn't know that? How come Lucifer is surprised to be punished? If he knows the story, how come he doesn't know the ending of the story?

One other thing that Lucifer also told Eve is that she would not die. But from Lucifer's perspective, this was a true statement also, because after Eve eats the fruit of the Tree of Knowledge of Good and Evil, then all she has to do is go over and take a bite of the Tree of Life and live forever. Satan had no idea that God will put cherubim and a flaming sword in front of the Tree of Life, because in all the previous Gardens of Eden, on all the previous earths, God never had to put cherubim and a flaming sword in front of the Tree of Life. That is why Satan told Eve she would not die; because the Tree of Life was right there in the Garden in plain sight.

The part of the story that is so perplexing is that Lucifer must not have known that the person giving the fruit to an Adam and an Eve would be punished. Now, why, why, why would Lucifer know the whole story but somehow forget that particular event? The answer is obvious if you just think logically. It is because God gave Adam and Eve the fruit in all the previous Gardens of Eden, in all the previous worlds. That is why Lucifer believes Eve will not die; because she always had access to the Tree of Life. God confirms this; God says,

> Lest he put forth his hand, and take also of the tree of life, and eat, and live for ever: *Genesis 3:22*

From Lucifer's perspective, he needs to build a rapport with Eve; he needs Eve to trust him, because she is the key to Satan's plan. In an attempt to gain her trust, he tells her she will be as the gods and she will not die. From Satan's perspective, once she eats of the Tree of Life, she will live forever. And when that happens, Eve will trust Satan more than she trusts God, because Satan's words would have become truth.

And Satan would always remind Eve; "Remember who was the one back in the Garden who told you that you would not die? It was me, so trust me, for I am the one who tells you the truth."

That is how Satan planned to get Eve to be on his team and gain her trust. But Satan did not realize God could change the game. Satan did not know the mind of God: "and he sought also to beguile Eve, for he knew not the mind of God..." (Moses 4:6).

God does two things that Lucifer was not expecting.

1. He punishes the person who gives the fruit to Adam and Eve.
2. He puts cherubim and a flaming sword to restrict access to the Tree of Life.

Those two things had never happened in the previous stories, and they are a surprise to Lucifer. He did not expect it. From Lucifer's point of view, the result should be the same, Adam and Eve both got the fruit! Who cares who gave it to them, or what time in their maturity that they received it? It should not matter who gave it to them. It just matters that they got it.

The element of long passages of time in Theory A and Theory B is that eventually God was supposed to give the fruit to Adam and Eve. Fathers do not give their children roast beef to eat before their children have any teeth. Therefore, God the Father would give Adam the fruit when he was ready to grow and handle the problems, challenges, and rewards associated with such risks.

Theory C

Theory C says that our world is different and unique from all the previous worlds. Where can we find evidence of this in the scriptures?
Here is one that says that Satan is the god of this world:

> In whom the god of this world hath blinded the minds of them which believe not...   *2 Corinthians 4:4*

Corinthians says that Satan is the god of this world, implying our world is not the same as the others.

Also, Moses establishes that the Lord God named all the other Eves in all the previous worlds, but on this world God did not name Eve; it was Adam who named Eve, inferring that our world is different than all the previous worlds.

> And Adam called his wife's name Eve, because she was the mother of all living; for thus have I, the Lord God, called the first of all women, which are many.
> *Moses 4:26*

Thus God named all Eves except for the Eve on our world. Conclusion: our world is unique. This next scripture also infers that our world is unique.

> Wherefore, I can stretch forth mine hands and hold all the creations which I have made; and mine eye can pierce them also, and among all the workmanship of mine hands there has not been so great wickedness as among thy brethren. *Moses 7:36*

This scripture shows us that out of all of God's creations, ours is the most wicked. Our world is unique. I want to focus on the word "unique" in that it means there are no others like it in all of God's creations. Our world was the only world wicked enough to crucify our own Lord and Savior. Why was our world wicked enough, why are we set apart from all of God's other creations? Because the story of the Garden of Eden plays out differently in our case than all the previous Gardens of Eden. Our world has Lucifer. Remember, our world was annihilated, except for eight people, by a great flood. Our world is so wicked that God Himself killed everyone on this world except for eight people. Wow!!! Double Wow! God didn't allow the people to war against each other and kill each other off. No, He didn't even allow that to happen. God Himself sent a flood and killed everyone. That's a pretty wicked world, even a world so wicked that the descendants from the eight lone survivors would eventually become so wicked again as to actually crucify and kill their own creator, even Jesus Christ. This proves that our world is unique.

If I am right, and our world is unique, then what made it unique? Jesus came to this earth because there is opposition in all things. Our world has a satan who is continually trying to encourage people to sin. That is why Jesus came to this world. Lucifer is unique to our world and therefore Jesus Christ being born to our world is also unique to our world.

The other worlds did have sin. However, they just weren't as evil as our world. There was sin on the other worlds, no doubt. You do not need Satan whispering in your ear to commit a sin.

This concept of previous worlds without Satan is difficult for some of my Mormon friends to accept. They believe that if there was no Satan then there would be no sin. This line of thought is simply wrong and I can prove it just by reminding them of the plan of salvation story. Just think about the story for a minute.

Doctrine and Covenants 76:25 says that Lucifer had been an angel with authority. Lucifer had been in the presence of God, but sinned while he was in the presence of God and was cast out of heaven. No one was compelling Lucifer to commit a sin; there wasn't a satan whispering in his ear to commit a sin, because it says in Doctrine and Covenants 76:25 that Lucifer was in the presence of God and still fell from heaven. Therefore, you do not have to have a satan whispering in your ear to sin. However, if you do have Satan whispering in everyone's ear, then he can compel a third part of heaven to sin. Having a satan whispering in your ear is a catalyst for sin, and becomes exponential to create such a wicked world that God Himself would send a flood and start over; only to have the remaining descendants become evil enough to crucify their own Lord and Master, their own Savior.

The previous worlds did have sin, murder, theft, etc., but just not to the extent that we have it. Our world is unique because Christ came to this world to atone, be crucified and become resurrected. Why did He come to our world? He came to our world because there was a satan here. An extra-ordinary amount of evil requires an extra-ordinary amount of goodness to counter balance. Opposition in all things!

To summarize, Lucifer gets punished for giving the fruit to Eve. Lucifer has a plan to get bodies for his followers. Satan is speeding up the time line because he is getting impatient and needs Eve to start producing children. Lucifer needs procreation to begin for his plan to work. Without this, Lucifer cannot get bodies for his followers. Satan is trying to obtain bodies for his followers to prove he is as powerful as God the Father. But God is onto his plan, and God knows exactly what He is doing in Genesis 3:15. Please read this next verse closely. This is God talking to Satan as He punishes him:

> And I will put enmity between thee and the woman, and between thy seed and her seed...   *Genesis 3:15*

Just to make sure I was reading the scripture correctly, I double-checked it in the Book of Moses. Remember, Genesis was written by Moses and the Book of Moses was written by Joseph Smith. The Book of Moses was not translated, but was written from direct inspiration from God to Joseph Smith. Therefore, in cross-referencing Genesis 3:15 with Moses 3:21, I find it says the same thing:

> And I will put enmity between thee and the woman, between thy seed and her seed...   *Moses 4:21*

Doctrine and Covenants 6:28 says, "in the mouth of two or three witnesses shall every word be established." So, here we have two scriptures written by two different prophets. Actually, they are two of the greatest prophets who have ever lived and they say the exact same thing, word for word, that God had to put something called "enmity" between the seed of Satan and the seed of Eve. Why did God have to punish Lucifer in that way? Why did God have to say that? Why was that his particular punishment?

It's because as soon as Eve eats the fruit, she can have children, and Lucifer needs a woman with seed to produce bodies for his angels. If it were not so, then God would not have had to say that in Genesis 3:15.

This is why Satan gives the fruit to Eve before she is ready to receive it. He is impatient. He is being pressured from his angels to get bodies for them. Satan is feeling the pressure. To speed the process up, he does not wait for God to give Adam and Eve the fruit. Satan wants to do the same things that God does, so Satan gives the fruit in an effort that will cause Eve the ability to have seed. Once she can have seed, then Satan will have bodies for his followers. God knows this is possible. If it were not so, then God would not have had to punish Satan in such a specific way. Think about how specific that punishment is. Wow, God gets right to the point.

Therefore, Satan's actions and choices are what makes this world unique from all the previous worlds and causes our world to have Jesus Christ come down and live among us: the same Jesus Christ who was crucified, resurrected three days later, and saved all the inhabitants of this earth (and all the other earths) from death.

I am not saying that Jesus Christ did, or did not live on another earth. I do not know, but I do believe, and my theory is, that He only lived on our earth, and that makes our earth unique. He not only saved our world but all worlds. I do not know the mechanics of how He was able to do it. I just believe that He did do it. The Savior came and lived on our world and that means our world is unique.

It could have been that the previous inhabitants of other worlds looked forward to a future world to which a savior would be born; just like everyone in the Old Testament had to look forward and be baptized in the name of a savior who would come in the future. They were baptized for a future savior that was to come. Everything the Old Testament inhabitants heard about the Savior Jesus Christ came by prophecy of future events.

This is in contrast to the people of the New Testament to whom a story that had happened in Jerusalem was told in the past tense. Reading what Jesus actually said is much easier to believe and follow than trying to live by a prophet telling you what Jesus will say in the future. I believe it is much easier to believe in Christ as a New Testament person, in the past tense, than it is for Old Testament people looking to a future story. Seems more difficult for the Old Testament people to believe, but that was the lot of the followers of God in the Old Testament. Therefore, it is my belief that our Savior atoned for all of the worlds in the Garden of Gethsemane and on the cross.

Some of you reading this might say that I am inferring that God did not see this all coming, and that God is not all-knowing. That is not true. God knew it would happen that way on one of His worlds.

My answer to that question is very simple; a question back to you. The question is, when God kicked Adam and Eve out of the Garden of Eden did He know that thousands of years in the future He was going to kill all of Adam's posterity except for eight? Is God all-knowing? If you said yes, then you have answered your own question. That is, He did know that He was eventually going to send a flood and kill all the inhabitants of the earth and start again with eight souls.

Just because a father knows what his children are going to do before they actually do that thing, does not mean the father has predestined his children. It means that some of his children have to actually do things before they can understand. There is no substitute for experience, which is a fact that Satan does not completely understand or comprehend.

Studying what it is like to have a body from reading a book is one thing, but actually living in and controlling that body; to not over-eat, over-drink, or withstand other bodily desires, this is a much different thing.

The flood was a result of the children of God using their agency to receive the harvest of the things they had planted. They were given their opportunity to have experience, of which there is no substitute. If your child plants wheat in the spring, the child should not expect orange trees to grow in the fall. But sometimes children do just that, even though their parents warn them that this course will not get them an orange tree. Some children just have to experience it for themselves to learn. This is a universal rule. God knows this, and He must painfully sit back and allow His children to fail so that they can learn. Sometimes there is no other way to transfer knowledge. Experience has no substitute.

Where there is a tremendous amount of opposition, then that enables a tremendous hero to arise, grow and "OVERCOME" the evil of the universe. God knew that in producing X number of worlds there would rise up a single angel who would become a satan. It was just a matter of time, God knew it would happen, and He just waited for the event to unfold. A single being from eons of previous creations would arise as an angel who was "a son of the morning" not "THE" son of the morning, but "A" son of the morning (D&C 76:26). An angel who would choose by his own accord to rebel and fall from heaven. The most difficult tests produce the most growth. We are all on this world because we have the opportunity to overcome extreme evil.

We have been placed in a world unlike all of the worlds before, and therefore have the opportunity to grow faster and to levels never before known. Once Lucifer chose his path, then God just implemented the plan that was previously thought out. It became time to make a unique world that had the ability to produce exalted children of God. If our world is the most evil, then the people who survive it and overcome always with charity in their hearts are, by definition, the most righteous and stalwart followers of God. This one unique earth, that is the most wicked of all the other earths, has the power and potential to produce not just humans who are saved, but humans who can become exalted. Becoming exalted is not an easy endeavor. It takes effort, leadership and self-control.

> He that humbleth himself shall be exalted.   *Luke 14:11*

Lucifer chose all by himself to become a satan. God did not manipulate him to do evil. Satan thought that he had a substitute for experience. His plan was to save everyone from sin by not giving anyone the choice to sin, and therefore, deprive everyone of growth. Because where there is no choice, there is no real risk. It sounds noble, but Satan really was in it for his own glory. He thought his plan was better than God's plan.

From Lucifer's perspective, he needed Eve to start having seed, so he wanted her to hurry up and eat the fruit.

From Lucifer's perspective, Eve would become like the gods and not die, because she had access to the Tree of Life and then she would trust him. It did not even enter his mind that giving the fruit to Eve was a punishable offence, because it was going to happen anyway and no one had ever been punished for giving the fruit before. He was showing off to his followers that he could obtain bodies for them and walk and talk like God by giving the fruit to Adam and Eve.

From Lucifer's perspective, the outcome of the story of the Garden of Eden was unchangeable because it had happened the same way for millions of earths before. He had no idea that God would change two things; (i) put cherubim and the flaming sword to protect the Tree of Life, and (ii) punish the person who gives the fruit to Adam and Eve, in a very, very specific way. Those two things had never happened before.

From our human perspective, the Garden of Eden was just a really, really, really nice but over-rated cage. It is a life with no risks involved. When something bad happens to me in life, I sometimes wish I were in a really nice cage, protected from the difficult things. But as that moment passes, I realize that I am grateful to not be in a really nice cage and that I have opportunity all around me.

Theory A: is about time. When you read the story of the Garden of Eden, consider very long periods of time passing between each event and imagine how time might affect the story.

Theory B: is that God was the one who was supposed to give the fruit to Adam and Eve.

Theory C: is that our earth is unique because Christ was born on our earth. There is opposition in all things because we have a satan, and people on this earth have a chance to become not just saved, but exalted.

Ok... Those are Theories A, B, and C. All three theories work in tandem, or you can just agree with one or two of them. I realize that many of you will not agree with my theories and that is OK, because it is just a theory, something to ponder on and think about.

I started off this chapter by comparing the spelling of the number one and number two to the pronunciation of the number one and number two. And unless a little child has someone to explain how to spell the first two numbers, they would never come up with the conclusion by themselves, by sounding out the words. They would need a clue or a guide to figure it out.

The same is true of the story in the first few chapters of the Bible. If there is not some additional information, like Theories A, B, and C, then the first few chapters of the Bible leave the reader a bit logically frustrated.

Adam's dilemma never made sense to me, but with Theories A, B and C, the story finally fits together. I might be totally wrong, but at least I have something that makes sense. I have read theories from great Bible scholars on this subject. They are all very smart people with much more insight than I have. But in the end, all their explanations did not logically fit together.

I am not saying that I am right. And whether my theories are correct or not; I do not know. However, these theories have expedited my pondering and spiritual yearnings to understand God and the scriptures again and again. They have inspired me to search scriptures and cross-references, which expanded my knowledge of God's Holy Books. I hope they do the same thing for you. Thanks for keeping an open mind for the last few minutes.

> Note: The epitome of ignorance is not believing in something simply because you know nothing about the subject. Talk about irony; that is truly the epitome or essence of ignorance.

The fun thing about this chapter is that, whether I am right or wrong, it makes no difference to anyone's salvation. It is just fun to talk about.

Jesus is the Christ and the Savior of the world. Allow Him into your life, all the way in, and your life will not be so thirsty and dry. You will be fulfilled, you will be able to overcome difficulties in life, and you will be numbered with the followers of Christ.

CHAPTER 13
EVOLUTION VS. CREATION

In Genesis Chapter 2, it gives us the ingredients God uses for life on earth. If you look at it closely, you might be able to pick them out. Ready? Here we go. Verse 9 reads, "out of the ground made the Lord God to grow every tree." But, for the animals in Verse 19 it reads, "out of the ground the Lord God formed every beast of the field." It also reads that out of the ground He formed every fowl in the air. Then we get to God's next-to-the-last creation, which is Adam. (Eve is actually the last creation.) The next-to-last creation is man. It also tells us in Verses 6 & 7 that God put up a mist from the earth, and watered the whole face of the ground and the Lord God formed man from the dust of the ground.

All right, did anyone catch that? Did you pick that up? Was it difficult to decipher the pre-created materials that God used? I will summarize; (i) the trees came from the ground, (ii) the beasts came from the ground, (iii) the fowl in the air came from the ground, and (iv) the man came from the ground or the dust of the ground with a little mist on top of the ground. The key ingredients are the ground and some water or mist.

I had a friend ask me one time, "Are you trying to tell me that all life on earth came from the same substance?"

And my reply was, "Hey, I didn't write the Bible; I'm just reading it. So it is not me that is telling you that all life on earth came from the same ingredients. It is the Bible telling you that all life came from the same ingredients."

The other ingredient is time. When many people read Genesis, they never put in the element of time as an ingredient. When I talk to my atheist friends about this, I always ask them, "How did Moses get this so right?" Atheists believe that Moses was just writing fiction. If that is true, then how did he guess so correctly? Genesis and the Book of Moses say that there were only six time periods of creation called days. Let's do the time line backwards:

Sixth day: On the sixth day God created cattle and creeping things and then God created Man and his last creation was Eve.

Fifth day: On the fifth day the waters brought forth moving creatures (whales) and fowl that may fly.

Fourth day: On the fourth day God created two great lights, the moon and the sun.

Third day: On the third day God created the plants.

Second day: On the second day God created the firmament in the midst that it divided the waters with some water below and some above the firmament.

First day: On the first day God created light.

I'm not sure if you have put this together but the order of creation in Genesis is accurate. The story of science and the story in Genesis coincide. Wow, when Moses wrote Genesis, he was pretty much in agreement with the order in which the earth and life on it has evolved. So I say to my atheist friends, how did

Moses do it? If he was writing fiction, then how did he get it so correct?

For instance, Moses says that on the first day God created light. But note that Moses also says that God did not create the moon or the sun until the fourth day. Please take note of what Moses does not say. He does not say that the sun was created in the first day. He says that light was created in the first day. Wow again. The Big Bang Theory says that the first thing that happened was a big bang of energy that created forms of light and energy. Then the Big Bang Theory says that the second thing that happened was that this light and energy created vast clouds of particles.

Now, compare that to Moses, because he says that the second thing to happen was that the firmament was created and that the firmament separated the water, with some water above the firmament and other water below the firmament. Firmament is another name for clouds. There are clouds of particles and two sections of water divided by the clouds. If Moses is just a man, writing some fictitious book, then why would he say that light was created four whole days before our sun and moon were created? How would he put that together if he was just making it up?

If my atheist friends are correct, and Moses was just making it all up, then they would have to conclude that Moses was sitting on some big rock and saw a majestic bird fly overhead, then guessed that the bird was made from the ground. After making that assumption, Moses then wrote it down to pass it off as a revelation from God. The question is, how does anyone look at a bird and conclude that it came from the ground? It is a correct statement, but how did Moses put that together? It is like watching a huge jet airplane fly overhead and you say that the jet came from the ground. You are correct, the metal came from the ground, the plastics came from the ground, the glass in the windows came from sand, or the ground, and the jet fuel came from the ground. So, to say that a jet airplane "came from the ground" is correct, but how would a man with a 1300BC education ever put all that together and be so right?

Let us put this into perspective. If I said to you, please write an essay summarizing the nearly fourteen billion-year history of the universe all the way down to how life started on earth and do it in four pages. Ready, go! Because that is exactly what Moses did; he summarized nearly fourteen billion years into the first two chapters of the Bible. And I think he did a really, really, really great job, considering he only had a few pieces of paper to cram in a lot of information. Are there parts missing? Of course, no one can explain a complete fourteen billion year-old story in four pages and think they are going to have every detail explained.

How did Moses determine that man, birds, beasts, trees, and all life, came from the same substance? But even more impressive is, how did he know that our sun and moon had not been created until the universe was almost nine billion years old? And how did he know that light was created almost nine billion years before our sun and moon had been created? The universe is almost fourteen billion years old. The sun and moon are only 4.5 to 5 billion years old. The Book of Genesis says that the sun and moon were created on the fourth day of a six-day creation schedule. It would seem like Moses got really, really, really lucky if my atheist friends are correct. What are the statistical odds that Moses would have guessed that part so precisely? It is pretty astonishing for a guy who is just making it all up, by writing fiction, as my atheist friends claim.

My atheist friends have never given me an answer to that question, I am still waiting. Over the years I have learned that creating doubt in an atheist is not as difficult as one might think. They have doubts.

The more I learn about science, the more I learn about God. I tell my atheist friends that science is helping me prove that

Moses did talk to God, because there is no other way that Moses could have obtained these historical facts on the creation of the universe and how all life on earth came from the same materials. Moses did an incredible job of summarizing almost fourteen billion years into just a few pages. Please read the first few chapters of Genesis from this perspective and see if you also come to the same conclusions.

> Note: Just to put the number one billion into context; if I gave you one dollar per second, $60 per minute, $3,600 per hour (wouldn't that be a great hourly wage), $86,400 per day. It would take me almost 31.9 years to give you a billion dollars. If you wanted to count to one billion at the pace of one number per second it would take you 31.9 years to count to one billion. A billion seconds is approximately 32 years.

God Could Not Have?

Now here is what I say to my Protestant, Catholic and Mormon friends when they tell me that God could not have...

Friends, when you say that God could not have used evolution to make the body of Adam, are you sure you are using the term "could not have" correctly? Or, are you saying that God "would not have" used evolution to create Adam's body? Or, maybe you mean that God could have used evolution to create Adam's body but you believe He did not use evolution to accomplish this outcome.

Well, if that is what you are saying, then what you just said and what I just heard was that you have admitted that it is possible that God could have used evolution to create the body of Adam. No one would ever say that God "could not" have done it that way. "Could not" is not the correct term when you are talking about the powers of God. One hundred percent of my

Protestant friends, one hundred percent of my Catholic friends and one hundred percent of my Mormon friends eventually agree with this statement.

Therefore, this means that the possibility exists; that God, if He had wanted to, could have made Adam's body evolve over time from the same substance as that from which the trees, the fowl and the beasts came.

I need to make a distinction here; the body that housed Adam's spirit was not created inside of the Garden of Eden. Let me repeat. Before Adam's spirit was placed into Adam's body, that body was not in the Garden of Eden; it was first created outside the Garden of Eden.

Here are a few scriptures that verify this:

> And the Lord God formed man of the dust of the ground, and breathed into his nostrils the breath of life; and man became a living soul. And the Lord God planted a garden eastward in Eden; and there he put the man whom he had formed. *Genesis 2:7-8*

Did you catch that? The Lord God formed the body of a man from the dust of the ground and once the body was ready, then, and only then, did God make it a living soul, and then God built the Garden and placed the man in the Garden.

What the Bible does not tell us is how long it took for God to make a body for Adam's spirit. God does not give us the details on the method and length of time it took Him to take some dust of the ground, with some water or mist over that ground and come up with a man's body. The Bible does not tell us.

It would be equally difficult for me to explain how a jet airplane came from the ground. It would take me volumes and volumes of books to explain how long and exactly how humans were ever able to create a jet airplane from the ground. So, Moses just summarizes the story.

God had some materials that He had previously created called the ground and mist. He used those materials over a long period of time. Finally, after He had created the plants, fish, beasts and fowl, then and only then did He create a body that was in His own image. After the body was formed properly and correct enough to receive a spirit child of God, once it was ready, then and only then did God put the spirit of Adam in that body. This all happened before the Garden of Eden.

Dust of the Ground and DNA?

The term "dust of the ground" is probably another summary phrase Moses decided to use. While writing the Book of Genesis, Moses uses the term "dust of the ground" for the elements that make up Adam's body. I am not sure if God told Moses exactly how the body was created. Maybe Moses did receive the exact knowledge, right down to the DNA and elements. Even so, Moses knew he was going to be presenting this concept to an uneducated audience. Therefore, he decided not to go into details because his audience would not understand. The smallest particle known to the people living in 1300BC was the term "dust."

So, rather than go into a detailed discussion on DNA, carbon, nitrogen, oxygen and the periodic table, etc. Moses selected a term that everyone would understand as the smallest known particle. Moses uses the word "dust," or the term, "dust of the ground" to convey the general overall message of where Adam's body came from and leaves it at that. He summarizes, because he has to; he only has four pages of the book in which to summarize nearly fourteen billion years—just as I would summarize the explanation of a jet airplane that comes from elements on the periodic table. If I only had four pages to do that, I doubt I could do a better job than Moses did.

Therefore, from a certain perspective, evolution and the Book of Genesis are in agreement on this one subject. Evolution says that our bodies originally came from the elements of carbon, nitrogen, etc., dirt, water and some burst of energy. Now compare that to Genesis. Genesis says we came from the dust of the ground mixed with water and the power of God. The main difference is that evolution tries to tell us exactly how long it took to create the body of man and the Bible gives us a time period called the sixth day. God just tells us that He made the body of man. He does not explain in detail the process or the time period that it took. He just says that He did it. This all happened before Adam was brought into the Garden of Eden.

The question is, what is the time period between the time God created the body of Adam and when man became a living soul and was introduced into the Garden? How much time passed while God was creating the body? When it says that, "the Lord God formed man of the dust of the ground" how long did that take? How much time passed while He was forming Adam's body from the dust of the ground?

The one ingredient that most people miss when reading the Book of Genesis is the ingredient of **time**. Most people never give God any time to work out His plan. I have Christian friends who believe that the time periods of the first day, the second day, the third day and so on, spoken of in the beginning of Genesis are referring to six, twenty-four hour periods of time. Some of my very orthodox Mormon, Protestant and Catholic friends believe that the whole universe was created in six consecutive twenty-four hour periods equaling one hundred and forty-four hours total. From the creation of light right up to the creation of Eve, they believe it took one hundred and forty-four hours.

I have two answers for this:

My first answer is, if God did create all the beasts, fowl and man in the sixth day, as Genesis says, and if that day was only twenty four hours and not hundreds of millions of years: if this list of living organisms was that easy to create, all in just twenty-four hours, then why did God need Noah? If God can create all animals, fowl and man in just twenty-four hours (the sixth day), then He would not have had Noah build an ark that took hundreds of years to complete. That would have been unnecessary because He could have just started over and been right back at the same place by tomorrow afternoon. The answer is that God knows it takes a long time to create beasts, fowl and then eventually man. It is a process that takes a lot of effort and time. And rather than truly just start over, He has Noah build an ark, because it takes great lengths of time to create an earth teeming with life, such as animals, birds and man.

My second answer, which is specifically designed for my Mormon friends, comes from a letter written on Christmas Day in the year 1844 from Joseph Smith's personal secretary, Mr. W. W. Phelps, who wrote this letter to Joseph Smith's brother, William Smith. Here is a quote from the letter of which I would like to glean a few interesting items regarding the element of time and how old our universe is. It says:

"Well, now, Brother William, when the house of Israel begin to come into the glorious mysteries of the kingdom, and find that Jesus Christ, whose goings forth, as the prophets said, have been from of old, from eternity; and **that eternity**, agreeably to the records found in the catacombs of Egypt, has been going on in this system (not this world) almost two thousand, five hundred and fifty-five millions of years," (Times and Seasons, vol.5, pg. 758).

Ok, if you did not catch that, the letter said that "eternity" (the word eternity) is almost 2.555 billion years (2 ½ billion years).

Some people use the word "eternity" as a synonym to the word "infinity." The first thing I want you to know from this letter is that "eternity" does not mean "infinity." Eternity is a fixed period of time.

The second thing that I want to point out from the letter is that I believe that W. W. Phelps (Joseph Smith's personal secretary) and William Smith (Joseph Smith's brother) did not come up with this idea on their own. My personal belief is that they are referencing something that Joseph Smith taught on an earlier date because the letter says, "agreeably to the records found in the catacombs of Egypt." This is in reference to some Egyptian translations that only Joseph Smith had a gift for doing. If this is true, then Joseph Smith is the first religious leader I know of using the word "billions" of years to describe the creation process. Most scientists in Joseph Smith's time were using the mere one hundred million-year figure when speaking about the age of the earth and the universe.

The modern-day apostles, Brother Bruce R. McConkie, commented on this letter in his book, *The Mortal Messiah* and Boyd K Packer commented on this letter in a general conference address. The point I am trying to make is that if you believe everything was created in just six consecutive twenty-four hour periods, then I believe you are probably not in sync with Bruce R. McConkie, Boyd K Packer, Joseph Smith, W. W. Phelps and William Smith on this subject; meaning if they were here today, they would probably disagree with you on this one item.

Eternity vs. Infinity

Commenting on this letter, Brother Bruce R. McConkie in his book *The Mortal Messiah*, (Book 1, p.32-33) says; "Joseph Smith and the early brethren in this dispensation knew much that we do not know" and "this matter of how long eternity has been going on in our portion of created things is one of these matters." From these statements it appears that Joseph Smith revealed that our universe, or system, was 2.555 billion years old. Therefore, Brother McConkie interpreted this letter to mean that our universe is 2.555 billion years old. I am not saying his interpretation is incorrect, but the way I read the letter from Joseph Smith's personal secretary to Joseph's brother, it does not say the universe is 2.555 billion years old. It says, in my opinion, that an "eternity" is a finite period of 2.555 billion years. Therefore, if the word "eternity" is defined as 2.555 billion years, or if "eternity" is just a set period of time, then finally the following scriptures now make sense to me:

> For I know that God is not a partial God, neither a changeable being; but he is unchangeable from all eternity to all eternity. *Moroni 8:18*

I used to think this scripture meant for all infinity to all infinity. Also, I used to think that infinity and eternity were synonymous. So, I started to test my hypothesis that the word "eternity," in the scriptures, is a set time frame. And placing the word "all" preceding the word "eternity" has a different meaning than the single word "eternity." For example, no one would ever say the phrase "all infinity" because it does not make much sense and it is pointless. Without a definition of what an "eternity" is, then the statement, "all eternity" appears to be a redundant statement.

However, if we insert the definition that an eternity is a set period of time, then the scripture (Moroni 8:18) says that God is unchangeable from all 2.555 billion-year time frames in the past and for all 2.555 billion-year time frames in the future.

Let us test my hypothesis on another scripture;

> This high priesthood being after the order of his Son, which order was from the foundation of the world; or in other words, being without beginning of days or end of years, being prepared from eternity to all eternity, according to his foreknowledge of all things. *Alma 13:7*

In this scripture, Alma first tells us that what he is talking about does not have a beginning days or end of years, and that "years" and "days" are earthly terms. Alma then says that what he is talking about was prepared from eternity to all eternity.

Saying; "from eternity to all eternity" is different from saying "from all eternity to all eternity." If my hypotheses is correct, this scripture basically means from the eternity that we are in right now, and for all future eternity, or all time periods of eternity in the future. The term "all eternity" would be the plural of eternity because it says "all" (all eternity = infinity).

Let us test it again.

> For they are vessels of wrath, doomed to suffer the wrath of God, with the devil and his angels in eternity;
> *Doctrine and Covenants 76:33*

What is interesting here is that eternity is singular not plural, as it does not have "all" preceding it. Therefore, the devil and his angels are suffering the wrath of God in this current 2.555 billion years that we are living in right now.

> And verily in this thing ye have done wisely, for it is required of the Lord, at the hand of every steward, to render an account of his stewardship, both in time and in eternity. *Doctrine and Covenants 72:3*

Again, this is for time and in eternity. So the time that is referred to is the "time" on earth and for the eternity that we are in right now. It is just another way of saying that you must render an account for your time on earth and the 2.555 billion years that you are currently living in right now.

Let's test it again:
> And again, verily I say unto you, if a man marry a wife, and make a covenant with her for time and for all eternity... *Doctrine and Covenants 132:18*

Again, if you insert the definition it makes sense. If the scripture said that you marry "from all eternity" and "for all eternity," it would mean that you would have been married since the beginning of the universe. But Doctrine and Covenants 132:18

does not say that. It says that you are married for "time," which means here on earth, and "for all eternity," which means for all of the 2.555 billion time periods to come in the future.

I have looked up and reviewed almost every scripture that uses the word "eternity" and when I replace it with 2.555 billion years in the scriptures, it almost always has the possibility of working with my hypothesis, thus making sense from a certain perspective and context.

For instance, when referring to Christ, it says He was from all eternity to all eternity. That statement makes sense. And when people marry in the temple for "time and all eternity," this statement now makes sense, as opposed to saying that they are married for "all infinity," which does not make sense.

Now, the following is the most interesting part of my hypothesis. When I tried to do the same type of substitution in the Bible dictionary or in the scripture study guide, my hypothesis does not work.

In any writings outside of the scriptures, the substitution of 2.555 billion years for the word "eternity" does not work. It does not fit. But in every place in the actual scriptures the new definition of "an eternity" does seem to work in all instances. Why would this be? Answer is: because prophets wrote the scriptures and men wrote the Bible dictionary.

After testing my theory in and outside of the scriptures, my conclusion is that "infinity" is not the same thing as "eternity." The two words are not synonyms when used within the Holy Scriptures. I have been using the term "eternity" to define infinity my whole life. But now that I read this letter and compared it to the scriptures, I believe the two words are not the same thing. I believe that Joseph Smith taught that the eternity that we are in is nearly 2.555 billion years. He is also the first religious leader I know of who used the notion of billions of years of creation. Even leading scientists in Joseph

Smith's time were only using the terms of a mere hundreds of thousands of years for the existence of the earth. No person that I can find, scientist or religious leader, was using the term billions in Joseph Smith's time to explain the origins of the earth. And Joseph was using, not just one billion, but multiples of billions of years. Once again, Joseph Smith was an amazing man. Please remember this concept and we will come back to it later in this chapter.

Creation by the Snap of the Finger

Here is a theoretical situation. OK, you exist in some way as a spirit billions and billions of years ago. Let's imagine that this is all before God created this universe. You're sitting there with God and God turns to you and asks if you have you ever felt the warmth of sunshine? You, of course, say no. Then He asks if you have ever swam across a river? You, of course, say no. He asks if you have ever tasted a hot apple pie right out of the oven with whip cream on the top? You say that you have never tasted anything, you are just a spirit and have no physical body.

God then says, "I'm going to make that happen. I am going to make (or create) an apple pie for you because I want you to have that experience of eating and tasting the delicious flavor of an apple pie with whip cream on top."

Here is a basic question that you need to answer as you contemplate the issue of evolution vs. creation. Do you think God then just snaps his fingers and there is an apple pie with whip cream right in front of you, that it appears right out of thin air? And not only is there an apple pie in front of you, but in a snap of a finger your spirit is thrust into a physical body with taste buds and palate so that you can now eat food and taste the apple pie? Who, reading this, right now, believes God would accomplish this goal by the snap of His finger? Or, do you believe that God would use natural laws to complete the task?

God might then say; "I am going to need an apple tree, some

wheat, some sugar, a cow, to make the cream from, and a heat source or fire to cook it. In order to get all of the items, I am going to need an earth type planet that can grow such food items, a man to till the ground, harvest the crops and build ovens to cook it in. To have an earth that can do all of this, it would require a warm and stable sun to give life to the plants and animals. That earth would need a large moon to give it balance as it spins to allow for regular temperatures, and so on and so on."

God would make a checklist using natural laws. Who reading this right now believes God might accomplish His goal this way and not use the snap of a finger method?

I'm not saying that God **could** not have done it that way but I am asking you if you think God **would** have done it that way?

The late astrophysicist Carl Sagan said, "If you want to make an apple pie from scratch you would first have to create the entire universe."

Now, let us continue on and talk about the science of evolution, and I use the word "science" as a precise description.

The controversy in science today is not if all life evolved from one "genesis" moment and all life can trace its existence back to one common microbial organism. The controversy in science is in determining exactly how life actually began on the planet. One group of scientists believes that life was delivered to earth on the back of an asteroid, and another group of scientists believes life began here on earth in a mixture of elements and some burst of energy. Almost as soon as the earth could foster life, it did. If life began here on earth then the elements of carbon, nitrogen, oxygen, water, and many others, somehow receive a burst of energy from somewhere. It might have been a lightening strike, a volcano at the bottom of the ocean, or heat from the sun. But some type of energy illuminates the pool of elements and life begins on earth.

Therefore, the question is, if the earth sprang forth life almost as soon as it could have sprung forth life and all current life can trace its existence back to one single event, then why didn't the earth spring forth life again and again? If the earth is so fertile that it can spring forth life almost as soon as it was even possible, then why doesn't the earth spring forth life today?

And if it sprang forth life four billion years ago, then why didn't it spring a new strain of life three billion years ago and another strain two billion years ago? Why is there only one "genesis" moment in the earth's history? Well, this question has caused some scientists to believe that the first microbial life did not begin on earth but was delivered to the earth on an asteroid.

If science one day proves that asteroids delivered microbial life to the earth, then Genesis stating that plants were created on the third day, before the moon and sun were created on the fourth day, would be proof and show once again how right Moses was. If that is proven, then my atheist friends will have one more question that they can't answer about Moses and how correct he was.

Many Christians—Catholics, Protestants and Mormons—believe it took no time at all to create the body that was eventually developed to house the spirit of Adam. Why do they believe God snapped His fingers and it was done? We never give God any time in the creation story. Most of us do not give God any time, ever. We pray for things and we want the answer right now; we want the answer today. We believe that God needs to answer our prayers and should do so without the consideration of any passage of time.

This is an error in surmising who God is and how He operates. When I read the scriptures I do not see that the verses and passages tell us anything that would lead us to believe that God works in this manner, but it is astounding that most of us believe in the "snap of a finger" theory. However, we have very few actual scripture stories upon which to base this assumption.

Look at these excerpts from the Book of Abraham, Chapter four as it discusses the creation when it says;

- The last sentence of Verse 9, "and it was so as they ordered."
- The last sentence of Verse 10, "and the Gods saw that they were obeyed."
- The last sentence of Verse 12, "and the Gods saw that they were obeyed."
- The last sentence of Verse 21, "and the Gods saw that they would be obeyed, and that their plan was good."

Now read the whole verse of Abraham, Chapter 4 Verse 18; this is where the whole time thing comes in:

> And the Gods watched those things which they had ordered until they obeyed. *Abraham 4:18*

Therefore, it is my assumption that if they watched until they were obeyed, then there must have been some passage of time while they were watching. The Book of Abraham is inferring that it took time. Therefore, was Adam in the Garden of Eden one day, one year, a hundred years, or a hundred million years, while the rest of the earth outside of the Garden was evolving? How long was Adam in the Garden of Eden? And also, how long did it take God to make the body of Adam before Adam was introduced into the Garden?

Copernicus, Galileo and Kepler

The following is an example of an erroneous interpretation of the Bible. At one time in history, most all of the Christian world believed that the earth was in the center of the universe and that the sun went around the earth. This is mainly because of the following Biblical references (Psalm 93:1, 96:10, and 1 Chronicles 16:30) which, include text that basically says; "the world is firmly established, it cannot be moved."

> Who laid the foundations of the earth, that it should not be removed for ever.   *Psalms 104:5*

> The sun also ariseth, and the sun goeth down, and hasteth to his place where he arose.   *Ecclesiastes 1:5*

These scriptures are all true from the context in which they were written. Then Copernicus came along in the mid-1500s and said that the earth travels around the sun.

This was in contrast to the interpretation of the above Biblical scriptures. Because of this theory, Copernicus' church threatened to excommunicate him for teaching things contrary to the Bible. Copernicus had evidence that his theory was correct.

So in reality, his church was going to excommunicate him for telling the truth. That is a perfect example of irony; a church threatening excommunication for teaching the truth.

Later in the early 1600s, Galileo supported the Copernican theory and he, too, was found guilty of heresy and threatened with torture to retract his theory.

Johannes Kepler, a contemporary of Galileo, mathematically proved elliptical orbits from which the movements of the planets could be predicted. But his writings were, for a time, locked up and banned from publication. This was all because of the incorrect interpretation of the Old Testament scriptures that we listed above regarding scientific issues. As we now know, Copernican theory became a fact with the evidence presented by Johannes Kepler and Galileo. The earth does orbit the sun. This is no longer a theory.

In the Image of God, or in the Image of Swine?

It is clear that before God could put Adam's spirit into that body, God needed to make sure the body was correct and right. The body had to be very particular in nature; it had to be in the image of God. There had to be a precise type of body that could house Adam's spirit or that could accept Adam's spirit.

Let's go to the Book of Mark in the Bible and review the story of the man named Legion who had many unclean spirits crammed inside of him. These were the unclean spirits that were from pre-earth life who, in following Lucifer's rebellion, lost the war in heaven. These are your brothers and sisters in spirit; they are all children spirits of God the Father, but they didn't get a body.

Because they lost the war in heaven, a bunch of these spirits somehow crammed themselves into the man named Legion. Jesus instructs the many spirits to leave the body of Legion. The interesting thing is that these spirits believed it would be possible to live inside a pig's body. I don't know how they came to that assumption, but they did. They asked Jesus to unlock the key or open the combination so that the pig's bodies would accept or allow their spirits to enter. Jesus basically said, "Sure go ahead, I will make it so your spirits can get inside the pigs' bodies." And the next thing that happened was that these spirits left Legion's body to inhabit the pigs' bodies. The Book of Mark says that once the spirits got into the swine, then the whole herd went crazy and ran right down the side of the mountain into the sea to drown. Therefore, the spirits occupying the pigs' bodies had to leave the bodies of the pigs.

When the Legion spirits were inside of the crazy man, why didn't he run down the hill and drown himself? The point is that the body of a pig is not sophisticated or complex enough to host a spirit child of God. But the interesting thing is that these spirits thought it was possible to live in such a body that was not in the image of God.

Summarizing:

Evolution says that all life was formed from water and elements, and some energy.

Genesis says that all life came from the ground and the dust of the ground with a mist of water and the power of God.

Evolution says that it took billions of years for life to evolve from one "genesis" event and the last creation was man.

Genesis says that it took six days for all of creation and all life was created in three of the six days. Joseph Smith taught it took billions of years.

Evolution says that life was created from very tiny elements and started with some burst of energy, lightening strike, volcano, or sunlight.

Genesis says that man was created from very tiny particles named "the dust of the ground" and God was the cause of that creation.

Genesis says that plants were created before the moon and sun.

Science says that microbial life may have come to earth on an asteroid and therefore existed before our moon and sun existed.

The Big Bang Theory says that the universe began almost fourteen billion years ago.

Six Multiplied by 2.555 Billion Years

Genesis puts a book end on each of the first six days of Creation when it says, "and this was the fourth day, and this was the fifth day and this was the sIxth day." However, on the seventh day there is no statement that says, "and that was the seventh day." It only says that God rested on the seventh day, therefore the seventh day is not finished. The seventh day remains open; there is nothing that says that the seventh day is finished and complete. Therefore, Genesis is inferring that the seventh day started right after Adam and Eve were created and is still going on and has not finished.

If that is true and also if the term "eternity" does not mean "infinity," then I have a possible time line, assuming that eternity is a period of time and that period is 2.555 billion years and all creation in the Bible came forth in the first six days or six time periods. And if we multiply 2.555 billion years with the six time periods, the total is 15.333 billion years. I realize that my calculations are over a billion years more than compared to the estimated 13.7 billion-year time line of the Big Bang Theory.

The Big Bang Theory never considers the time before the actual big bang and it does not address how long it took to generate enough energy to start the big bang explosion. Maybe from God's point of view, it may have taken a half of a day (which would be 1.25 billion years) to accumulate enough energy for the big bang to actually go bang. If that is true, then the 15.333 billion-year calculation would be very close. Six time periods, each being 2.555 billion years, with the big bang building up energy for a half a day before it ignited. This is just a thought of mine, it may fit and it may not fit, but it is sure something to think about. It is astonishing that Joseph Smith was using the term "billions" to describe the creation process and the beginning in the scriptures.

When I read the story in the Bible, everything fits together with science. All I need to do is differentiate the creation of the spirit of man from the creation of the physical body of Adam and then give God some time to allow things to be created.

What is strange to me is that there are people who believe in the Big Bang Theory and don't believe in God. If you believe in the Big Bang Theory, then you should believe in God. How can you believe in the Big Bang Theory and not see God everywhere? If the Big Bang Theory is true, then that is the best evidence that God does exist. Think about it: there was nothing in the universe and then there was an unimaginable burst of energy smaller than a head of a pin.

This pin head had so much energy that all that energy turned into matter within seconds and created all the basic elements and building blocks in the known universe today; all from an energy source smaller than the size of a pin head. That seems to me to prove that there is a God.

Let us go back to the Copernicus story. When his book first came out it was a theory, then other men, Galileo and Kepler, used scientific calculations to prove that his theory was a fact. It has mathematically and physically been proven so the theory of Copernicus stopped being a theory and became a fact.

Today we know the earth does go around the sun. Evolution has come to the same point. It was a theory and it no longer is a theory, there is no controversy.

The Ultimatum Is Wrong!

This is the part I'm worried about. I'm worried that our children are going off to college to learn about evolution and we have drilled into their heads that if they believe in evolution then they are not Christian. They return from college, then sort of stop going to church because they think it is an ultimatum. It is an "either-or" kind of choice. This line of thinking is false. I believe this is one of the reasons why many Christian denominations inside of the United States are dwindling in numbers; someone has told them that to be a Christian you cannot believe in evolution.

I am here to tell you that statement is not true. I am a Christian, I believe in Christ, and I also know that evolution has happened on planet earth.

Please remember, the epitome of ignorance is rejecting something solely on the basis that you know nothing about it. That is the epitome of the word "ignorance."

I live in the 21st century and looking back in time I wonder if my great, great, great, great grandfather was one of those people who ridiculed Copernicus for his theory without ever spending any serious time investigating his valid scientific observations. I think that if I had a chance to go back in time and talk to my great ancestor, I would say to him;

- You could see the moon.

- You could see that the moon is round.

- You could see with the shadows on the moon that it must have a spherical shape.

- You can see the sun in the sky and its round.

- You could observe or read about lunar eclipses.

- You could see the sun move across the sky each day.

But why did you not even consider the possibility that Copernicus was correct? You would have realized he was correct if you had investigated the evidence. The answer probably is that my great ancestor had read the Bible one way and would not consider anything that would contradict his assumption in the scriptures. Someone must have told him that the Bible said this or that. Therefore, he may have decided to condemn Copernicus rather than actually look at the evidence himself. I kind of chuckle and laugh at my great ancestor for not seeing that the earth really does go around the sun. It seems like a simple thing to get, once you have seen the evidence. Now switch your mind and don't think about Copernicus who is five hundred years in our past. Let's go forward five hundred years into the future, and let's talk with your great, great, great, great, grandson. Ask yourself, is my great, great, great, great grandson going to look back at me and chuckle at me regarding evolution? He might say to me, "Great, great, great, great grandfather, you had so much evidence that evolution did happen. Why did you not accept the evidence of evolution and then see how it could have fit into God's overall design?"

I want to say to my grandchildren who read this chapter; with the scientific knowledge that I have today, Moses is correct in his four-page summary of the fourteen- billion-year history of the universe. Jesus is the Christ, and this universe is fantastic. I do not care if you believe in evolution or not. What I do care about is your relationship with God, your belief in Christ and your earthly pursuit to truly master the full meaning of the word "charity." Never let anyone tell you that if you believe in evolution you cannot be a Christian. I am living proof that you can. It has made my understanding of God and the way He operates even more satisfying. Finding and digging in the words of Moses and Joseph Smith has elevated my understanding of God and His plan. Living a life as a Christian is a much better life than anything else, and following science to learn about God is a lifelong expedition of intrigue. Jesus is the Christ, and God the Father has a plan for each of you; and only you can find out what that means for you.

CHAPTER 14
JOSEPH SMITH'S GREATEST SPEECH

The King Follett Discourse was delivered by Joseph Smith on April 7, 1844, just a few months before he was killed. This discourse is the most controversial speech ever given by the prophet. Joseph Smith spoke for approximately two hours at a funeral sermon for a Mr. King Follett. The event was attended by at least eight thousand people and therefore the prophet probably had to shout most of the speech in order to be heard. Four men attempted to scribe the dictation as best as they could and then in the weeks after the speech they collaborated all of their notes. After Joseph Smith died, the first amalgamation of the speech was published in the *Times and Seasons* (August 1844). Joseph Smith was never able to review or edit the dictation of the discourse and there are obvious gaps and many inconsistencies that are not rounded out or made complete in the document. Therefore, please do not dissect this speech word for word like you would when reading the scriptures. Use it just to understand general themes of thought. To put this in context of the time period, it needs to be noted that Joseph Smith continued to receive multiple death threats and his safety and the safety of his family must have weighed heavy on his mind (as you can detect from some of the phases in the sermon). There are several versions of this discourse/speech and several amalgamations. The following amalgamation was published in the *Ensign* magazine in the year 1971. The author of *Mr. Mormon* has included this speech as a full chapter of this book because he believes this is Joseph Smith's greatest speech ever given. John S. Pennington Jr. made an audio version of the King Follett Discourse - please go to www.mrmormon.com to download.

The King Follett Discourse

Beloved Saints: I will call [for] the attention of this congregation while I address you on the subject of the dead. The decease of our beloved brother, Elder King Follett, who was crushed in a well by the falling of a tub of rock has more immediately led me to this subject. I have been requested to speak by his friends and relatives, but inasmuch as there are a great many in this congregation who live in this city as well as elsewhere, who have lost friends, I feel disposed to speak on the subject in general, and offer you my ideas, so far as I have ability, and so far as I shall be inspired by the Holy Spirit to dwell on this subject.

I want your prayers and faith that I may have the instruction of Almighty God and the gift of the Holy Ghost, so that I may set forth things that are true and which can be easily comprehended by you, and that the testimony may carry conviction to your hearts and minds of the truth of what I shall say. Pray that the Lord may strengthen my lungs, stay the winds, and let the prayers of the Saints to heaven appear, that they may enter into the ears of the Lord of Sabaoth, for the effectual prayers of the righteous avail much. There is strength here, and I verily believe that your prayers will be heard.

Before I enter fully into the investigation of the subject which is lying before me, I wish to pave the way and bring up the subject from the beginning, that you may understand it. I will make a few preliminaries, in order that you may understand the subject when I come to it.

I do not calculate or intend to please your ears with superfluity of words or oratory, or with much learning; but I calculate [intend] to edify you with the simple truths from heaven.

The Character of God

In the first place, I wish to go back to the beginning—to the morn of creation. There is the starting point for us to look to, in order to understand and be fully acquainted with the mind, purposes and decrees of the Great Eloheim, who sits in yonder heavens as he did at the creation of the world. It is necessary for us to have an understanding of God himself in the beginning. If we start right, it is easy to go right all the time; but if we start wrong we may go wrong, and it will be a hard matter to get right.

There are but a very few beings in the world who understand rightly the character of God. The great majority of mankind do not comprehend anything, either that which is past, or that which is to come, as it respects their relationship to God. They do not know, neither do they understand the nature of that relationship; and consequently they know but little above the brute beast, or more than to eat, drink and sleep. This is all man knows about God and His existence, unless it is given by the inspiration of the Almighty.

If a man learns nothing more than to eat, drink and sleep, and does not comprehend any of the designs of God, the beast comprehends the same things. It eats, drinks, sleeps, and knows nothing more about God; yet it knows as much as we, unless we are able to comprehend by the inspiration of Almighty God.

If men do not comprehend the character of God, they do not comprehend themselves. I want to go back to the beginning, and so lift your minds into more lofty spheres and a more exalted understanding than what the human mind generally aspires to.

I want to ask this congregation, every man, woman and child, to answer the question in their own hearts, what kind of a being God is? Ask yourselves; turn your thoughts into your hearts, and say if any of you have seen, heard, or communed with Him?

This is a question that may occupy your attention for a long time. I again repeat the question—What kind of being is God? Does any man or woman know? Have any of you seen Him, heard Him, or communed with Him? Here is the question that will, peradventure, from this time henceforth occupy your attention. The scriptures inform us that "this is life eternal, that they might know thee the only true God, and Jesus Christ, whom thou hast sent." (John 17:3)

If any man does not know God, and inquires what kind of a being He is—if he will search diligently his own heart—if the declaration of Jesus and the apostles be true, he will realize that he has not eternal life; for there can be eternal life on no other principle.

My first object is to find out the character of the only wise and true God, and what kind of a being He is; and if I am so fortunate as to be the man to comprehend God, and explain or convey the principles to your hearts, so that the Spirit seals them upon you, then let every man and woman henceforth sit in silence, put their hands on their mouths, and never lift their hands or voices, or say anything against the man of God or the servants of God again. But if I fail to do it, it becomes my duty to renounce all further pretensions to revelations and inspirations, or to be a prophet; and I should be like the rest of the world—a false teacher, be hailed as a friend, and no man would seek my life. But if all religious teachers were honest enough to renounce their pretensions to godliness when their ignorance of the knowledge of God is made manifest, they will all be as badly off as I am, at any rate; and you might just as well take the lives of other false teachers as that of mine. If any man is authorized to take away my life because he thinks and says I am a false teacher, then, upon the same principle, we should be justified in taking away the life of every false teacher, and where would be the end of blood? And who would not be the sufferer?

The Privilege of Religious Freedom

But meddle not with any man for his religion: all governments ought to permit every man to enjoy his religion unmolested. No man is authorized to take away life in consequence of difference of religion, which all laws and governments ought to tolerate and protect, right or wrong. Every man has a natural, and, in our country, a constitutional right to be a false prophet, as well as a true prophet. If I show, verily, that I have the truth of God, and show that ninety-nine out of every hundred professing religious ministers are false teachers, having no authority, while they pretend to hold the keys of God's kingdom on Earth, and was to kill them because they are false teachers, it would deluge the whole world with blood.

I will prove that the world is wrong, by showing what God is. I am going to inquire after God; for I want you all to know Him, and to be familiar with Him; and if I am bringing you to a knowledge of Him, all persecutions against me ought to cease. You will then know that I am His servant; for I speak as one having authority.

God an Exalted Man

I will go back to the beginning before the world was, to show what kind of a being God is. What sort of a being was God in the beginning? Open your ears and hear, all ye ends of the Earth, for I am going to prove it to you by the Bible, and to tell you the designs of God in relation to the human race, and why He interferes with the affairs of man.

God himself was once as we are now, and is an exalted man, and sits enthroned in yonder heavens! That is the great secret. If the veil were rent today, and the great God who holds this world in its orbit, and who upholds all worlds and all things by

... power, was to make himself visible—I say, if you were to see him today, you would see him like a man in form—like yourselves in all the person, image, and very form as a man; for Adam was created in the very fashion, image and likeness of God, and received instruction from, and walked, talked and conversed with Him, as one man talks and communes with another.

In order to understand the subject of the dead, for consolation of those who mourn for the loss of their friends, it is necessary we should understand the character and being of God and how He came to be so; for I am going to tell you how God came to be God. We have imagined and supposed that God was God from all eternity. I will refute that idea, and take away the veil, so that you may see.

These ideas are incomprehensible to some, but they are simple. It is the first principle of the gospel to know for a certainty the character of God, and to know that we may converse with Him as one man converses with another, and that He was once a man like us; yea, that God himself, the Father of us all, dwelt on an Earth, the same as Jesus Christ Himself did; and I will show it from the Bible.

Eternal Life to Know God and Jesus Christ

I wish I was in a suitable place to tell it, and that I had the trump of an archangel, so that I could tell the story in such a manner that persecution would cease forever. What did Jesus say? (Mark it, Elder Rigdon!) The scriptures inform us that Jesus said, as the Father hath power in himself, even so hath the Son power—to do what? Why, what the Father did. The answer is obvious—in a manner to lay down his body and take it up again. Jesus, what are you going to do?

To lay down my life as my Father did, and take it up again. Do you believe it? If you do not believe it you do not believe the Bible. The scriptures say it, and I defy all the learning and wisdom and all the combined powers of Earth and hell together to refute it. Here, then, is eternal life—to know the only wise and true God; and you have got to learn how to be gods yourselves, and to be kings and priests to God, the same as all gods have done before you, namely, by going from one small degree to another, and from a small capacity to a great one; from grace to grace, from exaltation to exaltation, until you attain to the resurrection of the dead, and are able to dwell in everlasting burnings, and to sit in glory, as do those who sit enthroned in everlasting power. And I want you to know that God, in the last days, while certain individuals are proclaiming His name, is not trifling with you or me.

The Righteous to Dwell in Everlasting Burnings

These are the first principles of consolation. How consoling to the mourners when they are called to part with a husband, wife, father, mother, child, or dear relative, to know that, although the Earthly tabernacle is laid down and dissolved, they shall rise again to dwell in everlasting burnings in immortal glory, not to sorrow, suffer, or die any more, but they shall be heirs of God and joint heirs with Jesus Christ. What is it? To inherit the same power, the same glory and the same exaltation, until you arrive at the station of a god, and ascend the throne of eternal power, the same as those who have gone before. What did Jesus do? Why, I do the things I saw my Father do when worlds came rolling into existence. My Father worked out His kingdom with fear and trembling, and I must do the same; and when I get my kingdom, I shall present it to My Father, so that He may obtain kingdom upon kingdom, and it will exalt Him in glory. He will then take a higher exaltation, and I will take His place, and thereby become exalted myself.

So that Jesus treads in the tracks of His Father, and inherits what God did before; and God is thus glorified and exalted in the salvation and exaltation of all His children.

It is plain beyond disputation, and you thus learn some of the first principles of the gospel, about which so much hath been said.

When you climb up a ladder, you must begin at the bottom, and ascend step by step, until you arrive at the top; and so it is with the principles of the gospel—you must begin with the first, and go on until you learn all the principles of exaltation. But it will be a great while after you have passed through the veil before you will have learned them.

It is not all to be comprehended in this world; it will be a great work to learn our salvation and exaltation even beyond the grave. I suppose I am not allowed to go into an investigation of anything that is not contained in the Bible. If I do, I think there are so many over-wise men here that they would cry "treason" and put me to death. So I will go to the old Bible and turn commentator today.

I shall comment on the very first Hebrew word in the Bible; I will make a comment on the very first sentence of the history of creation in the Bible—Berosheit. I want to analyze the word. Baith—in, by, through, and everything else. Rosh—the head, Sheit—grammatical termination. When the inspired man wrote it, he did not put the Baith there. An old Jew without any authority added the word; he thought it too bad to begin to talk about the head! It read first, "The head one of the Gods brought forth the Gods." That is the true meaning of the words. Baurau signifies to bring forth. If you do not believe it, you do not believe the learned man of God. Learned men can teach you no more than what I have told you. Thus the head God brought forth the Gods in the grand council.

I will transpose and simplify it in the English language. Oh, ye lawyers, ye doctors, and ye priests, who have persecuted me, I want to let you know that the Holy Ghost knows something as well as you do. The head God called together the Gods and sat in grand council to bring forth the world. The grand councilors sat at the head in yonder heavens and contemplated the creation of the worlds which were created at the time. When I say doctors and lawyers, I mean the doctors and lawyers of the scriptures. I have done so hitherto without explanation, to let the lawyers flutter and everybody laugh at them. Some learned doctors might take a notion to say the scriptures say thus and so; and we must believe the scriptures; they are not to be altered. But I am going to show you an error in them.

I have an old edition of the New Testament in the Latin, Hebrew, German and Greek languages. I have been reading the German, and find it to be the most [nearly] correct translation, and to correspond nearest to the revelations which God has given to me for the last fourteen years. It tells about Jacobus, the son of Zebedee. It means Jacob. In the English New Testament it is translated James. Now, if Jacob had the keys, you might talk about James through all eternity and never get the keys. In the 21st [verse] of the fourth chapter of Matthew, my old German edition gives the word Jacob instead of James.

The doctors (I mean doctors of law, not physic) say, "If you preach anything not according to the Bible, we will cry treason." How can we escape the damnation of hell, except God be with us and reveal to us? Men bind us with chains. The Latin says Jacobus, which means Jacob; the Hebrew says Jacob, the Greek says Jacob and the German says Jacob, here we have the testimony of four against one. I thank God that I have got this old book; but I thank him more for the gift of the Holy Ghost. I have got the oldest book in the world; but I have got the oldest book in my heart, even the gift of the Holy Ghost. I have all the four Testaments. Come here, ye learned men, and read, if you can.

I should not have introduced this testimony, were it not to back up the word rosh—the head, the Father of the Gods. I should not have brought it up, only to show that I am right.

A Council of the Gods

In the beginning, the head of the Gods called a council of the Gods; and they came together and concocted [prepared] a plan to create the world and people it.

When we begin to learn this way, we begin to learn the only true God, and what kind of a being we have got to worship. Having a knowledge of God, we begin to know how to approach Him, and how to ask so as to receive an answer.

When we understand the character of God, and know how to come to Him, he begins to unfold the heavens to us, and to tell us all about it. When we are ready to come to him, he is ready to come to us.

Now, I ask all who hear me, why the learned men who are preaching salvation, say that God created the heavens and the Earth out of nothing? The reason is, that they are unlearned in the things of God, and have not the gift of the Holy Ghost; they account it blasphemy in any one to contradict their idea. If you tell them that God made the world out of something, they will call you a fool. But I am learned, and know more than all the world put together. The Holy Ghost does, anyhow, and he is within me, and comprehends more than all the world; and I will associate myself with him.

Meaning of the Word Create

You ask the learned doctors why they say the world was made out of nothing, and they will answer, "Doesn't the Bible say he created the world?" And they infer, from the word create, that it must have been made out of nothing. Now, the word create came from the word baurau, which does not mean to create out of nothing; it means to organize; the same as a man would organize materials and build a ship.

Hence we infer that God had materials to organize the world out of chaos—chaotic matter, which is element, and in which dwells all the glory. Element had an existence from the time He had. The pure principles of element are principles which can never be destroyed; they may be organized and re-organized, but not destroyed. They had no beginning and can have no end.

I have another subject to dwell upon, which is calculated to exalt man; but it is impossible for me to say much on this subject. I shall therefore just touch upon it, for time will not permit me to say all. It is associated with the subject of the resurrection of the dead—namely, the soul—the mind of man—the immortal spirit. Where did it come from? All learned men and doctors of divinity say that God created it in the beginning; but it is not so: the very idea lessens man in my estimation. I do not believe the doctrine; I know better. Hear it, all ye ends of the world; for God has told me so; and if you don't believe me, it will not make the truth without effect. I will make a man appear a fool before I get through; if he does not believe it. I am going to tell of things more noble.

We say that God Himself is a self-existing being. Who told you so? It is correct enough; but how did it get into your heads? Who told you that man did not exist in like manner upon the same principles? Man does exist upon the same principles. God made a tabernacle and put a spirit into it, and it became a living soul. (Refers to the Bible.) How does it read in the Hebrew? It does not say in the Hebrew that God created the spirit of man. It says, "God made man out of the Earth and put into him Adam's spirit, and so became a living body."

The mind or the intelligence which man possesses is co-equal [co-eternal] with God himself. I know that my testimony is true; hence, when I talk to these mourners, what have they lost?

Their relatives and friends are only separated from their bodies for a short season: their spirits which existed with God have left the tabernacle of clay only for a little moment, as it were; and they now exist in a place where they converse together the same as we do on the Earth.

I am dwelling on the immortality of the spirit of man. Is it logical to say that the intelligence of spirits is immortal, and yet that it has a beginning? The intelligence of spirits had no beginning, neither will it have an end. That is good logic. That which has a beginning may have an end.

There never was a time when there were not spirits; for they are co-equal [co-eternal] with our Father in heaven.

I want to reason more on the spirit of man; for I am dwelling on the body and spirit of man—on the subject of the dead. I take my ring from my finger and liken it unto the mind of man—the immortal part, because it had no beginning.

Suppose you cut it in two; then it has a beginning and an end; but join it again, and it continues one eternal round. So with the spirit of man. As the Lord liveth, if it had a beginning, it will have an end. All the fools and learned and wise men from the beginning of creation, who say that the spirit of man had a beginning, prove that it must have an end; and if that doctrine is true, then the doctrine of annihilation would be true. But if I am right, I might with boldness proclaim from the housetops that God never had the power to create the spirit of man at all. God himself could not create himself.

Intelligence is eternal and exists upon a self-existent principle. It is a spirit from age to age and there is no creation about it. All the minds and spirits that God ever sent into the world are susceptible of enlargement.

The first principles of man are self-existent with God. God himself, finding he was in the midst of spirits and glory, because he was more intelligent, saw proper to institute laws whereby the rest could have a privilege to advance like himself. The relationship we have with God places us in a situation to advance in knowledge. He has power to institute laws to instruct the weaker intelligences, that they may be exalted with Himself, so that they might have one glory upon another, and all that knowledge, power, glory, and intelligence, which is requisite in order to save them in the world of spirits.

This is good doctrine. It tastes good. I can taste the principles of eternal life, and so can you. They are given to me by the revelations of Jesus Christ; and I know that when I tell you these words of eternal life as they are given to me, you taste them, and I know that you believe them. You say honey is sweet, and so do I. I can also taste the spirit of eternal life. I know that it is good; and when I tell you of these things which were given me by inspiration of the Holy Spirit, you are bound to receive them as sweet, and rejoice more and more.

The Relation of Man to God

I want to talk more of the relation of man to God. I will open your eyes in relation to the dead. All things whatsoever God in his infinite wisdom has seen fit and proper to reveal to us, while we are dwelling in mortality, in regard to our mortal bodies, are revealed to us in the abstract, and independent of affinity of this mortal tabernacle, but are revealed to our spirits precisely as though we had no bodies at all; and those revelations which will save our spirits will save our bodies. God reveals them to us in view of no eternal dissolution of the body, or tabernacle. Hence the responsibility, the awful responsibility, that rests upon us in relation to our dead; for all the spirits who have not obeyed the gospel in the flesh must either obey it in the spirit or be damned. Solemn thought!—dreadful thought!

Is there nothing to be done?—no preparation—no salvation for our fathers and friends who have died without having had the opportunity to obey the decrees of the Son of Man? Would to God that I had forty days and nights in which to tell you all! I would let you know that I am not a "fallen prophet."

Our Greatest Responsibility

What promises are made in relation to the subject of the

salvation of the dead? and what kind of characters are those who can be saved, although their bodies are mouldering and decaying in the grave?

When His commandments teach us, it is in view of eternity; for we are looked upon by God as though we were in eternity; God dwells in eternity, and does not view things as we do.

The greatest responsibility in this world that God has laid upon us is to seek after our dead. The apostle says, "They without us cannot be made perfect"; for it is necessary that the sealing power should be in our hands to seal our children and our dead for the fulness of the dispensation of times—a dispensation to meet the promises made by Jesus Christ before the foundation of the world for the salvation of man.

Now, I will speak of them. I will meet Paul half way. I say to you, Paul, you cannot be perfect without us. It is necessary that those who are going before and those who come after us should have salvation in common with us; and thus hath God made it obligatory upon man. Hence, God said, "I will send you Elijah the prophet before the coming of the great and dreadful day of the Lord: he shall turn the heart of the fathers to the children, and the heart of the children to their fathers, lest I come and smite the Earth with a curse."

The Unpardonable Sin

I have a declaration to make as to the provisions which God hath made to suit the conditions of man—made from before the foundation of the world. What has Jesus said? All sins, and all blasphemies, and every transgression, except one, that man can be guilty of, may be forgiven; and there is a salvation for all men, either in this world or the world to come, who have not committed the unpardonable sin, there being a provision either in this world or the world of spirits. Hence God hath made a provision that every spirit in the eternal world can be ferreted out and saved unless he has committed that unpardonable sin which cannot be remitted to him either in this world or the world of spirits.

God has wrought out a salvation for all men, unless they have committed a certain sin; and every man who has a friend in the eternal world can save him, unless he has committed the unpardonable sin. And so you can see how far you can be a savior.

A man cannot commit the unpardonable sin after the dissolution of the body, and there is a way possible for escape. Knowledge saves a man; and in the world of spirits no man can be exalted but by knowledge. So long as a man will not give heed to the commandments, he must abide without salvation. If a man has knowledge, he can be saved; although, if he has been guilty of great sins, he will be punished for them. But when he consents to obey the gospel, whether here or in the world of spirits, he is saved.

A man is his own tormentor and his own condemner. Hence the saying, They shall go into the lake that burns with fire and brimstone. The torment of disappointment in the mind is as exquisite as a lake burning with fire and brimstone. I say, so is the torment of man.

I know the scriptures and understand them. I said, no man can commit the unpardonable sin after the dissolution of the body, nor in this life, until he receives the Holy Ghost; but they must do it in this world. Hence the salvation of Jesus Christ was wrought out for all men, in order to triumph over the devil; for if it did not catch him in one place, it would in another; for he stood up as a Savior. All will suffer until they obey Christ himself.

The contention in heaven was—Jesus said there would be certain souls that would not be saved; and the devil said he would save them all, and laid his plans before the grand council, who gave their vote in favor of Jesus Christ. So the devil rose up in rebellion against God, and was cast down, with all who put up their heads for him. (Book of Moses—Pearl of Great Price, Ch. 4:1–4; Book of Abraham, Ch. 3:23–28) [Moses 4:1–4; Abr. 3:23–28].

The Forgiveness of Sins

All sins shall be forgiven, except the sin against the Holy Ghost; for Jesus will save all except the sons of perdition. What must a man do to commit the unpardonable sin? He must receive the Holy Ghost, have the heavens opened unto him, and know God, and then sin against him. After a man has sinned against the Holy Ghost, there is no repentance for him. He has got to say that the sun does not shine while he sees it; he has got to deny Jesus Christ when the heavens have been opened unto him, and to deny the plan of salvation with his eyes open to the truth of it; and from that time he begins to be an enemy. This is the case with many apostates of The Church of Jesus Christ of Latter-day Saints.

When a man begins to be an enemy to this work, he hunts me, he seeks to kill me, and never ceases to thirst for my blood. He gets the spirit of the devil—the same spirit that sins against the Holy Ghost. You cannot save such persons; you cannot bring them to repentance; they make open war, like the devil, and awful is the consequence.

I advise all of you to be careful what you do, or you may by-and-by find out that you have been deceived. Stay yourselves; do not give way; don't make any hasty moves, you may be saved. If a spirit of bitterness is in you, don't be in haste. You may say, that man is a sinner. Well, if he repents, he shall be forgiven. Be cautious: await. When you find a spirit that wants bloodshed,—murder, the same is not of God, but is of the devil. Out of the abundance of the heart of man the mouth speaketh.

The best men bring forth the best works. The man who tells you words of life is the man who can save you. I warn you against all evil characters who sin against the Holy Ghost; for there is no redemption for them in this world nor in the world to come.

I could go back and trace every object of interest concerning the relationship of man to God, if I had time. I can enter into the mysteries; I can enter largely into the eternal worlds; for Jesus said, "In my Father's house are many mansions; if it were not so, I would have told you. I go to prepare a place for you." (John 14:2). Paul says, "There is one glory of the Sun, and another glory of the moon, and another glory of the stars; for one star differeth from another star in glory. So also is the resurrection of the dead." (1 Cor. 15:41). What have we to console us in relation to the dead? We have reason to have the greatest hope and consolation for our dead of any people on the Earth; for we have seen them walk worthily in our midst, and seen them sink asleep in the arms of Jesus; and those who have died in the faith are now in the celestial kingdom of God. And hence is the glory of the Sun.

You mourners have occasion to rejoice, speaking of the death of Elder King Follett; for your husband and father is gone to wait until the resurrection of the dead—until the perfection of the remainder; for at the resurrection your friend will rise in perfect felicity and go to celestial glory, while many must wait myriads of years before they can receive the like blessings; and your expectations and hopes are far above what man can conceive; for why has God revealed it to us?

I am authorized to say, by the authority of the Holy Ghost, that you have no occasion to fear; for he [Brother Follett] is gone to the home of the just. Don't mourn, don't weep. I know it by the testimony of the Holy Ghost that is within me; and you may wait for your friends to come forth to meet you in the morn of the celestial world.

Rejoice, O Israel! Your friends who have been murdered for the truth's sake in the persecutions shall triumph gloriously in the celestial world, while their murderers shall welter for ages in torment, even until they shall have paid the uttermost farthing. I say this for the benefit of strangers.

I have a father, brothers, children, and friends who have gone to a world of spirits. They are only absent for a moment. They are in the spirit, and we shall soon meet again. The time will soon arrive when the trumpet shall sound. When we depart, we shall hail our mothers, fathers, friends, and all whom we love, who have fallen asleep in Jesus. There will be no fear of mobs, persecutions, or malicious lawsuits and arrests; but it will be an eternity of felicity.

A question may be asked—"Will mothers have their children in eternity?" Yes! Yes! Mothers, you shall have your children; for they shall have eternal life, for their debt is paid. There is no damnation awaiting them for they are in the spirit. But as the child dies, so shall it rise from the dead, and be for ever living in the learning of God.

It will never grow [in the grave]; it will still be the child, in the same precise form [when it rises] as it appeared before it died out of its mother's arms, but possessing all the intelligence of a God.

I will leave this subject here, and make a few remarks on the subject of baptism. The baptism of water, without the baptism of fire and the Holy Ghost attending it, is of no use; they are necessarily and inseparably connected. An individual must be born of water and the spirit in order to get into the kingdom of God. In the German, the text bears me out the same as the revelations which I have given and taught for the past fourteen years on that subject. I have the testimony to put in their teeth. My testimony has been true all the time. You will find it in the declaration of John the Baptist. (Reads from the German). John says, "I baptize you with water, but when Jesus comes, who has the power (or keys) He shall administer the baptism of fire and the Holy Ghost." Great God! Where is now all the sectarian world? And if this testimony is true, they are all damned as clearly as anathema can do it. I know the text is true. I call upon all you Germans who know that it is true to say, Eye. (Loud shouts of "Aye").

Alexander Campbell, how are you going to save people with water alone? For John said his baptism was good for nothing without the baptism of Jesus Christ. "Therefore, not leaving the principles of the doctrine of Christ, let us go on unto perfection; not laying again the foundation of repentance from dead works, and of faith towards God, of the doctrine of baptism, and of laying on of hands, and of resurrection of the dead, and of eternal judgment. And this will we do, if God permit." (Heb. 6:1–3).

There is one God, one Father, one Jesus, one hope of our calling, one baptism. All these three baptisms only make one. Many talk of baptism not being essential to salvation; but this kind of teaching would lay the foundation of their damnation. I have the truth, and am at the defiance of the world to contradict me, if they can.

I have now preached a little Latin, a little Hebrew, Greek, and German; and I have fulfilled all. I am not so big a fool as many have taken me to be. The Germans know that I read the German correctly.

The Second Death

Hear it, all ye ends of the Earth —all ye priests, all ye sinners, and all men. Repent! Repent! Obey the gospel. Turn to God; for your religion won't save you, and you will be damned. I do not say how long. There have been remarks made concerning all men being redeemed from hell; but I say that those who sin against the Holy Ghost cannot be forgiven in this world or in the world to come; they shall die the second death. Those who commit the unpardonable sin are doomed to Gnolom—to dwell in hell, worlds without end. As they concocted scenes of bloodshed in this world, so they shall rise to that resurrection which is as the lake of fire and brimstone. Some shall rise to the everlasting burnings of God; for God dwells in everlasting burnings and some shall rise to the damnation of their own filthiness, which is as exquisite a torment as the lake of fire and brimstone.

I have intended my remarks for all, both rich and poor, bond and free, great and small. I have no enmity against any man. I love you all; but I hate some of your deeds. I am your best friend, and if persons miss their mark it is their own fault. If I reprove a man, and he hates me, he is a fool; for I love all men, especially these my brethren and sisters.

I rejoice in hearing the testimony of my aged friends. You don't know me; you never knew my heart. No man knows my history. I cannot tell it: I shall never undertake it. I don't blame anyone for not believing my history. If I had not experienced what I have, I would not have believed it myself. I never did harm any man since I was born in the world. My voice is always for peace.

I cannot lie down until all my work is finished. I never think any evil, nor do anything to the harm of my fellow-man. When I am called by the trump of the archangel and weighed in the balance, you will all know me then. I add no more. God bless you all. Amen.

ABOUT THE AUTHOR

John S. Pennington, Jr. is the creator and author of the audio book series, *Mr. Mormon,* which has been downloaded over 20,000 times, in twenty eight different countries via the website www.mrmormon.com. The inspiration for the *Mr. Mormon* book came when John made several CD recordings answering gospel questions and gave these recordings to his three sons. If, for some reason, he died early in life, John wanted his children to know of his testimony of the gospel of Jesus Christ. Eventually a few friends listened to the recordings and encouraged John to put a book together.

John was born in Nashville, Tennessee in 1964 and grew up in Las Vegas, Nevada, where at the age of seventeen, he joined The Church of Jesus Christ of Latter-day Saints and served a full-time mission in the State of Alabama, USA. After returning home from his mission, he attended Brigham Young University and met his wife, Jane, who is from Alberta, Canada. John and Jane were married in the Cardston, Alberta Temple in 1985. John graduated from the University of Utah with a Bachelor of Science Degree in Economics, class of 1988.

In the business world, John Pennington is a fund manager and a Co-Founder of a family of real estate related investment funds that currently manage over $4.3 billion of Assets Under Management (AUM), and employs over one thousand people across eighteen states.

He has served on the Advisory Board of the Westminster College School of Business in Salt Lake City, Utah, and also as a Director of Fundraising for the Utah Special Olympics program.

He is currently a high priest in The Church of Jesus Christ of Latter-day Saints and has served in several ward bishoprics as 1st and 2nd counselor, with over twenty years of experience instructing priesthood quorums and young adult Sunday school classes. John repeatedly says, "I am not a Bible scholar by any measurement, but I do love studying the scriptures, and I retain the right to change my opinion or my thoughts on any gospel topic at any time in the future."

To download the Mr. Mormon audio book series please visit www.mrmormon.com

Made in the USA
Lexington, KY
01 June 2017